GAME ENGINE GEMS 3

GAME ENGINE GEMS 3

Edited by Eric Lengyel

CRC Press
Taylor & Francis Group
Boca Raton   London   New York

CRC Press is an imprint of the
Taylor & Francis Group, an **informa** business

AN A K PETERS BOOK

CRC Press
Taylor & Francis Group
6000 Broken Sound Parkway NW, Suite 300
Boca Raton, FL 33487-2742

© 2016 by Taylor & Francis Group, LLC
CRC Press is an imprint of Taylor & Francis Group, an Informa business

No claim to original U.S. Government works

Printed and bound in India by Replika Press Pvt. Ltd.

Printed on acid-free paper
Version Date: 20160201

International Standard Book Number-13: 978-1-4987-5565-8 (Hardback)

This book contains information obtained from authentic and highly regarded sources. Reasonable efforts have been made to publish reliable data and information, but the author and publisher cannot assume responsibility for the validity of all materials or the consequences of their use. The authors and publishers have attempted to trace the copyright holders of all material reproduced in this publication and apologize to copyright holders if permission to publish in this form has not been obtained. If any copyright material has not been acknowledged please write and let us know so we may rectify in any future reprint.

Except as permitted under U.S. Copyright Law, no part of this book may be reprinted, reproduced, transmitted, or utilized in any form by any electronic, mechanical, or other means, now known or hereafter invented, including photocopying, microfilming, and recording, or in any information storage or retrieval system, without written permission from the publishers.

For permission to photocopy or use material electronically from this work, please access www.copyright.com (http://www.copyright.com/) or contact the Copyright Clearance Center, Inc. (CCC), 222 Rosewood Drive, Danvers, MA 01923, 978-750-8400. CCC is a not-for-profit organization that provides licenses and registration for a variety of users. For organizations that have been granted a photocopy license by the CCC, a separate system of payment has been arranged.

Trademark Notice: Product or corporate names may be trademarks or registered trademarks, and are used only for identification and explanation without intent to infringe.

Visit the Taylor & Francis Web site at
http://www.taylorandfrancis.com

and the CRC Press Web site at
http://www.crcpress.com

Contents

Preface xiii

Part I Graphics and Rendering 1

Chapter 1   The Open Game Engine Exchange Format 3
Eric Lengyel
    1.1 Introduction 3
    1.2 OpenDDL 8
    1.3 Scene Structure 12
    1.4 Object Data 14
    1.5 Animation 18
    References 21

Chapter 2   Realistic Blending of Skies, Water, and Terrain 23
Frank Kane
    2.1 The Problem 23
    2.2 Blending Terrain with the Sky 26
    2.3 Applying Visibility Effects to Distant Clouds 30
    2.4 Creating Realistic Ocean Horizons 31
    2.5 Putting it All Together 33
    References 34

Chapter 3   Fog with a Linear Density Function 37
Eric Lengyel
    3.1 Introduction 37

3.2	Fog Factor Calculation	38
3.3	Visibility Culling	44
	References	52

Chapter 4 Vegetation Management in Leadwerks Game Engine 4   53
Josh Klint

4.1	Introduction	53
4.2	The Problem	54
4.3	The Idea	55
4.4	Culling	56
4.5	Rendering	61
4.6	Level of Detail	62
4.7	Physics	65
4.8	Future Development	70
	References	71

Chapter 5 Smooth Horizon Mapping   73
Eric Lengyel

5.1	Introduction	73
5.2	Horizon Map Generation	75
5.3	Rendering with Horizon Maps	79
	References	83

Chapter 6 Buffer-Free Generation of Triangle Strip Cube Vertices   85
Don Williamson

6.1	Introduction	85
6.2	Generating Cube Vertices	86
6.3	Wireframe Cubes	89

Chapter 7 Edge-Preserving Smoothing Filter for Particle Based Rendering   91
Kin-Ming Wong and Tien-Tsin Wong

7.1	Introduction	91
7.2	Guided Image Filtering	91
7.3	GLSL Implementation	94
7.4	Results and Performance	97
	Acknowledgements	99
	References	99

Chapter 8	**Variable Precision Pixel Shading for Improved Power Efficiency**	**101**

Rahul P. Sathe

8.1 Introduction and Background	101
8.2 Algorithm	102
8.3 Results	107
8.4 Discussion	107
Acknowledgements	109
References	109

Chapter 9	**A Fast and High-Quality Texture Atlasing Algorithm**	**111**

Manny Ko

9.1 Introduction	111
9.2 Background	112
9.3 Chart Segmentation	113
9.4 Atlas Packing	115
9.5 Atlas-Aware Filtering	118
Acknowledgements	119
References	120

Part II Physics   121

Chapter 10	**Rotational Joint Limits in Quaternion Space**	**123**

Gino van den Bergen

10.1 Introduction	123
10.2 3D Rotations	124
10.3 Unit Quaternions	128
10.4 Quaternions vs. Exponential Map	129
10.5 Swing-Twist Limits	130
10.6 Volumetric Limits	137
References	138

Chapter 11	**Volumetric Hierarchical Approximate Convex Decomposition**	**141**

Khaled Mamou

11.1 Introduction	141
11.2 Convex Approximation	142
11.3 Volumetric Hierarchical Approximate Convex Decomposition	145

    References   157

Chapter 12   Simulating Soft Bodies Using Strain Based Dynamics   159
Muhammad Mobeen Movania

    12.1 Introduction   159
    12.2 Position Based Dynamics   160
    12.3 Strain based Dynamics   162
    12.4 Implementation Details   166
    12.5 Implementing Cloth Simulation   169
    12.6 Implementing Tetrahedral Mesh Simulation   172
    12.7 Barycentric Interpolation   175
    12.8 Experimental Evaluation   176
    12.9 Future Work   179
    References   181

Part III   General Programming   183

Chapter 13   Generic, Lightweight, and Fast Delegates in C++   185
Stefan Reinalter

    13.1 Background   186
    13.2 The Delegate Technique   188
    13.3 Toward a Generic Solution   191
    13.4 Embracing C++11   193
    13.5 Extensions   195
    13.6 Source Code   195

Chapter 14   Compile-Time String Hashing in C++   197
Stefan Reinalter

    14.1 Background   198
    14.2 The Hash Technique   199
    14.3 Toward a Generic Hash Function   201
    14.4 Implementation Notes   204
    14.5 Source Code   205

Chapter 15   Static Reflection in C++ Using Tuples   207
Nicolas Guillemot

    15.1 Rethinking Composition Using Tuples   208

	15.2 Recursive Member Iteration	210
	15.3 Practical Concerns	215

Chapter 16   Portable SIMD Programs Using ISPC — 219
Nicolas Guillemot and Marc Fauconneau Dufresne

	16.1 The Problem	220
	16.2 ISPC Basics	222
	16.3 ISPC Example Programs	222
	16.4 Integration in a Game Engine	224
	16.5 Tips & Tricks	227
	References	228

Chapter 17   Shared Network Arrays as an Abstraction of Network Code from Game Code Logic — 229
João Lucas Guberman Raza

	17.1 Introduction	229
	17.2 How SNAs Work	230
	17.3 How a Gameplay Programmer Uses SNAs	232
	17.4 How a Network Programmer Uses SNAs	234
	17.5 Further Discussion	236
	References	236

Part IV   Character Control and Artificial Intelligence — 237

Chapter 18   Vision Based Local Collision Avoidance — 239
Teófilo Bezerra Dutra, Ricardo Marques, Julien Pettré, and Jan Ondřej

	18.1 Introduction	239
	18.2 Local Path Planning in Games	240
	18.3 Vision Based Obstacle Avoidance	242
	18.4 Purely Reactive Technique	244
	18.5 Gradient Based Technique	247
	18.6 Final Considerations	250
	Acknowledgements	252
	References	252

Chapter 19 A Programming Framework for Autonomous NPCs — 255

Artur de Oliveira da Rocha Franco, José Gilvan Rodrigues Maia, and Fernando Antonio de Carvalho Gomes

19.1 Introduction	255
19.2 CordéIS Overview	257
19.3 Implementing CordéIS for Electronic RPGs	261
19.4 About the Demo	265
References	265

Chapter 20 Beyond Smart Objects: Behavior-Oriented Programming for NPCs in Large Open Worlds — 267

Martin Černý, Tomáš Plch, and Cyril Brom

20.1 Introduction	267
20.2 A Little Bit of Context	269
20.3 Behavior Objects	270
20.4 Integration Within an AI System	271
20.5 Implementation in *Kingdom Come: Deliverance*	273
20.6 Lessons Learned	277
Acknowledgements	279
References	279

Chapter 21 A Control System for Enhancing Entity Behavior — 281

Mike Ramsey

21.1 Controller Basics	282
21.2 PID Implementation	284
21.3 Use Cases and Strategies for a PID Controller	285
References	288

Chapter 22 A Control System Based Approach to Entity Behavior — 289

Mike Ramsey

22.1 A Single Control System	289
22.2 Hierarchical Control System Basics	291
22.3 A Hierarchical Control System for Following	291
References	294

Contributor Biographies 295

Index 305

Preface

This book is the third volume of the *Game Engine Gems* series, and it contains a new collection of clever techniques and practical advice on the subject of game engine development. A group of 26 experienced professionals, several of whom also contributed to the first or second volume, have written the 22 chapters that follow and have filled them with expert knowledge and wisdom.

The topics covered in this book vary somewhat widely within the subject of game engine development and have been divided into the following four broad categories:

- Graphics and rendering,
- Physics,
- General programming, and
- Character control and artificial intelligence.

Audience

The intended audience for this book includes professional game developers, students of computer science programs, and practically anyone possessing an interest in how the pros tackle specific problems that arise during game engine development. Many of the chapters assume a basic knowledge of computer architecture as well as some knowledge of the high-level design of current-generation game consoles, such as the PlayStation 4 and Xbox One. The level of mathematics used in the book rarely exceeds that of basic trigonometry and calculus.

The Website

The official website for the *Game Engine Gems* series can be found at the following address:

http://www.gameenginegems.com/

Supplementary materials for many of the gems in this book are posted on this website, and they include demos, source code, and examples. For chapters that include project files, the source code can be compiled using Microsoft Visual Studio.

Any corrections to the text that may arise will also be posted on the website. Announcements about the next volume in the *Game Engine Gems* series will appear here as well.

Part I

Graphics and Rendering

1

The Open Game Engine Exchange Format

Eric Lengyel
Terathon Software

1.1 Introduction

The Open Game Engine Exchange (OpenGEX) format is a text-based file format designed to facilitate the transfer of complex scene data between applications such as modeling tools and game engines. OpenGEX was created in order to provide a clean, well-specified format that supports the modeling and animation features needed by game developers while retaining conciseness and generality. The OpenGEX specification [Lengyel 2015] was first released in September 2013 along with export plugins for Maya and 3ds Max. OpenGEX version 1.1.2, the latest as of this writing, was released in December 2014 along with updated plugins for Maya, 3ds Max, and Blender.

OpenGEX directly supports the following concepts, and it has an extension mechanism that can be used to add new application-specific types of information to an OpenGEX file.

- Hierarchical scene organization through the use of node trees.
- Factored node transforms that may, for example, be split into position, rotation, and scale to assist animation.
- Object instancing, meaning that multiple nodes can reference the same object and share its data.
- Geometry objects, light objects, and camera objects.
- Multiple materials per mesh with independent binding per instance.
- Multiple vertex colors and texture coordinate sets per mesh.
- Skinned meshes, including support for skeletons, bind-pose transforms, and bone influence data.

- Morphed meshes, also known as blend shapes or shape keys.
- Key frame animation for all node transforms and morph weights.
- Linear, Bézier, and tension-continuity-bias (TCB) animation curves.
- Standard material colors and textures (diffuse, specular, normal, emission, opacity, and transparency).
- Texture coordinate transforms.

This chapter provides an overview of the design of OpenGEX, the structures that compose an OpenGEX file, and the basic syntax upon which those structures are built. At the most basic level, an OpenGEX file consists of a node hierarchy, a set of objects, a set of materials, and some additional information about global units and axis orientation. The various node, object, and material structures contain all of the details such as geometric data and animation tracks within a hierarchy of additional types of structures defined by OpenGEX. The relationships among all of these structures are shown in Figure 1.1. The data itself is formatted using the syntax defined by the Open Data Description Language (OpenDDL), which arose during the process of developing OpenGEX.

A near-minimal example of a complete OpenGEX file describing a green cube is shown in Listing 1.1. It begins with a group of `Metric` structures that define the units of measurement and the global up direction. Those are followed by a single `GeometryNode` structure that provides the name and transform for the cube. The geometric data for the cube is stored in the `GeometryObject` structure that is referenced by the geometry node. The geometry object structure contains a single mesh of triangle primitives that includes per-vertex positions, normals, and texture coordinates. Finally, the `Material` structure at the end of the file contains the green diffuse reflection color.

Additional Information

More detailed information about OpenGEX can be found on the official website at the following address:

   http://opengex.org/

This website is home to the latest specification and export plugins for the various supported modeling applications. It also hosts a generic import template written in C++ that can be used as a starting point for the development of an OpenGEX import module for a game engine's art pipeline.

1.1 Introduction

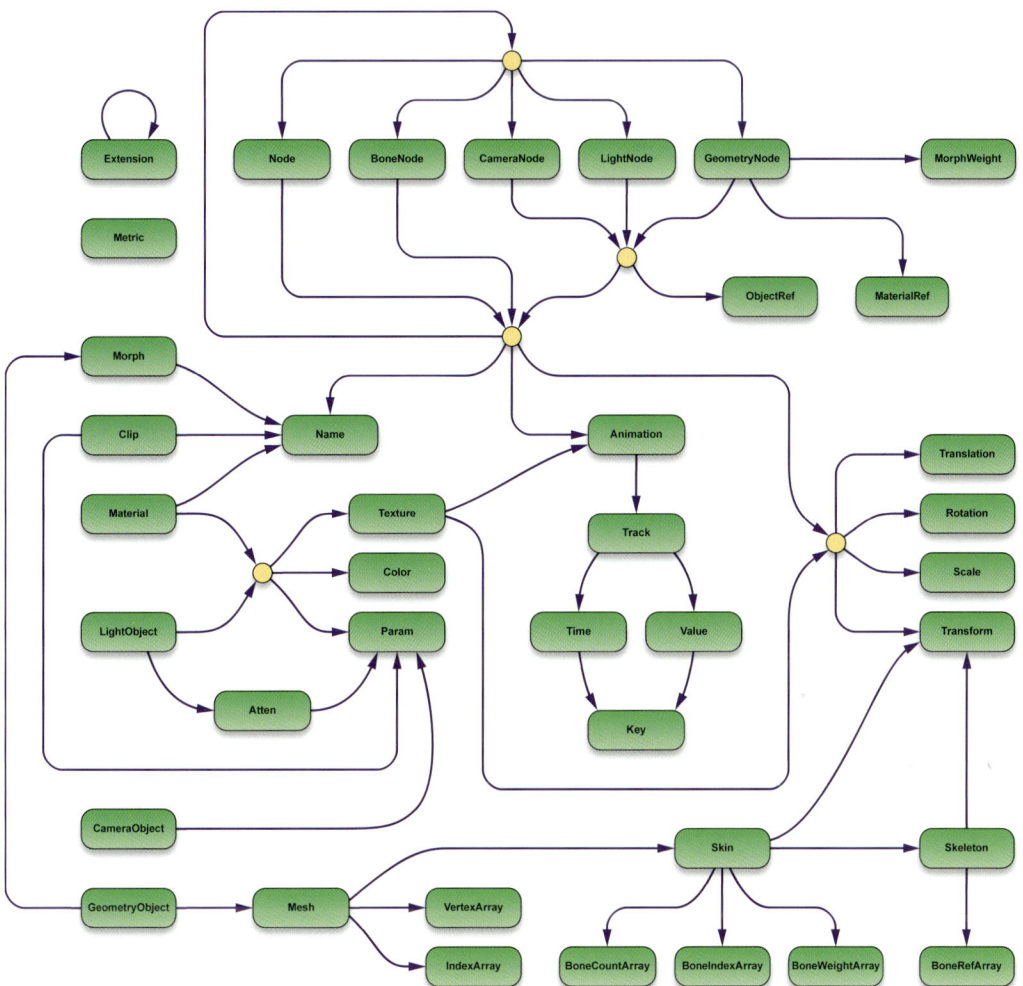

Figure 1.1. This diagram illustrates the relationships among the structures defined by the OpenGEX format. The purple arrows point from each of the structures to the specific substructures they are allowed to contain. (Substructures that are simply OpenDDL data types have been omitted.) The circular orange nodes serve only to combine paths in order to simplify the diagram where common relationships exist.

Listing 1.1. This is an example of a very simple OpenGEX file containing the data for a green cube. It consists of a single geometry node that references a geometry object and a material.

```
Metric (key = "distance") {float {0.01}}
Metric (key = "angle") {float {1}}
Metric (key = "time") {float {1}}
Metric (key = "up") {string {"z"}}

GeometryNode $node1
{
    Name {string {"Cube"}}
    ObjectRef {ref {$geometry1}}
    MaterialRef {ref {$material1}}

    Transform
    {
        float[16]
        {
            {0x3F800000, 0x00000000, 0x00000000, 0x00000000,    // {1, 0, 0, 0
             0x00000000, 0x3F800000, 0x00000000, 0x00000000,    //  0, 1, 0, 0
             0x00000000, 0x00000000, 0x3F800000, 0x00000000,    //  0, 0, 1, 0
             0x42480000, 0x42480000, 0x00000000, 0x3F800000}    //  50, 50, 0, 1}
        }
    }
}

GeometryObject $geometry1        // Cube
{
    Mesh (primitive = "triangles")
    {
        VertexArray (attrib = "position")
        {
            float[3]
            {
                {0xC2480000, 0xC2480000, 0x00000000}, {0xC2480000, 0x42480000, 0x00000000},
                {0x42480000, 0x42480000, 0x00000000}, {0x42480000, 0xC2480000, 0x00000000},
                {0xC2480000, 0xC2480000, 0x42C80000}, {0x42480000, 0xC2480000, 0x42C80000},
                {0x42480000, 0x42480000, 0x42C80000}, {0xC2480000, 0x42480000, 0x42C80000},
                {0xC2480000, 0xC2480000, 0x00000000}, {0x42480000, 0xC2480000, 0x00000000},
                {0x42480000, 0xC2480000, 0x42C80000}, {0xC2480000, 0xC2480000, 0x42C80000},
                {0x42480000, 0xC2480000, 0x00000000}, {0x42480000, 0x42480000, 0x00000000},
                {0x42480000, 0x42480000, 0x42C80000}, {0x42480000, 0xC2480000, 0x42C80000},
                {0x42480000, 0x42480000, 0x00000000}, {0xC2480000, 0x42480000, 0x00000000},
                {0xC2480000, 0x42480000, 0x42C80000}, {0x42480000, 0x42480000, 0x42C80000},
                {0xC2480000, 0x42480000, 0x42C80000}, {0xC2480000, 0x42480000, 0x00000000},
                {0xC2480000, 0xC2480000, 0x00000000}, {0xC2480000, 0xC2480000, 0x42C80000}
            }
        }

        VertexArray (attrib = "normal")
```

1.1 Introduction

```
                {
                    float[3]
                    {
                        {0x00000000, 0x00000000, 0xBF800000}, {0x00000000, 0x00000000, 0xBF800000},
                        {0x00000000, 0x00000000, 0xBF800000}, {0x00000000, 0x00000000, 0xBF800000},
                        {0x00000000, 0x00000000, 0x3F800000}, {0x00000000, 0x00000000, 0x3F800000},
                        {0x00000000, 0x00000000, 0x3F800000}, {0x00000000, 0x00000000, 0x3F800000},
                        {0x00000000, 0xBF800000, 0x00000000}, {0x00000000, 0xBF800000, 0x00000000},
                        {0x00000000, 0xBF800000, 0x00000000}, {0x80000000, 0xBF800000, 0x00000000},
                        {0x3F800000, 0x00000000, 0x00000000}, {0x3F800000, 0x00000000, 0x00000000},
                        {0x3F800000, 0x00000000, 0x00000000}, {0x3F800000, 0x00000000, 0x00000000},
                        {0x00000000, 0x3F800000, 0x00000000}, {0x00000000, 0x3F800000, 0x00000000},
                        {0x00000000, 0x3F800000, 0x00000000}, {0x80000000, 0x3F800000, 0x00000000},
                        {0xBF800000, 0x00000000, 0x00000000}, {0xBF800000, 0x00000000, 0x00000000},
                        {0xBF800000, 0x00000000, 0x00000000}, {0xBF800000, 0x00000000, 0x00000000}
                    }
                }

                VertexArray (attrib = "texcoord")
                {
                    float[2]
                    {
                        {0x3F800000, 0x00000000}, {0x3F800000, 0x3F800000}, {0x00000000, 0x3F800000},
                        {0x00000000, 0x00000000}, {0x00000000, 0x00000000}, {0x3F800000, 0x00000000},
                        {0x3F800000, 0x3F800000}, {0x00000000, 0x3F800000}, {0x00000000, 0x00000000},
                        {0x3F800000, 0x00000000}, {0x3F800000, 0x3F800000}, {0x00000000, 0x3F800000},
                        {0x00000000, 0x00000000}, {0x3F800000, 0x00000000}, {0x3F800000, 0x3F800000},
                        {0x00000000, 0x3F800000}, {0x00000000, 0x00000000}, {0x3F800000, 0x00000000},
                        {0x3F800000, 0x3F800000}, {0x00000000, 0x3F800000}, {0x00000000, 0x00000000},
                        {0x3F800000, 0x00000000}, {0x3F800000, 0x3F800000}, {0x00000000, 0x3F800000}
                    }
                }

                IndexArray
                {
                    unsigned_int32[3]
                    {
                        {0, 1, 2}, {2, 3, 0}, {4, 5, 6}, {6, 7, 4}, {8, 9, 10},
                        {10, 11, 8}, {12, 13, 14}, {14, 15, 12}, {16, 17, 18},
                        {18, 19, 16}, {20, 21, 22}, {22, 23, 20}
                    }
                }
            }
        }
    }

Material $material1
{
    Name {string {"Green"}}
    Color (attrib = "diffuse") {float[3] {{0, 1, 0}}}
}
```

1.2 OpenDDL

During the development of OpenGEX, a generic syntax for expressing different types of data arose and became known as the Open Data Description Language (OpenDDL). This language is designed to store strongly-typed data in a human-readable text format that is similar to the variable initialization syntax of C/C++. The data can be composed of arrays of values and arrays of arrays, making it very suitable for storing information that arises in 3D graphics, such as vertex positions, texture coordinates, and transformation matrices.

An OpenDDL file is composed of a sequence of *structures*. A single structure consists of a type identifier followed by an optional name, an optional list of properties, and then its data payload enclosed in braces. This general syntax is illustrated by the railroad diagram shown in Figure 1.2. There are two general types of structures, those with built-in types that contain primitive data such as integers or strings, and those that represent custom data structures defined by a derivative file format such as OpenGEX. As an example, suppose that a particular format defined a data type called Vertex that contains the 3D coordinates of a single vertex position. This could be written as follows.

```
Vertex
{
    float {1.0, 2.0, 3.0}
}
```

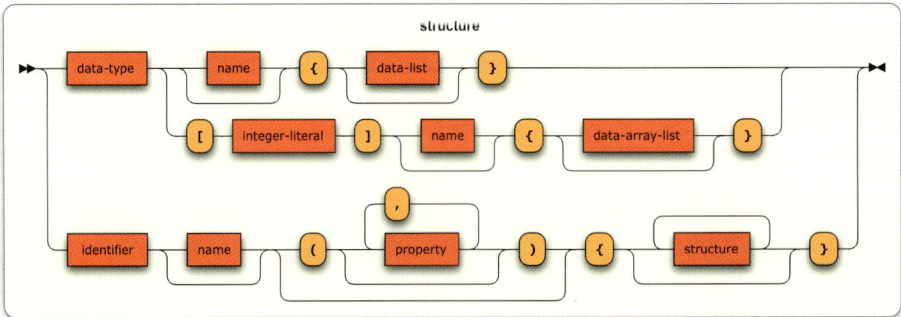

Figure 1.2. An OpenDDL file contains a sequence of structures that follow the production rule shown here.

The `Vertex` identifier represents a custom data structure defined by the file format, and it contains another structure of type `float`, which is a built-in primitive data type. The data in the `float` structure consists of the three values 1.0, 2.0, and 3.0. In general, raw data values in a primitive data structure are always specified as a comma-separated array of unbounded size. In the case that only a single value needs to be specified, the array simply has a size of one element.

The raw data inside a primitive data structure may also be specified as a comma-separated array of *subarrays* of values. Each subarray has the same size, and this size is specified by placing a positive integer value inside brackets immediately following the primitive type identifier, preceding the structure's name if it has one. Each value contained in the primitive data structure is then written as a comma-separated array of values enclosed in braces. The OpenGEX format defines a structure called `VertexArray` that contains an array of vertex attributes. In the case that the attribute is the position of the vertex, each subarray would typically contain three floating-point values that are written as follows.

```
VertexArray (attrib = "position")
{
    float[3]
    {
        {1.0, 2.0, 3.0}, {0.5, 0.0, 0.5}, {0.0, -1.0, 4.0}
    }
}
```

OpenDDL defines the primitive data types listed in Table 1.1. When used as the identifier for a data structure, each entry in this table indicates that the structure is a primitive structure and that its data payload is composed of an array of literal values. Any other identifier used for a data structure indicates that it does not contain primitive data, but instead that it contains other data structures as allowed by the particular format. The identifier itself can be composed of uppercase and lowercase letters, numerical digits, and the underscore character, but it cannot begin with a number. The OpenGEX format defines 39 specific data structure identifiers to organize the information that it supports.

Any structure in an OpenDDL file can have a *name* assigned to it. Names are used when it is necessary to refer to one structure from another structure. For example, an animation track in the OpenGEX format specifies the transform that it modifies by referencing the name of the target structure containing the transform data. When a structure has a name, that name begins with either a dollar sign or

Type	Description
bool	A boolean type that can have the value true or false.
int8	An 8-bit signed integer that can have values in the range $[-2^7, 2^7-1]$.
int16	A 16-bit signed integer that can have values in the range $[-2^{15}, 2^{15}-1]$.
int32	A 32-bit signed integer that can have values in the range $[-2^{31}, 2^{31}-1]$.
int64	A 64-bit signed integer that can have values in the range $[-2^{63}, 2^{63}-1]$.
unsigned_int8	An 8-bit unsigned integer that can have values in the range $[0, 2^8-1]$.
unsigned_int16	A 16-bit unsigned integer that can have values in the range $[0, 2^{16}-1]$.
unsigned_int32	A 32-bit unsigned integer that can have values in the range $[0, 2^{32}-1]$.
unsigned_int64	A 64-bit unsigned integer that can have values in the range $[0, 2^{64}-1]$.
half	A 16-bit floating-point type conforming to the S1-E5-M10 format.
float	A 32-bit floating-point type conforming to the S1-E8-M23 format.
double	A 64-bit floating-point type conforming to the S1-E11-M52 format.
string	A double-quoted character string with contents encoded in UTF-8.
ref	A sequence of structure names, or the keyword null.
type	A type having values that are type names in the first column of this table.

Table 1.1. These are the primitive data types defined by OpenDDL.

percent sign and is written immediately after the structure identifier as in the following example taken from the OpenGEX format.

```
Rotation %xrot (kind = "x")
{
    float {1.5708}
}
```

Here, the name of this particular Rotation structure is "xrot". The percent sign indicates that it is a local name, meaning that it is only visible within the scope containing the Rotation structure. Names that begin with a dollar sign, on the other hand, have global scope and are visible throughout the entire file.

A *reference* value is used to form a link to a specific structure within an OpenDDL file. If the target structure has a global name, then the value of a reference to it is simply the name of the structure, beginning with the dollar sign character. If the target structure has a local name, then the value of a reference to it depends on the scope in which the reference appears. If the reference appears in a structure that is a sibling of the target structure, then its value is the name of the target structure, beginning with the percent sign character. Continuing with the previous example, a `Track` structure that is part of an OpenGEX animation can reference the above `Rotation` structure as follows.

```
Animation (begin = 0.0, end = 2.0)
{
    Track (target = %xrot)
    {
        ...
    }
}
```

In this case, the reference to "xrot" appears in a property of the `Track` structure. (Properties are described below.) References can also appear in the data payloads of `ref` structures, and this is used in OpenGEX when a node refers to the object that it instances, as in the following example.

```
GeometryNode $node5
{
    Name {string {"Cylinder"}}
    ObjectRef {ref {$geometry2}}
    ...
}
```

A non-primitive data structure may define one or more *properties* that can be specified separately from the data that the structure contains. Every property has a specific type that is defined by the derivative file format but not explicitly included in the file itself. Properties are written in a comma-separated list inside parentheses following the name of the structure, or just following the structure identifier if there is no name. Each property is composed of a property identifier followed by an equals character (=) and the value of the property. In the above examples, the `Rotation` structure has a `kind` property of type `string`, and the `Track` structure has a `target` property of type `ref`.

The exact format of the various primitive data types supported by OpenDDL are described in detail on the openddl.org website and in the OpenGEX specification. The formats are intended to be unsurprising to those familiar with popular programming languages such as C++.

1.3 Scene Structure

In OpenGEX (and in many modeling programs), an individual item in a scene is represented by a *node*, and the raw data referenced by any particular item appearing in the scene is encapsulated inside an *object*. The relationships among nodes and objects form the overall scene structure.

Nodes and Objects

Nodes are organized into trees that form a transformation hierarchy, and references between nodes and objects form an instance graph. An OpenGEX file may contain any number of nodes at the root level, and each node may contain any number of child nodes. There is no limit to how many nodes may reference a particular object.

The OpenGEX structures that participate in scene organization are listed in Table 1.2. The types of nodes that can be present in a scene include geometry nodes, light nodes, camera nodes, and bone nodes. OpenGEX also supports generic nodes that are used only for grouping other nodes in the scene and transforming them as a whole.

The geometric data and other parameters belonging to geometries, lights, and cameras without regard for placement in the scene are stored in a flat set of object structures. An OpenDDL reference is used to make the connection between each node and the object that it instances. Material information is stored in a flat set of material structures that can be referenced by geometry nodes.

Transforms

Each node in the hierarchy may contain one or more of the transformation structures listed in Table 1.3. The set of these transformation structures contained directly inside a particular node structure collectively defines that node's local transform.

Each transformation structure can be designated as either a node transform or an object transform (based on the value of its `object` property), and these divide

1.3 Scene Structure

Structure	Description
Node	A generic node used only for grouping other nodes and transforming the group as a whole.
GeometryNode	A node that references a geometry object. This node may also reference materials and contain morph weights.
LightNode	A node that references a light object.
CameraNode	A node that references a camera object.
BoneNode	A node that represents a bone belonging to a skeleton used by a skinned mesh.
ObjectRef	Inside a geometry node, light node, or camera node, contains a reference to a geometry object, light object, or camera object.
MaterialRef	Inside a geometry node, contains a reference to a material.
GeometryObject	An object that contains mesh data for a geometry.
LightObject	An object that contains parameters for an infinite light, point light, or spot light.
CameraObject	An object that contains parameters for a camera.

Table 1.2. These are the OpenGEX structures that define the node hierarchy and specify the objects that appear in a scene.

the complete local transform into two factors. The node transform is inherited by subnodes, meaning that the local transform of a subnode is relative only to the node transform factor of its parent node. The object transform is applied only to the node to which it belongs and is not inherited by any subnodes. This is a special feature of OpenGEX that supports concepts such as pivot points in a general manner.

The node transform is calculated by converting all of the transforms having an `object` property value of `false` to a 4×4 matrix and multiplying them together in the order that they appear inside the node structure. Similarly, the object transform is calculated by multiplying matrices together for the transforms having an `object` property value of `true` in the order that they appear inside the node structure. Any interleaving of transforms having different object property values has no meaning.

Structure	Description
Transform	Contains a 4×4 transformation matrix.
Translation	Contains a three-dimensional translation vector.
Rotation	Contains a rotation that is expressed as a quaternion, an angle about a given axis, or an angle about the x, y, or z axis.
Scale	Contains either a three-dimensional scale applied to all three axes or a one-dimensional scale applied to the x, y, or z axis.

Table 1.3. These are the OpenGEX structures that specify transformations.

1.4 Object Data

There are three types of objects defined by OpenGEX: geometry objects, light objects, and camera objects. These structures contain the data that defines the appearance and properties of these items in their own local coordinate systems without regard for how they might be transformed by the nodes that reference them.

Geometry Objects

Geometry objects contain a set of mesh structures, one for each level of detail, that each contain vertex and primitive information as well as optional skinning data. Each mesh structure typically contains several arrays of per-vertex data and one or more index arrays as shown in Listing 1.2.

Listing 1.2. This mesh structure contains per-vertex positions, normals, and texture coordinates, and it contains an index array that determines how triangle primitives are assembled. The letters appearing in the arrays are placeholders for what would actually be numerical data in a real file.

```
Mesh (primitive = "triangles")
{
    VertexArray (attrib = "position")
    {
        float[3] {{x, y, z}, {x, y, z}, ...}
    }

    VertexArray (attrib = "normal")
```

```
    {
        float[3] {{x, y, z}, {x, y, z}, ...}
    }

    VertexArray (attrib = "texcoord")
    {
        float[2] {{u, v}, {u, v}, ...}
    }

    IndexArray (material = 0)
    {
        unsigned_int16[3] {{i, j, k}, {i, j, k}, ...}
    }
}
```

A mesh may be segmented into multiple pieces to which different materials can be applied by including multiple index arrays having different values for their material properties. The materials themselves are specified by the geometry nodes referencing the geometry object that contains the mesh. This makes it possible to apply different materials to different instances of the same geometry object.

Skinning

A mesh structure may include skinning information, in which case it contains all of the structures listed in Table 1.4. A typical skin structure is shown in Listing 1.3, and it exemplifies how the skeleton and per-vertex bone influences are specified. The details about how this information is used to calculate skinned vertex positions and normals are provided in the OpenGEX specification.

The skeleton contains a list of references to the nodes in the scene that act as the bones, and it specifies an array of transformation matrices that represent the configuration of those bones in the bind pose. The skinning calculations require the *inverses* of the bind-pose matrices, so other exchange formats typically store those instead. However, it is common for scale adjustments and coordinate axis permutations (such as changing the up direction) to be applied when importing data into a game engine, and these would need to be applied to the non-inverted matrices, so for this reason, OpenGEX does not store the inverses.

Structure	Description
`Skin`	Contains information about a skeleton and the per-vertex bone influence data.
`Skeleton`	Inside a skin structure, contains information about the bones belonging to a skeleton.
`BoneRefArray`	Inside a skeleton structure, contains a list of references to the bone nodes.
`BoneCountArray`	Inside a skin structure, contains an array of bone counts specifying how many bones influence each vertex.
`BoneIndexArray`	Inside a skin structure, contains an array of bone indexes specifying which bones influence each vertex.
`BoneWeightArray`	Inside a skin structure, contains an array of weights specifying how strongly each bone influences each vertex.

Table 1.4. These are the OpenGEX structures that specify the skeleton and bone influence data for a skinned mesh.

Listing 1.3. A `Skin` structure is required to contain the substructures shown here.

```
Skin
{
    Skeleton
    {
        BoneRefArray    // References to the bone nodes.
        {
            ref {$bone1, $bone2, ...}
        }

        Transform       // Bind-pose transforms for all bones.
        {
            float[16]
            {
                ...
            }
        }
    }
```

1.4 Object Data

```
    BoneCountArray    // Number of bones influencing each vertex.
    {
        unsigned_int8 {...}
    }

    BoneIndexArray    // Bone index per influence per vertex.
    {
        unsigned_int8 {...}
    }

    BoneWeightArray   // Weight per influence per vertex.
    {
        float {...}
    }
}
```

Morphing

Each vertex array stored in a mesh structure may specify a morph target index. This makes it possible to define multiple shapes with the same number of vertices but different positions, normals, colors, texture coordinates, etc., for each morph target. Morph targets are blended together using morph weights that are stored with the geometry nodes that reference the geometry object containing the morph data. Different geometry nodes can blend the morph targets in different ways and may even utilize different subsets of the available morph targets. The details about how morphed vertex attributes are calculated are provided by the OpenGEX specification.

Materials

Each geometry node in a scene can reference a set of materials that are applied to the geometry object that it instances. OpenGEX defines several basic material parameters, colors, and texture maps that can be used to construct a proper shader to be applied when rendering a geometry. This information is stored in a material structure. An exporter may also include custom properties that are not explicitly defined by OpenGEX. A game engine has considerable freedom in how it chooses to utilize the information included in a material structure.

The standard set of colors defined by the OpenGEX specification are diffuse, specular, emission, opacity, and transparency. There is one standard scalar parameter defined by the specification, and that is the specular power appearing in the conventional Phong shading model. This parameter, and each of the standard colors listed above are also defined as standard texture maps along with one more texture map that contains tangent-space normal vectors.

A texture map structure may contain a set of transformation structures. These specify a transform to be applied to a mesh's texture coordinates before they are used to sample the texture map.

Light Objects

OpenGEX supports three types of light sources: infinite (directional) lights, points lights, and spot lights. Light objects contain information about a light's color, intensity, and attenuation functions. In the case of a spot light, a light object may also specify a texture map to be used as a projection.

For point lights and spot lights, OpenGEX supports a variety of general attenuation functions that are designed to fit intensity fall-off models commonly used by game engines and various modeling applications. These functions are specified by one or more attenuation structures contained within the light object. If more than one attenuation structure is present, then the effective intensity fall-off model is given by the product of the individual functions at any particular distance from the light source.

Camera Objects

A camera object contains a small amount of information about a camera having a perspective projection. A camera object can specify the horizontal field of view angle and the distance to the near and far clipping planes. When any of these are missing, an application is free to use its own default values.

1.5 Animation

Node transformations, morph weights, and texture coordinate transformations may all be animated through the inclusion of animation structures inside node structures and texture structures. A complete transformation may be decomposed into multiple components, such as rotations about one or more axes followed by a translation, and an animation may contain several tracks that animate each component separately. An OpenGEX file may contain multiple animation clips, and each animation structure identifies which clip it belongs to. Information about a complete animation clip is stored inside a clip structure that can appear at the top level of the file. The OpenGEX structures involved in animation are summarized in Table 1.5.

1.5 Animation

Structure	Description
Animation	Contains a set of animation tracks that control one or more target structures.
Clip	Contains information about a single animation clip.
Track	Inside an animation structure, contains animation key data for a single transformation structure or morph weight structure.
Time	Inside a track structure, contains key time data.
Value	Inside a track structure, contains key value data.
Key	Inside a time or value structure, contains the data that defines an animation curve.

Table 1.5. These are the OpenGEX structures that contain animation data.

All animation data in OpenGEX is specified in terms of *key frames* in which information about the overall shape of an animation curve is given at many discrete times. The values of the animation curve in between consecutive time keys are determined by a specific method of interpolation. OpenGEX supports three widely used interpolation methods: linear, Bézier, and TCB (tension-continuity-bias). The Bézier and TCB methods require additional information beyond the curve's value at each time key. The details about the exact calculations used to implement each interpolation method are provided in the OpenGEX specification.

The example shown in Listing 1.4 demonstrates how animation tracks are typically used to modify the position and rotation of a node over a short time interval. The values of the animation curves are specified at three key times, and the transforms at other times are determined through Bézier interpolation using the control point data supplied in the track structures.

Listing 1.4. The animation tracks in this example move the node along the *x* axis while rotating it about the *z* axis, and then they move the node along the *z* axis.

```
GeometryNode
{
    Translation %xpos (kind = "x")
    {
        float {-0.47506}
    }

    Translation %zpos (kind = "z")
    {
        float {0}
    }

    Rotation %zrot (kind = "z")
    {
        float {0}
    }

    Animation (begin = 0, end = 1)
    {
        Track (target = %xpos)
        {
            Time (curve = "bezier")
            {
                Key {float {0, 0.666667, 1}}
                Key (kind = "-control") {float {0, 0.444467, 0.8889}}
                Key (kind = "+control") {float {0.2222, 0.777767, 1}}
            }

            Value (curve = "bezier")
            {
                Key {float {-0.47506, 413.657, 413.657}}
                Key (kind = "-control") {float {-0.47506, 413.657, 413.657}}
                Key (kind = "+control") {float {-0.47506, 413.657, 413.657}}
            }
        }

        Track (target = %zpos)
        {
```

```
            Time (curve = "bezier")
            {
                Key {float {0, 0.666667, 1}}
                Key (kind = "-control") {float {0, 0.444467, 0.8889}}
                Key (kind = "+control") {float {0.2222, 0.777767, 1}}
            }

            Value (curve = "bezier")
            {
                Key {float {0, 0, 158.682}}
                Key (kind = "-control") {float {0, 0, 158.682}}
                Key (kind = "+control") {float {0, 0, 158.682}}
            }
        }

        Track (target = %zrot)
        {
            Time (curve = "bezier")
            {
                Key {float {0, 0.666667, 1}}
                Key (kind = "-control") {float {0, 0.444467, 0.8889}}
                Key (kind = "+control") {float {0.2222, 0.777767, 1}}
            }

            Value (curve = "bezier")
            {
                Key {float {0, 3.14582, 3.14582}}
                Key (kind = "-control") {float {0, 3.14582, 3.14582}}
                Key (kind = "+control") {float {0, 3.14582, 3.14582}}
            }
        }
    }
}
```

References

[Lengyel 2015] Eric Lengyel. *Open Game Engine Exchange Specification, Version 1.1.2.* Terathon Software, 2015.

2

Realistic Blending of Skies, Water, and Terrain

Frank Kane
Sundog Software LLC

Atmospheric scattering is often applied inconsistently between dynamic skies, terrain, water, and clouds, leading to unrealistic horizons and distant scenery in large, expansive outdoor scenes. Shaders tend to be specialized for these different scene elements, making it difficult to produce realistic results when they come together in the background. This chapter explains the origin of the problem, offers several solutions, and discusses the tradeoffs they entail.

2.1 The Problem

Figure 2.1 illustrates one manifestation of the problem. In this scene, fog is applied to the terrain, but the fog color on the distant mountains is inconsistent with the sky color behind them. This leads to the unnatural result of mountains looking like out-of-place cutouts against the sky.

Skies are often prerendered sky boxes or sky domes. In this case, if the fog density of the scene is known to be fixed, the sky textures may be retouched to better match the terrain. However, many engines built for outdoor scenes will include a procedural sky shader (such as one using the Preetham model [Preetham et al. 1999] or Hosek-Wilkie model [Hosek et al. 2012]) that can handle continual changes in time of day. These sky models produce sky colors from a function of the sun position, atmospheric turbidity, and position on the sky derived from fitting functions to experimentally obtained data. This is likely a very different approach from the algorithm used to apply fog or atmospheric scattering to your terrain, and the two are unlikely to produce consistent results on their own. Simpler models that just darken or color-shift skies based on time of day suffer from the same problem, as they still assume a given visibility.

2. Realistic Blending of Skies, Water, and Terrain

Figure 2.1. Atmospheric scattering on terrain without a matching sky color looks unnatural.

Figure 2.2 illustrates the challenges of handling reduced visibility on 3D clouds in the sky. Fundamentally, this is the same issue seen with terrain. The fog equation applied to the clouds doesn't match how the sky model handles visibility. As a result, the clouds appear to take on an unnatural color. Even if their fog color is physically realistic, if it doesn't match the sky behind them, your brain latches onto that discontinuity and declares the scene to be unreal.

Figure 2.3 shows an even more challenging problem in ocean scenes. In addition to the fog problem we described with terrain, the color of water is highly dependent on local surface normal vectors that determine the blend of reflection and refraction based on the Fresnel equations. Near the horizon, this detail is lost or averaged out in unrealistic manners. This can lead to distant water appearing overly reflective and matching the sky above it, while in real life there is a distinct line visible at the horizon of the ocean in clear conditions. Only a perfectly calm ocean, which doesn't exist in nature, would blend smoothly into the sky at the horizon when visibility is high.

Fortunately, several methods of varying complexity exist to smoothly blend distant terrain and clouds with the sky. Proper shading of distant water waves also has a simple solution.

2.1 The Problem

Figure 2.2. Poorly chosen fog colors results in distant clouds being more visible, instead of less.

Figure 2.3. Incorrect handling of distant surface normal vectors yields an indistinct horizon line.

2.2 Blending Terrain with the Sky

The sky behind your terrain is not a fixed color, and this is the fundamental problem. Especially at sunrise and sunset, there can be very sharp gradients in sky color as a function of sky elevation and sky azimuth. The reddest parts of the sky will be near the sun and near the horizon. A realistic sky model must simulate the location of the sun and how much atmosphere direct sunlight passes through in order to reach you (the *atmospheric mass*) as well as the molecules and particles that scatter that sunlight along the way. Figure 2.4 illustrates how the amount of atmosphere sunlight must traverse can vary greatly depending on the time of day due to the nature of our atmosphere and the curvature of Earth.

If you are applying a simple exponential fog equation to your terrain, it assumes a fixed fog color $\mathbf{C}_f$ and produces a final color $\mathbf{C}$ using the equation

$$\mathbf{C} = f\mathbf{C}_i + (1-f)\mathbf{C}_f$$

where $f = e^{-\rho d}$. Here, d is the distance from the eye-point to the terrain, ρ is a constant that controls the density of the fog, and $\mathbf{C}_i$ is the incident, unfogged terrain color. This fog equation has no hope of blending with a realistic sky, which may vary in color from light blue to deep orange around the horizon at sunset.

More sophisticated atmospheric scattering approaches simulate Rayleigh scattering as light passes from terrain to the eye, and blend your terrain color with the sky color in a more realistic manner [Ebert 2003]. However, there is still the problem of choosing an appropriate sky color at each vertex or fragment that matches the sky behind it.

One may be tempted to just use the same atmospheric scattering model for both the terrain and the sky to resolve these discrepancies. However, that's much easier said than done. Fog models intended for terrain will degrade to a constant color given large distances, so you can't simply treat your sky as an infinitely distant object because you'll end up with a flat, fog-colored sky. Trying to figure out the distance a ray of light will traverse before "leaving the atmosphere" of your sky won't do you any good, either. Because the density of the atmosphere changes as a function of altitude, it's not that simple. Recall from Figure 2.4 that the shape of the atmosphere also matters. Even if you could properly account for those effects, realistic sky colors also depend on modeling the scattered sunlight, reflections from the ground, air pollution, Mie scattering, amount of water vapor, and many other factors. This is why procedural sky shaders must resort to nonlinear regressions for realistic results, instead of actually trying to model these

2.2 Blending Terrain with the Sky

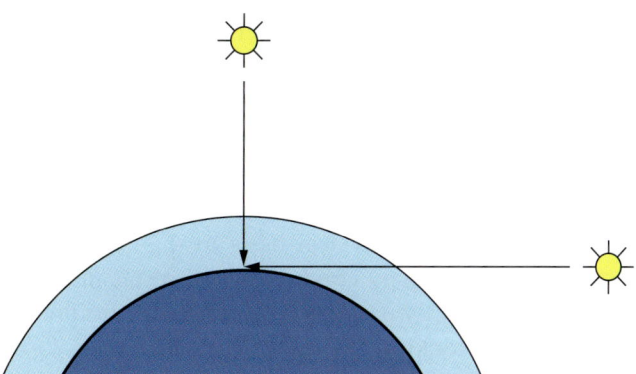

Figure 2.4. Sunlight arriving near the horizon must pass through more atmosphere than sunlight from overhead, yielding different sky colors.

different phenomena in real time. These procedural models are only appropriate for skies, and not terrain.

Still, one of the earliest analytic models of the sky attempted to use the same algorithms to apply atmospheric scattering to the terrain. It looks good under certain visibility conditions, but not in the general case. In fact, Figure 2.1 implements the Preetham / Hoffman model for atmospheric extinction [Hoffman and Preetham 2002] on terrain that accompanies the Preetham sky model used. But hand-tuning of constants is still required to produce good results for a given visibility condition.

All hope is not lost, however. There are some simple solutions that may produce visually satisfying results.

Blending the Sky Toward a Fixed Horizon Color

The simplest solution is to force a constant color in the sky near the horizon, which matches the fog color used for your terrain. Our SilverLining Sky SDK [Sundog] applies this in its sky shaders like this:

```
float fogDistance = volumeDistance / costheta;
float f = exp(-(fogDensity * fogDistance));
finalColor = mix(fogColor, skyColor, min(f, 1.0));
```

Here, `volumeDistance` represents the modeled visibility distance at the horizon, and `costheta` is the cosine of the angle between the zenith and a given point on the sky dome. This has the effect of fading in the desired fog color near the horizon in a reasonably realistic manner. The result is a more consistent sky color near the horizon, which does not vary with azimuth and varies little with elevation behind distant mountains. A good choice for the fog color is the computed sky color near the horizon in the view direction, before this additional fog is applied.

There is some physical basis to this approach. Fog tends to settle near the ground, and so foggy conditions will result in heavy scattering near the horizon but less so directly overhead. As a result, your brain will accept the resulting scene as natural looking.

This is a simple and fast way to eliminate anomalies resulting from fogged terrain against a realistic sky, but it does give up some realism at sunrise and sunset when you would expect the sky to look different at different azimuths. It is, however, the lesser of two evils.

Choosing a Better Fixed Fog Color

Another solution is to still use a completely analytic model for the sky, but choose your fixed fog color for the terrain more wisely. If your field of view isn't unrealistically wide, the variation in sky color as a function of azimuth usually won't be all that much within your view frustum. You can take advantage of this to still use a single fog color for your scene that matches your sky well enough in most situations.

What's needed is to implement the same algorithms in your sky shader on the CPU, so you can query the sky color for a given point on the sky and use that for the fog color in your scene. Choosing the correct point on the sky to sample is often the hard part in this approach. Analytic models can reach a discontinuity exactly at the horizon, which should be avoided. The distant mountains you are blending with the sky will be drawn just above the horizon line, not exactly on it, so you'll want to choose a point that is a degree or so above the horizon in the direction the camera is facing. Here's our code for choosing an azimuth angle to sample from the sky dome, given a view matrix:

```
Color Sky::GetAverageHorizonColor(double elevation)
{
    Matrix4    mv;
    Vector3    lookAt;

    Renderer::GetInstance()->GetModelviewMatrix(&mv);
```

2.2 Blending Terrain with the Sky

```
    mv = mv * Renderer::GetInstance()->GetInverseBasis4x4();

    if (Renderer::GetInstance()->GetIsRightHanded())
    {
        lookAt = Vector3(-mv.elem[2][0], -mv.elem[2][1], -mv.elem[2][2]);
    }
    else
    {
        lookAt = Vector3(mv.elem[2][0], mv.elem[2][1], mv.elem[2][2]);
    }

    double azimuth = DEGREES(atan2(lookAt.x, -lookAt.z));
    return GetAverageHorizonColor(azimuth, elevation);
}
```

This code assumes the presence of our own framework, but it conveys the general idea. The "inverse basis" matrix this code references simply handles differences between the sky's native coordinate system and the coordinate system used by the scene, if any. The *z* vector is extracted from the resulting view matrix, and the `atan2()` function is used to determine the azimuth angle the view is pointing towards.

While this approach may produce satisfying results during most times of day, it will still present problems near sunset and sunrise. If you're rotating the camera, the fog color will change noticeably as the camera goes across the area where the sun is because this is the part of the sky that changes the most as a function of azimuth. Seeing the fog color on the same bit of terrain change as a function of view angle isn't right. You can mitigate this by instead sampling several sky colors above the horizon from a range of azimuths centered on the view direction, and averaging them together. We've gotten satisfactory results by averaging eight sky colors across the scene's field of view. This smooths out fog color changes enough in most cases while still providing a good match between the sky and terrain for the scene as a whole.

This technique may be combined with the previous one. The fog color chosen in this manner may also be blended into your sky near the horizon to avoid any color inconsistencies at the horizon.

Using a Cube Map

The most accurate solution is to render your sky to a cube map, and modify your terrain shaders to sample this cube map to determine the best fog color at each vertex or fragment. All you need is the world-space vector from the eye to the terrain point to properly sample this cube map. When used with Rayleigh scattering shaders on terrain, this can produce wonderful results, as the "sky color" you are blending toward is known and consistent with the actual sky being displayed behind it.

This approach isn't always practical, though. Rendering the sky to six faces of a cube map can be expensive enough to cause dropped frames in some situations. If your application features continuous time of day changes, then the sky's cube map needs to be updated frequently, and that cost is incurred constantly. Rendering only one face per frame is one way to help spread out that cost.

One saving grace is that any 3D clouds in your scene, which would be the most expensive part of your sky, aren't needed for the purpose of creating a cube map for fog colors. So, any clouds in your scene may be omitted while generating the cube map. Not only does this make the cube map generation faster, but it also removes objects in the sky that move relative to the eye-point in your cube map. So you don't need to regenerate it as the camera moves, and you may use the same cube map to compute the fog colors for any object in your scene regardless of its position.

Your engine may already maintain a cube map of the sky for use as an environment map for reflections. If so, reusing this cube map to drive your fog colors is a simple choice.

2.3 Applying Visibility Effects to Distant Clouds

If your engine features 3D volumetric clouds, fogging them in a realistic manner against a dynamic sky background is even more challenging than with terrain. You can't assume they're near the horizon like your terrain is, plus they're at an altitude where atmospheric scattering behaves differently than it does near the ground.

The same issue seen with terrain exists when choosing an appropriate fog color for your clouds. You may use the same trick of sampling the sky color on the CPU at the location of each cloud and using that for the fog color, but there's an even better and simpler trick.

Assuming there are no large objects above the clouds in your scene, don't use a fog color at all on your clouds. Instead, fade them out as a function of their fog value. This gives you a perfect match with the sky colors behind them.

We compute a simple exponential-squared fog equation for our clouds. But instead of using the resulting fog value to interpolate between the cloud color and the fog color, we compute (1.0 - fog) and apply the result as the alpha value on the clouds.

It is worth noting that you generally don't want to apply the same fog density value to your clouds as you do to your terrain. Cumulus clouds are generally around 6 km high, and so typical fog density values seen near the ground would result in the clouds disappearing entirely with our scheme. While mathematically correct, it's not physically correct. The fog that affects your terrain may not exist at all, or at least be much thinner, at the altitude the clouds are at. As such, it's entirely reasonable to use a much smaller fog density value for your clouds than you use on your terrain.

In practice, choosing a separate fog density for your clouds by hand will yield the desired results with the least effort. But a slightly more principled approach may be followed if we assume that the fog affecting your terrain is uniform and underneath a fixed altitude. For example, the following code models a fog volume up to a given altitude, and assumes that typical eye points will be viewing the clouds at roughly a 45-degree angle through it. It then computes an appropriate adjusted fog density value for the clouds, which becomes smaller as the eye moves up toward the top of the fog volume. In the case where the eye is above the fog, a sufficiently small fog density for the clouds of your choosing should be applied as a default.

```
double distanceToEdgeOfFog = (fogHeight- eyeAltitude) * 1.414;
if (distanceToEdgeOfFog > 0.0)
{
    double cloudFogDensity = distanceToEdgeOfFog * fogDensity
            / cloudLayerAltitude;

    // Apply this fog density to your clouds, instead of some
    // small default density.
}
```

2.4 Creating Realistic Ocean Horizons

The same techniques discussed above for choosing realistic fog colors for terrain apply to oceans as well. But there's more to realistic ocean colors near the horizon than just fog. In addition to fog, the color of water is driven by a combination of reflected and refracted light, as given by the Fresnel equations. The reflectivity of the water may be accurately computed by the following GLSL code.

```
const float IOR = 1.33333;

vec3 P = reflect(vNorm, nNorm);
vec3 S = refract(P, nNorm, 1.0 / IOR);

float cos_theta1 = dot(P, nNorm);
float cos_theta2 = -dot(S, nNorm);

float Fp = (cos_theta1 - IOR * cos_theta2) /
           (IOR * cos_theta2 + cos_theta1);
float Fs = (cos_theta2 - IOR * cos_theta1) /
           (IOR * cos_theta1 + cos_theta2);

Fp = Fp * Fp;
Fs = Fs * Fs;

float reflectivity = clamp((Fs + Fp) * 0.5, 0.0, 1.0);
```

Here, `vNorm` is the normalized view vector to a fragment on the water, and `nNorm` is the surface normal. The resulting reflectivity value is used to blend between the color of reflected and refracted light at each fragment of the ocean surface.

As you can see, this result is highly dependent on the surface normal at each fragment. The refracted color in a deep ocean is usually a dark blue, while the reflected color is a lighter blue or gray sky color. Different surface normals can result in highly contrasting water colors.

What does this have to do with blending water into the sky? Well, think about just how quickly the surface normals on an ocean change. Every little wave has a huge effect on these normals, and as the water gets further away toward the horizon, these waves will be even smaller than your fragments or the resolution of your surface normal data. As such, properly averaging these normals when shading distant fragments is crucial to realistic results.

For color information, that's what mipmapping is for. But mipmaps don't work as well for normal maps. Unless the normals are all identical, averaging or interpolating normals will result in a vector with a length less than one. However, there's a simple fix:

1. Make sure your surface normals on the ocean are stored as simple (x, y, z) normal vectors applied to the RGB channels of a texture.

2. Enable mipmapping on that normal map.
3. When sampling the normal map in your shader, just renormalize the resulting vectors before using them in the Fresnel equations.

While this may all seem like an obvious thing to do, ocean rendering that is based on fast Fourier transforms (such as that described by [Tessendorf 2001]) actually lends itself to storing surface normals not as unit-length normal vectors, but instead as slopes in the x and y directions. Mipmapping that information doesn't produce the correct results at all and ends up producing perfectly reflective water in the distance even in rough seas. When using real normal maps instead and renormalizing their mipmapped samples, the water at the horizon will get darker as the waves get rougher, which is what happens in the real world as more refracted light is seen from the waves that are facing you.

Incidentally, you want to use the raw, mipmapped normal vector in your lighting equations without rescaling to unit length, or else aliasing may result from specular highlights. Having smaller normal vectors in the distance is a desirable effect when doing things like bump-mapping because bumpy surfaces should appear smoother when viewed from very far away. The problem of specular aliasing is treated in much more detail by Nvidia [Toksvig 2005] and by the LEAN Mapping technique [Olano and Baker 2010], if you're interested. It is also relevant to the topic of realistic depictions of distant objects.

2.5 Putting it All Together

Figure 2.5 shows the end result of applying all of these techniques. Note the smooth blending of clouds, terrain, and sky as well as the distinct horizon line over the ocean.

Inconsistent application of visibility effects on outdoor scenes is one of those things that lead to scenes just looking "wrong" even if the user can't quite articulate why. By paying attention to these details, your expansive terrains, skies, and oceans will become more believable and immersive.

Figure 2.5. Consistent visibility effects on distant terrain, clouds, and water yields believable scenes with reduced visibility.

References

[Ebert 2003] David S. Ebert. *Texturing & Modeling: A Procedural Approach*. Morgan Kaufmann, 2003.

[Hoffman and Preetham 2002] Nathaniel Hoffman and Arcot J. Preetham. "Rendering outdoor light scattering in real time". *Proceedings of Game Developers Conference 2002*, pp. 337–352.

[Hosek et al. 2012] Lukas Hosek and Alexander Wilkie. "An analytic model for full spectral sky-dome radiance". *ACM Transactions on Graphics*, Vol. 31, No. 4 (July 2012), Article 95.

[Olano and Baker 2010] Marc Olano and Dan Baker. "LEAN mapping". *Proceedings of the 2010 ACM SIGGRAPH symposium on Interactive 3D Graphics and Games*, pp. 181–188.

[Preetham et al. 1999] Arcot J. Preetham, Peter Shirley, and Brian Smits. "A practical analytic model for daylight". *Proceedings of the 26th annual conference on computer graphics and interactive techniques*, 1999, pp. 91–100.

[Sundog] Sundog Software website, http://www.sundog-soft.com/

References

[Tessendorf 2001] Jerry Tessendorf. "Simulating ocean water". *Proceedings of SIGGRAPH 2001*.

[Toksvig 2005] Michael Toksvig. "Mipmapping normal maps". *Journal of graphics, GPU, and game tools*, Vol. 10, No. 3 (2005), pp. 65–71.

3

Fog with a Linear Density Function

Eric Lengyel
Terathon Software

3.1 Introduction

In this chapter, we consider a fog volume inside which the density of the fog is a linear function of distance along some given direction. This naturally gives rise to a halfspace bounded by a plane where the density function is zero. On one side of the plane, the fog grows thicker as the distance from the plane increases, and on the other side of the plane, there is no fog at all. Such a fog volume has many uses in games ranging from heavy mist trapped in a valley to murky waters in a swamp. An example outdoor scene is shown in Figure 3.1.

We first derive a unified formula that allows us to render halfspace fog for all possible configurations in which the camera position and point being shaded are inside or outside the fog volume. Then, we examine the problem of determining which objects in the scene can be skipped when rendering because they are either too deep or too far away inside the fog volume to be visible.

The mathematics in this chapter are written in terms of four-dimensional Grassmann algebra. This means that we are using homogeneous coordinates and making a distinction between vectors and points. A vector $\mathbf{V} = (V_x, V_y, V_z, 0)$ is written in bold style and always has a w coordinate of zero. A point $\mathcal{P} = (P_x, P_y, P_z, 1)$ is written in script style and always has a w coordinate of one. A plane is represented by a trivector $\mathbf{F} = (F_x, F_y, F_z, F_w)$ that we also write in the bold style. A plane $\mathbf{F}$ can be multiplied by a vector $\mathbf{V}$ or a point $\mathcal{P}$ using the wedge product to produce a scalar as follows:

$$\mathbf{F} \wedge \mathbf{V} = F_x V_x + F_y V_y + F_z V_z$$
$$\mathbf{F} \wedge \mathcal{P} = F_x P_x + F_y P_y + F_z P_z + F_w. \tag{3.1}$$

Figure 3.1. This is an example of a fog volume that uses a linear density function. The fog plane (at which the density is zero) lies at a small distance above the camera position.

If the plane **F** is normalized, meaning that $F_x^2 + F_y^2 + F_z^2 = 1$, then the product $\mathbf{F} \wedge \mathcal{P}$ gives the signed perpendicular distance between the plane **F** and the point $\mathcal{P}$. As illustrated in Figure 3.2, the normal direction of our fog plane points outward from the fog volume, so $\mathbf{F} \wedge \mathcal{P} < 0$ for points $\mathcal{P}$ below the fog plane in the fogged halfspace, and $\mathbf{F} \wedge \mathcal{P} > 0$ for points $\mathcal{P}$ above the fog plane in the unfogged halfspace.

3.2 Fog Factor Calculation

The fog factor f determines how the shaded color calculated on a surface is mixed with the fog color before it is finally output from a fragment shader. For fog having a constant density ρ, the fog factor is typically calculated with the formula

$$f = e^{-\rho d}, \tag{3.2}$$

where d is the distance between the point being shaded and the camera position. Once the fog factor has been calculated, it is clamped to the range $[0,1]$, and the

3.2 Fog Factor Calculation

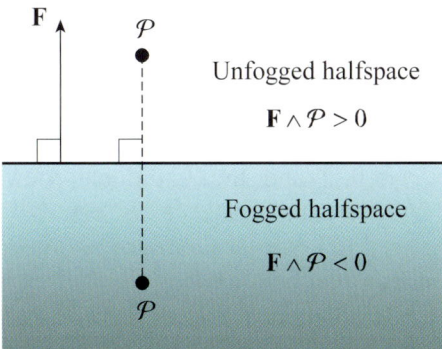

Figure 3.2. A point $\mathcal{P}$ in the fogged halfspace forms a negative wedge product with the fog plane **F**, and a point $\mathcal{P}$ in the unfogged halfspace forms a positive wedge product.

fragment's final color K_{final} is blended with a constant fog color K_{fog} to produce the color K that is written the frame buffer using the formula

$$K = fK_{\text{final}} + (1-f)K_{\text{fog}}. \tag{3.3}$$

What follows is the derivation for the case that a linear density function $\rho(\mathcal{P})$, depending on the point $\mathcal{P}$ being shaded, is used instead of a constant density [Lengyel 2007]. We account for the fact that the distance d is no longer necessarily equal to the total distance to the camera because the point $\mathcal{P}$ and the camera position may lie on opposite sides of the fog plane.

Derivation

Let the density function $\rho(\mathcal{P})$ be defined as

$$\rho(\mathcal{P}) = -a(\mathbf{F} \wedge \mathcal{P}) \tag{3.4}$$

for some positive constant a, and let dg represent the contribution to the fog factor exponent along a differential length ds, given by the product

$$dg = \rho(\mathcal{P})ds. \tag{3.5}$$

By integrating over the portion of the path that lies beneath the fog plane between the shaded point $\mathcal{P}$ and the camera position C, we obtain a function $g(\mathcal{P})$ that can be substituted for the product ρd in Equation (3.2).

Let the function

$$Q(t) = \mathcal{P} + t\mathbf{V} \qquad (3.6)$$

represent the line segment connecting the shaded point $\mathcal{P}$ with the camera position C, where $t \in [0,1]$ and the traditional view direction $\mathbf{V}$ is defined as $\mathbf{V} = C - \mathcal{P}$. The differential distance ds can be expressed in terms of t as $ds = \|\mathbf{V}\|dt$. We need to consider the four possible configurations of the points $\mathcal{P}$ and C with respect to the boundary plane, as illustrated in Figure 3.3. Of course, if $\mathbf{F} \wedge \mathcal{P}$ and $\mathbf{F} \wedge C$ are both positive, then no part of the line segment travels through the fog volume, and $g(\mathcal{P}) = 0$. In the case that $\mathbf{F} \wedge \mathcal{P} < 0$ and $\mathbf{F} \wedge C < 0$, we integrate over the entire distance between $\mathcal{P}$ and C to obtain

$$g(\mathcal{P}) = \int_{\mathcal{P}}^{C} dg = \int_{0}^{1} \rho(Q(t)) \|\mathbf{V}\| dt$$

$$= -\frac{a}{2} \|\mathbf{V}\| (\mathbf{F} \wedge \mathcal{P} + \mathbf{F} \wedge C). \qquad (3.7)$$

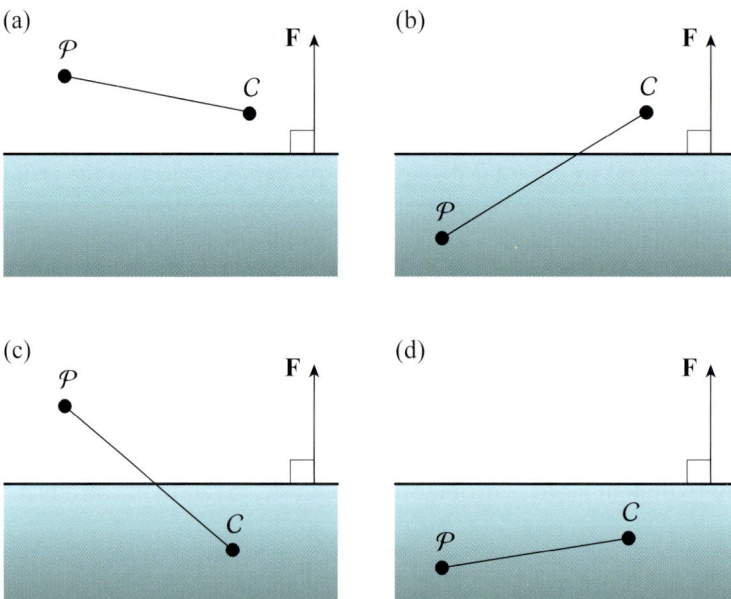

Figure 3.3. For a surface point $\mathcal{P}$ and a camera position C, there are four distinct configurations to consider when integrating over the portion of the path between them that lies within the fogged halfspace.

3.2 Fog Factor Calculation

In the two remaining cases, in which $\mathbf{F} \wedge \mathcal{P}$ and $\mathbf{F} \wedge C$ have opposite signs, we must integrate over only the part of the path that lies inside the fog volume. The parameter t_{plane} at which the line segment $Q(t)$ passes through the fog plane is given by

$$t_{\text{plane}} = -\frac{\mathbf{F} \wedge \mathcal{P}}{\mathbf{F} \wedge \mathbf{V}}, \tag{3.8}$$

and this becomes one of the limits of integration. In the case that only $\mathbf{F} \wedge \mathcal{P} < 0$, we have

$$g(\mathcal{P}) = \int_0^{t_{\text{plane}}} \rho(Q(t)) \|\mathbf{V}\| dt$$

$$= \frac{a}{2} \|\mathbf{V}\| \frac{(\mathbf{F} \wedge \mathcal{P})^2}{\mathbf{F} \wedge \mathbf{V}}, \tag{3.9}$$

and in the case that only $\mathbf{F} \wedge C < 0$, we have

$$g(\mathcal{P}) = \int_{t_{\text{plane}}}^1 \rho(Q(t)) \|\mathbf{V}\| dt$$

$$= -\frac{a}{2} \|\mathbf{V}\| \left(\mathbf{F} \wedge \mathcal{P} + \mathbf{F} \wedge C + \frac{(\mathbf{F} \wedge \mathcal{P})^2}{\mathbf{F} \wedge \mathbf{V}} \right). \tag{3.10}$$

The following table summarizes the fog functions $g(\mathcal{P})$ for the four possible cases shown in Figure 3.3. Our goal is to combine these into a single formula that produces the correct fog function in all cases without expensive branches or other conditional code in a fragment shader.

Case	$\mathbf{F} \wedge \mathcal{P}$	$\mathbf{F} \wedge C$	Fog Function $g(\mathcal{P})$
(a)	Positive	Positive	0
(b)	Negative	Positive	$\frac{a}{2} \|\mathbf{V}\| \frac{(\mathbf{F} \wedge \mathcal{P})^2}{\mathbf{F} \wedge \mathbf{V}}$
(c)	Positive	Negative	$-\frac{a}{2} \|\mathbf{V}\| \left(\mathbf{F} \wedge \mathcal{P} + \mathbf{F} \wedge C + \frac{(\mathbf{F} \wedge \mathcal{P})^2}{\mathbf{F} \wedge \mathbf{V}} \right)$
(d)	Negative	Negative	$-\frac{a}{2} \|\mathbf{V}\| (\mathbf{F} \wedge \mathcal{P} + \mathbf{F} \wedge C)$

First, we can make use of the fact that $\mathbf{F} \wedge \mathbf{V}$ is always positive in case (b) and always negative in case (c). By applying an absolute value to $\mathbf{F} \wedge \mathbf{V}$, we can merge cases (b) and (c) into one formula and write $g(\mathcal{P})$ as

$$g(\mathcal{P}) = -\frac{a}{2}\|\mathbf{V}\|\left[k(\mathbf{F} \wedge \mathcal{P} + \mathbf{F} \wedge C) - \frac{(\mathbf{F} \wedge \mathcal{P})^2}{|\mathbf{F} \wedge \mathbf{V}|}\right], \quad (3.11)$$

where the constant k is defined as

$$k = \begin{cases} 1, & \text{if } \mathbf{F} \wedge C \leq 0; \\ 0, & \text{otherwise.} \end{cases} \quad (3.12)$$

In order to incorporate case (d) into this formula, we need to eliminate the last term inside the brackets whenever $\mathbf{F} \wedge \mathcal{P}$ and $\mathbf{F} \wedge C$ have the same sign. This can be accomplished by replacing $\mathbf{F} \wedge \mathcal{P}$ with $\min((\mathbf{F} \wedge \mathcal{P})\operatorname{sgn}(\mathbf{F} \wedge C), 0)$ in the last term to arrive at the formula

$$g(\mathcal{P}) = -\frac{a}{2}\|\mathbf{V}\|\left[k(\mathbf{F} \wedge \mathcal{P} + \mathbf{F} \wedge C) - \frac{[\min((\mathbf{F} \wedge \mathcal{P})\operatorname{sgn}(\mathbf{F} \wedge C), 0)]^2}{|\mathbf{F} \wedge \mathbf{V}|}\right]. \quad (3.13)$$

This formula also works for case (a) because both terms are eliminated when $\mathbf{F} \wedge \mathcal{P}$ and $\mathbf{F} \wedge C$ are both positive, so we have found a single unified fog function that can be used in all cases. It may look complicated, but it is inexpensive to evaluate in a shader because $\mathcal{P}$ and $\mathbf{V}$ are the only values that vary.

Note that in Equation (3.13), if the quantity $\mathbf{F} \wedge \mathbf{V}$ is zero, then it is always true that the numerator of the last term is also zero. Although in practice a zero-divided-by-zero situation is rare enough to be ignored, a small positive ε can be added to $|\mathbf{F} \wedge \mathbf{V}|$ in the denominator to guarantee that a NaN is not produced without affecting the fog function's value significantly.

Implementation

A fragment shader implementation of the unified fog function $g(\mathcal{P})$ given by Equation (3.13) is shown in Listing 3.1. We can calculate the quantities $\mathbf{V}$, $\mathbf{F} \wedge \mathbf{V}$, $k(\mathbf{F} \wedge \mathcal{P} + \mathbf{F} \wedge C)$, and $(\mathbf{F} \wedge \mathcal{P})\operatorname{sgn}(\mathbf{F} \wedge C)$ in the vertex shader and interpolate them during triangle rasterization. This leaves only a somewhat small amount of computation to be performed in the fragment shader. The fog factor f is calculated as

$$f = \operatorname{sat}\left(2^{-g(\mathcal{P})/\ln 2}\right), \quad (3.14)$$

3.2 Fog Factor Calculation

Listing 3.1. This GLSL fragment shader code implements the unified fog function given by Equation (3.13), calculates the fog factor using Equation (3.14), and uses the fog factor to interpolate between the shader's final color and the fog color.

```
uniform float density;    // a / (2 ln 2)
uniform vec3 fogColor;

in vec3 V;                // V = C - P
in float FV;              // F ^ V
in float c1;              // k * (F ^ P + F ^ C)
in float c2;              // (F ^ P) * sgn(F ^ C)

void main()
{
   vec4 color = ...;      // Final shaded surface color.

   // Calculate g(P) using Equation (3.13).
   float g = min(c2, 0.0);
   g = length(V) * (c1 - g * g / abs(FV)) * density;

   // Calculate fog factor and apply.
   float f = clamp(exp2(g), 0.0, 1.0);

   color.rgb = color.rgb * f + fogColor * (1.0 - f);
   ...
}
```

where the sat function clamps to the range $[0,1]$. The negative signs appearing in front of the right side of Equation (3.13) and in the exponent of Equation (3.14) cancel each other, so neither appears in the code.

Infinite Geometry

For geometry rendered at infinity, such as a skybox, vertices are no longer represented by homogeneous points $\mathcal{P}$ having an implicit one in the w coordinate, but are instead given by direction vectors $\mathbf{D}$ having an implicit zero in the w coordinate. In this case, a fragment is always fully fogged whenever $\mathbf{F} \wedge \mathbf{D} < 0$, regardless of the value of $\mathbf{F} \wedge C$, because the ray given by

$$\mathcal{R}(t) = C + t\mathbf{D} \tag{3.15}$$

travels an infinite distance through the fog volume. The only nontrivial case is the one in which $\mathbf{F} \wedge \mathbf{D} > 0$ and $\mathbf{F} \wedge C < 0$, where the camera is inside the fog volume, and the direction $\mathbf{D}$ to the fragment being rendered points upward out of the fog volume.

To formulate the function $g(\mathcal{P})$ for infinite geometry, we need to integrate from the camera position C to the point where $\mathcal{R}(t)$ crosses the fog plane. This point is given by the parameter

$$t_{\text{plane}} = -\frac{\mathbf{F} \wedge C}{\mathbf{F} \wedge \mathbf{D}}, \tag{3.16}$$

and thus, the integral defining our fog function is

$$g(\mathcal{P}) = \int_0^{t_{\text{plane}}} \rho(\mathcal{R}(t)) \|\mathbf{D}\| dt$$

$$= \frac{a}{2} \|\mathbf{D}\| \frac{(\mathbf{F} \wedge C)^2}{\mathbf{F} \wedge \mathbf{D}}. \tag{3.17}$$

In order to use this function in all cases, we can clamp the fog factor calculation using bounds derived from $\mathbf{F} \wedge C$ and $\mathbf{F} \wedge \mathbf{D}$ to obtain

$$f = \text{clamp}\left(2^{-g(\mathcal{P})/\ln 2}, u, v\right), \tag{3.18}$$

where u and v are defined as

$$u = \begin{cases} 1, & \text{if } \mathbf{F} \wedge C > 0 \text{ and } \mathbf{F} \wedge \mathbf{D} > 0; \\ 0, & \text{otherwise;} \end{cases}$$

$$v = \begin{cases} 1, & \text{if } \mathbf{F} \wedge \mathbf{D} > 0; \\ 0, & \text{otherwise.} \end{cases} \tag{3.19}$$

If $\mathbf{F} \wedge \mathbf{D} \leq 0$, in which case the ray $\mathcal{R}(t)$ must enter the fog volume at some point, then both u and v are zero, and the pixel being shaded is always fully fogged. If $\mathbf{F} \wedge \mathbf{D} > 0$, then the fog factor can be less than one only if $\mathbf{F} \wedge C \leq 0$, corresponding to the case that the camera is inside the fog volume.

3.3 Visibility Culling

When rendering a scene with fog, objects can be far enough away from the camera to become imperceptible even though the fog factor f never reaches zero in a strictly mathematical sense. For example, a fog factor of 1/256 is too small for the light reflected from an object to make any difference when the display uses 8-bit color channels, and the rendered output would be 100% fog color. If we can calculate the distance at which the fog factor becomes this small, then we can cull any objects lying beyond that distance because they won't be visible. Due to the way the human visual system works, a significantly larger factor can be used to calculate the cutoff distance when the fog color has a bright intensity.

If we calculate the exact surface at which the fog factor reaches some small constant for a given camera position, then we get a shape such as the one shown in Figure 3.4, with some variation depending on the camera depth in the fog volume. (The formula for this curve is derived below.) Culling objects directly against this surface would be impractical, so we instead calculate the maximum distances at which objects would be visible in a couple different directions and place culling planes at those locations relative to the camera. First, we determine the vertical depth beneath the camera position within the fog volume at which objects become fully fogged and place a culling plane there that is parallel to the fog plane. This involves a simple, straightforward calculation. Second, we determine the horizontal distance (parallel to the fog plane) at which objects would be culled at *all* depths and place a culling plane at that distance from the camera aligned to be perpendicular to the camera's view direction. This calculation turns out to be much more complicated, but it has an elegant solution [Lengyel 2015].

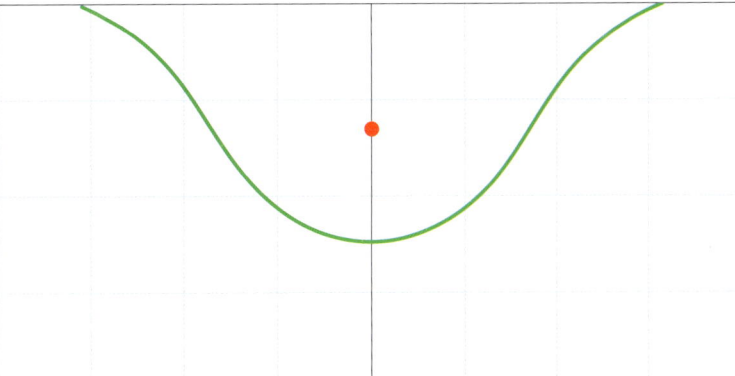

Figure 3.4. The green curve represents the exact surface at which the fog factor reaches a small constant value given the camera position (red dot) beneath the fog plane at the top of the graph.

In both cases, we determine the distance to the culling plane by setting the fog factor $f = e^{-g(\mathcal{P})}$ to a constant c small enough to be considered the cutoff value for perceptibility (such as $c = 1/256$). This means that $g(\mathcal{P})$ can be treated as the constant value

$$g(\mathcal{P}) = -\ln c \tag{3.20}$$

in any of the fog function equations in the previous section.

Vertical Depth

To cull objects by vertical depth, we need to find the distance d directly beneath the camera, opposite the normal direction of the fog plane, at which an object becomes completely fogged within the tolerance set by Equation (3.20). We assume that the camera is inside the fog volume, which means $\mathbf{F} \wedge C \leq 0$. In the case that the camera is above the fog plane, we can just set $\mathbf{F} \wedge C = 0$ because it wouldn't change the amount of fog through which a ray pointing straight down from the camera would pass.

Starting with Equation (3.7) and recognizing that $\|\mathbf{V}\| = d$, we have

$$g(\mathcal{P}) = -\frac{a}{2} d (\mathbf{F} \wedge \mathcal{P} + \mathbf{F} \wedge C). \tag{3.21}$$

For a point $\mathcal{P}$ lying directly below the camera position such that the vector $C - \mathcal{P}$ is perpendicular to the fog plane, we have $d = \mathbf{F} \wedge C - \mathbf{F} \wedge \mathcal{P}$, and we can thus make the substitution

$$\mathbf{F} \wedge \mathcal{P} + \mathbf{F} \wedge C = 2(\mathbf{F} \wedge C) - d. \tag{3.22}$$

This leads us to the quadratic equation

$$d^2 - 2d(\mathbf{F} \wedge C) - m = 0, \tag{3.23}$$

where we have set $m = 2g(\mathcal{P})/a$. The solution providing a positive distance d is then given by

$$d = \mathbf{F} \wedge C + \sqrt{(\mathbf{F} \wedge C)^2 + m}. \tag{3.24}$$

A plane parallel to the fog plane can be placed at this distance below the camera position to safely cull objects that are too deep in the fog volume to be visible.

3.3 Visibility Culling

Horizontal Distance

To cull objects in the horizontal direction, we need to find the minimum distance parallel to the fog plane beyond which objects are completely fogged (again, within tolerance) at all depths in the fog volume. This requires that we somehow find the maximum horizontal distance d for which Equation (3.7) holds true for a given constant $g(\mathcal{P})$, where d is the length of the projection of $\mathbf{V}$ onto the fog plane. Some examples of the distance d are shown in Figure 3.5, which also illustrates how the culling surfaces can be classified into three general varieties that are discussed below.

The problem of finding the correct culling distance d becomes much easier to tackle if we write $\mathbf{F} \wedge \mathcal{P}$ as a multiple of $\mathbf{F} \wedge C$ so we can make the substitution

$$\mathbf{F} \wedge \mathcal{P} = t(\mathbf{F} \wedge C). \tag{3.25}$$

Equation (3.7) can then be written as

$$g(\mathcal{P}) = -\frac{a}{2}\|\mathbf{V}\|(t+1)(\mathbf{F} \wedge C). \tag{3.26}$$

The vector $\mathbf{V}$ still depends on the point $\mathcal{P}$, but its length can be expressed in terms of the horizontal distance d and the depth of the camera position C by considering the right triangle shown in Figure 3.6, giving us

$$\|\mathbf{V}\|^2 = d^2 + (1-t)^2 (\mathbf{F} \wedge C)^2. \tag{3.27}$$

We can now rewrite Equation (3.26) as

$$g(\mathcal{P}) = -\frac{a}{2}(t+1)(\mathbf{F} \wedge C)\sqrt{d^2 + (1-t)^2 (\mathbf{F} \wedge C)^2}, \tag{3.28}$$

and this depends only on the known quantities $g(\mathcal{P})$ and $\mathbf{F} \wedge C$.

Solving Equation (3.28) for d^2 produces the function

$$d^2 = \frac{m^2}{(t+1)^2 (\mathbf{F} \wedge C)^2} - (1-t)^2 (\mathbf{F} \wedge C)^2 \tag{3.29}$$

that returns the squared culling distance for any input t representing the depth of a point $\mathcal{P}$, where we have again set $m = 2g(\mathcal{P})/a$. We can find the local maxima for the squared distance by taking a derivative of this function with respect to t and setting it equal to zero. After some simplification, we end up with the quartic equation

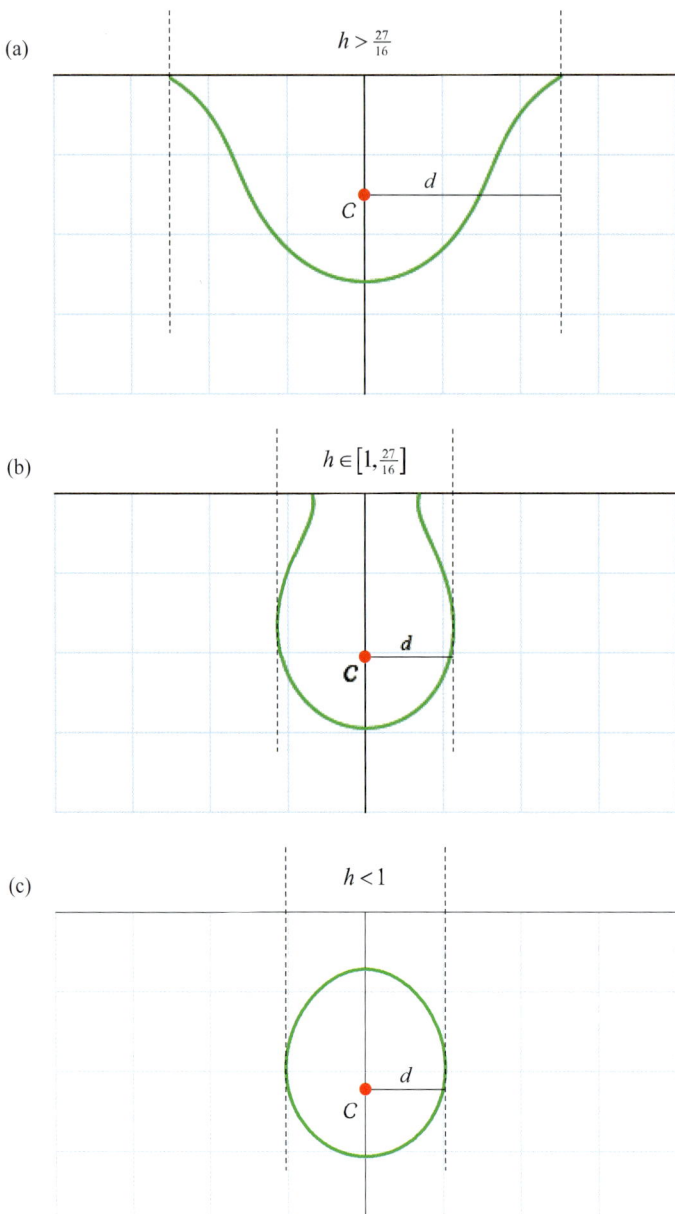

Figure 3.5. The horizontal culling distance *d* is equal to the maximum distance parallel to the fog plane beyond which objects are completely fogged. The green curves represent the exact culling surfaces that can be classified into three cases depending on the value of *h*, defined by Equation (3.31).

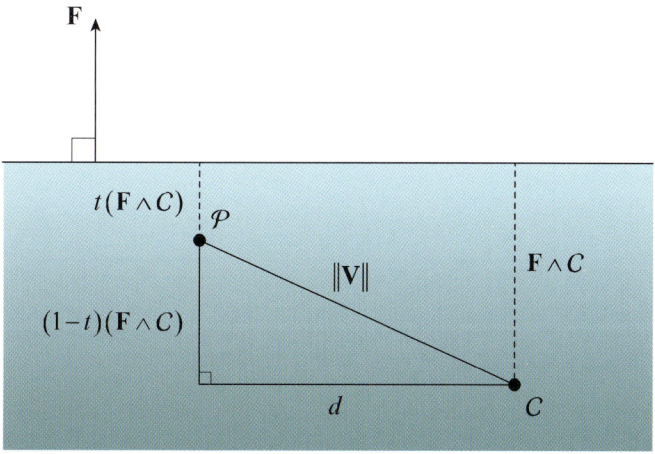

Figure 3.6. The length of the vector $\mathbf{V}$ can be expressed in terms of the distance d and the depths of the points C and $\mathcal{P}$.

$$q(t) = t^4 + 2t^3 - 2t + h - 1 = 0, \qquad (3.30)$$

where we have named the polynomial $q(t)$ and defined

$$h = \frac{m^2}{(\mathbf{F} \wedge C)^4}. \qquad (3.31)$$

A typical plot of the quartic function $q(t)$ in Equation (3.30) is shown in Figure 3.7. There are a couple of important properties that we can identify about this function. First, it is always the case that $q(1) = h$, and h is a positive number. Second, if we take a derivative to get

$$q'(t) = 4t^3 + 6t^2 - 2, \qquad (3.32)$$

then we see that $q'(\frac{1}{2}) = 0$, which means that $q(t)$ always has a local minimum at $t = \frac{1}{2}$. If the actual value of $q(t)$ is negative at $t = \frac{1}{2}$, then $q(t)$ must have a root in the range $(\frac{1}{2}, 1)$, and this is the value of t that we are looking for. By evaluating $q(\frac{1}{2})$, we see that this root exists precisely when $h < 27/16$, and this corresponds to cases (b) and (c) in Figure 3.5.

It may be tempting to find the roots of $q(t)$ by using an analytical solution, but in this case, the root in which we are interested can be found much more efficiently and accurately by using Newton's method with an initial value of $t_0 = 1$.

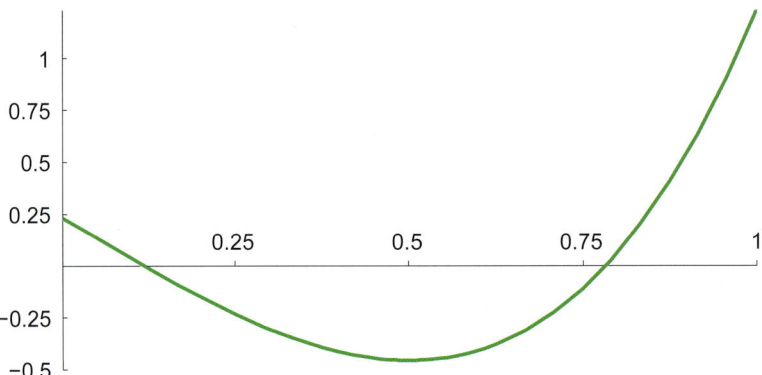

Figure 3.7. This is a plot of the function $q(t) = t^4 + 2t^3 - 2t + h - 1$ with $g(\mathcal{P}) = \ln 256$, $a = 0.1$, and $\mathbf{F} \wedge C = -10$, giving an approximate value of $h = 1.23$.

Recall that Newton's method refines an approximation t_i of a root using the formula

$$t_{i+1} = t_i - \frac{q(t_i)}{q'(t_i)}. \qquad (3.33)$$

We know right at the beginning that $q(1) = h$ and $q'(1) = 8$, so the first iteration of Newton's method can be explicitly calculated with ease to obtain

$$t_1 = 1 - \frac{h}{8}. \qquad (3.34)$$

One or two more iterations are all that are needed to produce an extremely accurate result that can be plugged back into Equation (3.29) to calculate the culling distance d.

If $h > 1$, then $d^2 > 0$ when $t = 0$, and it may be the case that the largest horizontal distance to the culling surface occurs on the fog plane itself. This corresponds to cases (a) and (b) in Figure 3.5. When $t = 0$, the distance d is given by

$$d = -(\mathbf{F} \wedge C)\sqrt{h-1}, \qquad (3.35)$$

where we have been careful to negate $\mathbf{F} \wedge C$ when factoring it out of the radical after taking square roots of both sides in Equation (3.29).

If $h \in [1, \frac{27}{16}]$, then the distance given by the root of Equation (3.30) and the distance given directly by Equation (3.35) are both valid, and the larger must be

3.3 Visibility Culling

chosen as the horizontal culling distance. This corresponds to case (b) in Figure 3.5. Otherwise, only one of the distances can be calculated and is thus the only choice for the horizontal culling distance. Listing 3.2 implements the distance calculations and handles all three of the possible cases.

Listing 3.2. This C++ code implements the horizontal culling distance calculations for a given value of $\mathbf{F} \wedge C$ passed in the `F_wedge_C` parameter. The constant `kFogCutoff` is the value of c in Equation (3.20), and the constant `kFogDensity` is the value of a in Equation (3.4).

```cpp
float CalculateHorizontalCullingDistance(float F_wedge_C)
{
    // Calculate m using Equation (3.20) for g(P).
    float m = -2.0F * log(kFogCutoff) / kFogDensity;
    float m2 = m * m;

    float d = 0.0F;
    float z2 = F_wedge_C * F_wedge_C;
    float zinv = 1.0F / F_wedge_C;
    float zinv2 = zinv * zinv;

    // Calculate h using Equation (3.31).
    float h = m2 * zinv2 * zinv2;
    if (h < 1.6875F)
    {
        // Here, h < 27/16, so a root to q(t) exists.

        // Explicitly calculate first iteration of Newton's method.
        float t = 1.0F - h * 0.125F;
        float t2 = t * t;

        // Apply Newton's method one more time.
        t -= (((t + 2.0F) * t2 - 2.0F) * t + (h - 1.0F)) /
             ((t * 4.0F + 6.0F) * t2 - 2.0F);

        // Plug root back into Equation (3.29).
        float tp = t + 1.0F;
        float tm = t - 1.0F;
        d = sqrt(m2 * zinv2 / (tp * tp) - tm * tm * z2);
    }
```

```
    if (h > 1.0F)
    {
        // Calculate the distance on the fog plane using Equation (3.35).
        // If both solutions exist, take the larger distance.
        d = max(-F_wedge_C * sqrt(h - 1.0F), d);
    }

    return (d);
}
```

References

[Lengyel 2007] Eric Lengyel. "Unified Distance Formulas for Halfspace Fog". *Journal of Graphics Tools*, Vol. 12, No. 2 (2007), pp. 23–32.

[Lengyel 2015] Eric Lengyel. "Game Math Case Studies". Game Developers Conference, 2015. Available at http://www.terathon.com/gdc15_lengyel.pdf.

4

Vegetation Management in Leadwerks Game Engine 4

Josh Klint
Leadwerks Software

4.1 Introduction

Although rendering capabilities of graphics hardware have increased substantially over the last generation, a specialized system for managing vegetation rendering and physics still performs an order of magnitude faster than a general purpose object management system and can use a small fraction of the memory that would otherwise be required. These optimizations are possible due to the unique characteristics of vegetation.

First, trees, bushes, and plants tend to be highly repetitive in nature, at least to the casual observer. One pine tree looks pretty much like any other. Variations in rotation, scale, and color are enough to convince the viewer that an entire forest made up of only a few unique tree models contains infinite variety.

Second, plants tend to be distributed in a roughly uniform manner. Areas with optimal conditions for growth tend to be filled with plant life, while inhospitable conditions (e.g., a steep cliff side) tend to be barren. Individual instances of plants repel one another as they compete for resources, resulting in a roughly uniform distribution. An extreme manmade example of this is an orchard where trees are planted in rows of equal spacing to make maximum use of the earth.

Finally, plants grow along the surface of the earth, which for practical purposes can be considered a 2D plane with a height offset. This means that their position in 3D space can be predicted and described in a compact manner.

These characteristics provide the opportunity for unique optimizations that can manage a larger volume of plant instances than a general-purpose object management system is capable of. This chapter describes our implementation of

Figure 4.1. A sample scene demonstrating several vegetation layers for different types of objects. This scene is included with the demo on the book's website.

such a system to handle both rendering and physics of large volumes of vegetation. The visual results of our implementation are shown in Figure 4.1, rendered in real time.

4.2 The Problem

In Leadwerks Game Engine 2, vegetation instances were stored in the scene file as a sequence of 4×4 matrices. Instances were read into memory and placed into a quadtree data structure. Chunks of instances were merged into single surfaces made of quads. A series of 2D images of the vegetation object was rendered at run time and displayed on the merged surfaces when the quadtree node reached a certain distance from the camera. Quadtree nodes closer than the billboard distance were iterated through, and all instances were individually culled and displayed as full-resolution 3D models. For physics, a specialized collision type was employed that accepted an array of 4×4 matrices and a scale factor for each axis.

This system allowed large, expansive landscapes to be rendered in real time with fast performance, but it also presented two problems. First, the rendering system involved significant CPU overhead. This was particularly taxing when performing frustum culling on quadtree nodes that were closer than the billboard LOD distance because each instance had to be tested individually. Second, each vegetation instance required the storage of a 4×4 matrix in two places (for physics and in the quadtree structure) plus a scaling factor for physics. Although 140 bytes per instance may seem minimal, the memory requirements became quite large in densely packed scenes and could grow to several hundred megabytes of data. This requirement seemed unnecessary, and it limited the ability of our vegetation system to scale.

Since our future plans involve expanded game worlds beyond the bounds of 32-bit floating point precision, it makes sense to build a more scalable vegetation management system now. At the beginning of our implementation of a new vegetation management system for Leadwerks Game Engine 4, we set out with the following design parameters:

- Fast rendering and physics performance.
- Low-or-no marginal memory consumption per instance.
- Ability to dynamically add and remove vegetation instances instantly (to provide better support for farm simulators and other games that alter the landscape).

We targeted hardware that supports OpenGL 4.0, which is equivalent to DirectX 11 and includes both discrete and integrated GPUs from Nvidia, AMD, and Intel.

4.3 The Idea

The Sierra Nevada mountain range in the western United States provides ample opportunities for hiking, mountain biking, and camping, with nine national forests and three national parks to visit. If you've ever hiked through the Sierras, you know that the view is pretty much "trees, everywhere". Trees do not grow directly on top of each other, and no good spot goes bare for long before something grows there.

The simplest approximation of this experience we could design would be a grid of tree instances that surround the camera, stretching out to the maximum view distance. This arrangement of trees lacks the apparent randomness found in nature, but if we use the tree's (x,z) position as a seed value, it should be possible to procedurally generate a rotation and scale for a more natural appearance. An additional offset can be generated to break up the appearance of the grid distribution and make it appear more random while retaining the roughly constant density of natural vegetation. A texture lookup on the terrain height map can then be used to retrieve the y (vertical) position of the tree on the landscape.

An initial test application was easily implemented and indicated that this gave a satisfactory appearance, but a full vegetation system with culling, LOD, and physics based on this idea was quite another thing to implement. The first challenge was to devise a system that would produce identical procedural noise on both the GPU and CPU.

The first attempt used a pseudorandom noise function in GLSL to generate unique results from each instance's (x, z) position. There were two problems with this idea. First, the performance penalty for using this to generate rotated 4×4 matrices for each vertex would be significant. Second, it was feared that small discrepancies in floating-point computations between different graphics hardware and CPU architectures could result in a misalignment of the procedural data calculated for graphics and physics.

To solve these issues, a small grid of instance data was generated. Each grid space stores a 4×4 matrix with the color contained in the right-hand column as follows.

$$\begin{bmatrix} m_{00} & m_{01} & m_{02} & brightness \\ m_{10} & m_{11} & m_{12} & m_{13} \\ m_{20} & m_{21} & m_{22} & m_{23} \\ m_{30} & m_{31} & m_{32} & scale \end{bmatrix}$$

This data is enough to provide a rotation, scale, color, and a small offset value to add to the position. The data is sent to the culling and rendering shaders as a texture. The data was tiled repeatedly across the vegetation field, in the same manner as a tiling texture applied to a surface. It was found that a 16×16 grid was sufficient to eliminate any tiling appearance, especially when variations in the terrain height were present. With this completed, the second requirement for our design was met because the memory usage of additional instances was zero.

Originally, we planned to combine this procedural distribution with the quadtree design of the Leadwerks 2 vegetation system. However, another technique came to our attention that promised to entirely eliminate the CPU overhead of the vegetation rendering system.

4.4 Culling

Instance cloud reduction is an established technique for modern hardware that efficiently culls large numbers of objects entirely on the GPU [Rákos 2010,

4.4 Culling

Shopf et al. 2008]. The technique works by passing all possible instances to the GPU and discarding instances that are culled by the camera frustum in a geometry shader (see Figure 4.2). Unlike a traditional shader, no fragment output is generated, and the results of the geometry shader are output to a texture buffer. A GPU query is used to retrieve the number of rendered primitives, which corresponds to the number of rendered instances. Visible geometry is rendered in a second pass by using the results of the query as the number of instances drawn and by reading the texture buffer that was populated in the culling pass. This technique seemed to offer the greatest promise for eliminating the overhead of our vegetation rendering system.

Rather than passing transformation data to the culling shader, we wanted to generate the transformation data entirely on the GPU. Our repeating grid technique detailed in the previous section was easily integrated into the culling

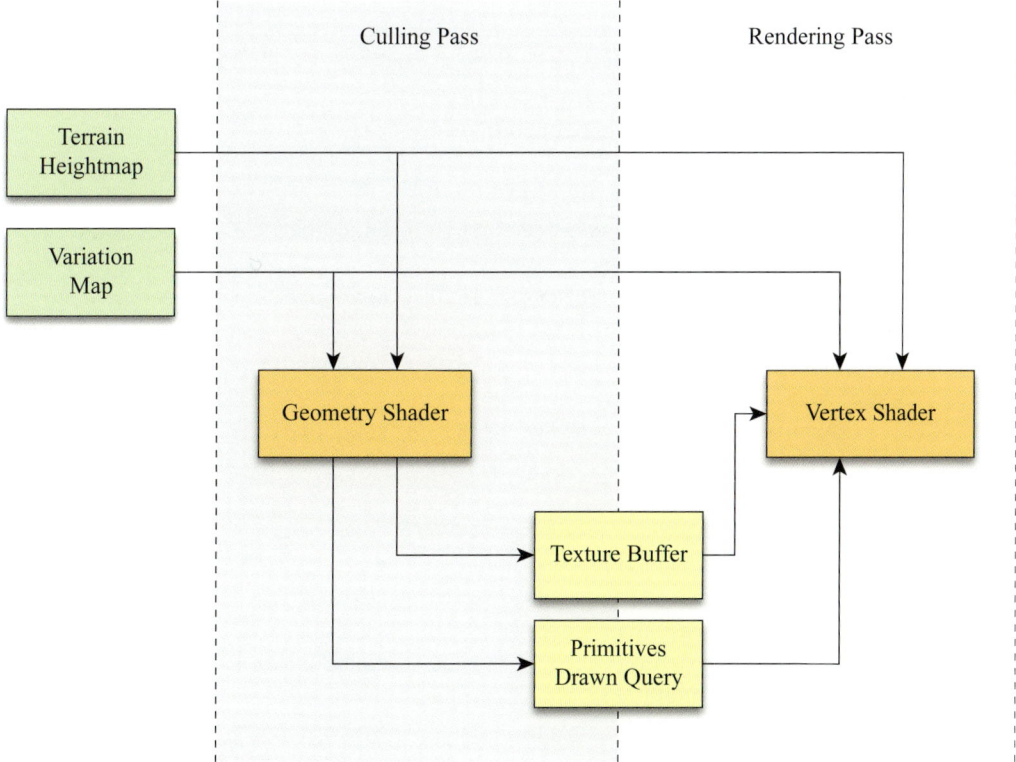

Figure 4.2. Instance cloud reduction is a GPU culling technique that works by writing visible instance IDs into a texture buffer, and then rendering visible objects in an additional pass.

shader. Unlike previous implementations that outputted a 4×4 matrix into the texture buffer, we instead wrote out a 32-bit unsigned integer specifying the instance ID.

Uniform values are sent to the culling shader to specify the grid position, size, and distribution density. The instance ID is used to calculate the x and z coordinates of each instance according to the following formula.

```
float x = floor(gl_InstandID / gridsize.x);
float z = gl_InstandID - x * gridsize.y;
x += gridoffset.x;
z += gridoffset.y;
```

The instance 4×4 matrix is then calculated according to the following formula, where texture5 is the 16×16 pixel variation map that we generated.

```
mat4    mat;

float sy = 1.0 / variationmapresolution;
float sx = sy * 0.0625;

mat[0][0] = texture(texture5, vec2((x * 16.0 + texcoord.x + 0.0) * sx,
        texcoord.y + z * sy)).r;
mat[0][1] = texture(texture5, vec2((x * 16.0 + texcoord.x + 1.0) * sx,
        texcoord.y + z * sy)).r;
mat[0][2] = texture(texture5, vec2((x * 16.0 + texcoord.x + 2.0) * sx,
        texcoord.y + z * sy)).r;
mat[0][3] = texture(texture5, vec2((x * 16.0 + texcoord.x + 3.0) * sx,
        texcoord.y + z * sy)).r;

mat[1][0] = texture(texture5, vec2((x * 16.0 + texcoord.x + 4.0) * sx,
        texcoord.y + z * sy)).r;
mat[1][1] = texture(texture5, vec2((x * 16.0 + texcoord.x + 5.0) * sx,
        texcoord.y + z * sy)).r;
mat[1][2] = texture(texture5, vec2((x * 16.0 + texcoord.x + 6.0) * sx,
        texcoord.y + z * sy)).r;
mat[1][3] = texture(texture5, vec2((x * 16.0 + texcoord.x + 7.0) * sx,
        texcoord.y + z * sy)).r;

mat[2][0] = texture(texture5, vec2((x * 16.0 + texcoord.x + 8.0) * sx,
```

4.4 Culling

```
            texcoord.y + z * sy)).r;
mat[2][1] = texture(texture5, vec2((x * 16.0 + texcoord.x + 9.0) * sx,
            texcoord.y + z * sy)).r;
mat[2][2] = texture(texture5, vec2((x * 16.0 + texcoord.x + 10.0) * sx,
            texcoord.y + z * sy)).r;
mat[2][3] = texture(texture5, vec2((x * 16.0 + texcoord.x + 11.0) * sx,
            texcoord.y + z * sy)).r;

mat[3][0] = texture(texture5, vec2((x * 16.0 + texcoord.x + 12.0) * sx,
            texcoord.y + z * sy)).r;
mat[3][1] = texture(texture5, vec2((x * 16.0 + texcoord.x + 13.0) * sx,
            texcoord.y + z * sy)).r;
mat[3][2] = texture(texture5, vec2((x * 16.0 + texcoord.x + 14.0) * sx,
            texcoord.y + z * sy)).r;
mat[3][3] = texture(texture5, vec2((x * 16.0 + texcoord.x + 15.0) * sx,
            texcoord.y + z * sy)).r;

mat[3][0] += x * density;
mat[3][2] += z * density;

vec2 texcoords = vec2((mat[3][0] + TerrainSize * 0.5) / TerrainSize +
        1.0 / TerrainResolution * 0.5, (mat[3][2] + TerrainSize * 0.5) /
        TerrainSize + 1.0 / TerrainResolution * 0.5);

mat[3][1] = texture(texture6, texcoords).r * TerrainHeight;
```

This shader could be optimized further by using an RGBA floating-point texture that combines matrix rows into a single texture lookup.

The first three elements of the fourth matrix row holds the instance's position in global space. We first check to see if the instance position is beyond the bounds of the terrain as follows.

```
if (mat[3][0] < -TerrainSize * 0.5) return;
if (mat[3][0] > TerrainSize * 0.5) return;
if (mat[3][2] < -TerrainSize * 0.5) return;
if (mat[3][2] > TerrainSize * 0.5) return;
```

We then calculate the distance to the camera and discard instances that are too far away from the camera to be seen:

```
if (dist >= viewrange.y) return;
```

We added slope and height constraints. This can be used to ensure that trees only appear above sea level, or to prevent plants from growing on steep cliff faces.

```
if (slope < sloperange.x) return;
if (slope > sloperange.y) return;
if (mat[3][1] < heightrange.x) return;
if (mat[3][1] > heightrange.y) return;
```

Finally, we calculate the actual center of the object's axis-aligned bounding box (AABB) and radius as follows.

```
vec3 scale = vec3(length(mat[0].xyz), length(mat[1].xyz),
      length(mat[2].xyz));
scale = scalerange.x + (scale - 1.0) * (scalerange.y - scalerange.x);

vec3 aabbcenter = aabbmin + (aabbmax - aabbmin) * 0.5;
size = aabbmax - aabbmin;
float radius = length(size * scale);

vec3 center = mat[3].xyz;
center.x += aabboffset.x * scale.x;
center.y += aabboffset.y * scale.y;
center.z += aabboffset.z * scale.z;
```

Then, we perform an intersection test between the camera frustum and a sphere that completely encloses the instance. The PADDING macro can be set to 1.0 to shift the sides of the frustum volume inward and visually confirm that the algorithm is working correctly. The frustum plane uniforms are the six planes that define the camera frustum volume. If a point lies outside of any of these planes, then by definition it does not intersect the camera frustum volume and is not visible.

```
#define PADDING 0.0

if (PlaneDistanceToPoint(frustumplane0, center) > radius - PADDING) return;
```

```
if (PlaneDistanceToPoint(frustumplane1, center) > radius - PADDING) return;
if (PlaneDistanceToPoint(frustumplane2, center) > radius - PADDING) return;
if (PlaneDistanceToPoint(frustumplane3, center) > radius - PADDING) return;
if (PlaneDistanceToPoint(frustumplane4, center) > radius - PADDING) return;
if (PlaneDistanceToPoint(frustumplane5, center) > radius - PADDING) return;
```

Finally, once all our tests have passed, we write the instance ID into the texture buffer and emit a vertex:

```
transformfeedback0 = ex_instanceID[0];
EmitVertex();
```

The outputted instance IDs are read by the vertex shader during the next step.

4.5 Rendering

Visible rendering of the instances takes place in a second pass. The results of the primitive count query are retrieved, and this tells us the number of instances to render. The texture buffers written in the culling pass are used to retrieve the ID of each rendered instance.

By default, our system uses two levels of detail, one that draws the full polygonal models (the *near* instances) and another that displays billboard representations of the models (the *far* instances). It quickly became apparent to us that two culling passes are necessary, one to collect the IDs of all near instances, and another for all far instances. The results are written into two separate texture buffers. A separate query object is used during each pass to retrieve the number of rendered primitives.

The necessity to synchronize with the GPU is a potential problem with this design. To reduce this problem, we perform vegetation culling at the beginning of the camera render function, and we perform the visible render pass toward the end, leaving as much activity between the two steps as possible. We found it was possible to reverse this order in the shadow rendering pass, so that rendering results were always one frame behind. This could also be done in the visible rendering pass, but quick movements of the camera resulted in very noticeable glitches, so this was reverted.

The demo accompanying this chapter on the book's website shows our system using three vegetation layers for trees, bushes, and grass. Source code for the vegetation class is included. Performance on discrete Nvidia and AMD GPUs

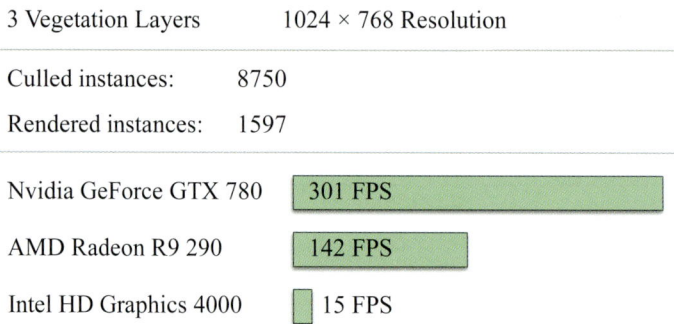

Figure 4.3. Performance is shown for the example scene running on Nvidia, AMD, and Intel graphics hardware.

was surprisingly fast with heavy loads in spite of the synchronization issue (Figure 4.3). Intel hardware performed at a comparatively slower speed, but this is to be expected for an integrated graphics chip. The use of atomic counters (available in GLSL 4.3) promises to provide a mechanism to avoid CPU/GPU synchronization, but this was not implemented in our first pass since our minimum system requirements are OpenGL 4.0 hardware.

4.6 Level of Detail

An efficient culling system capable of managing hundreds of thousands of vegetation instances requires an equally efficient detail reduction system, since so many objects can be drawn at once, and the vast majority of them are far away from the viewer. In Leadwerks 4, we opted to use a simple billboard system to draw vegetation instances that were positioned an adjustable distance from the camera. Instances closer than the billboard distance are rendered as full polygonal meshes with no intermediate LOD stages. This simplifies the engine workflow and limits the number of required culling passes to two, or to a single pass for layers that do not use billboarding (e.g., small plants and rocks).

We started by performing a series of 16 orthographic renders of the vegetation model. The diffuse, normal, and emission channels of the camera buffer provided a convenient mechanism to store the billboard data. Render results were copied into a single texture as shown in Figure 4.4. To provide some depth to the billboards when viewed from above, we performed an additional top-down render of the object and added a second upwards-facing quad to each billboard.

4.6 Level of Detail

Figure 4.4. A series of 16 orthographic views are rendered to the billboard texture. The closest two views are interpolated between based on camera position.

This remains stationary and provides a better appearance than camera-facing billboards.

The Leadwerks 2 vegetation system suffered from severe "popping" when models transitioned to billboard and when billboard views were switched based on the camera viewing angle. Creating a smooth transition between detail levels and billboard faces was a priority.

In the following billboard vertex shader, the relative angle of the camera position to the billboard's local space is calculated with the code below. The varying output `stage` represents the index of the billboard image to display, and the `blend` value is used to interpolate between the current and next stage.

```
float a = (atan(hdiff.y, hdiff.x) + pi) / (2.0 * pi) - 0.25;
a -= GetYaw(id);
a = mod(a, 1.0);
float stage = floor(a * billboardviews);
blend = a * billboardviews - stage;
```

Texture coordinates for the two nearest stages are calculated and outputted in varying `vec2` values as follows.

```
ex_texcoords0 = vertex_texcoords0;
ex_texcoords0.x /= billboardviews;
ex_texcoords0.x += stage / billboardviews;

stage = ceil(a * billboardviews);
if (stage >= billboardviews) stage = 0.0;
ex_texcoords1 = vertex_texcoords0;
ex_texcoords1.x /= billboardviews;
ex_texcoords1.x += stage / billboardviews;
```

In the following fragment shader, a dissolve effect is used to smoothly transition between billboard stages based on the `blend` varying value. This works by generating a pseudorandom floating-point value using the screen coordinate as a seed value, and comparing it to the `blend` value. The same technique is also used to smoothly fade billboards in and out with distance. When combined with multisampling, this produces results similar to alpha blending but retains accurate lighting information for the deferred renderer.

```
// Generate psuedorandom value
float f = rand(gl_FragCoord.xy / buffersize * 1.0 +
        gl_SampleID * 37.45128 + ex_normal.xy);

// Diffuse
vec4 outcolor = ex_color;
vec4 color0 = texture(texture0, ex_texcoords0);
vec4 color1 = texture(texture0, ex_texcoords1);

vec4 normalcolor;
vec4 normalcolor0 = texture(texture1, ex_texcoords0);
vec4 normalcolor1 = texture(texture1, ex_texcoords1);

vec4 emission;
vec4 emission0 = texture(texture2, ex_texcoords0);
vec4 emission1 = texture(texture2, ex_texcoords1);

// Dissolve blending
if (f > blend)
{
    outcolor = color0;
    normalcolor = normalcolor0;
    emission = emission0;
}
else
{
    outcolor = color1;
    normalcolor = normalcolor1;
    emission = emission1;
}
```

4.7 Physics

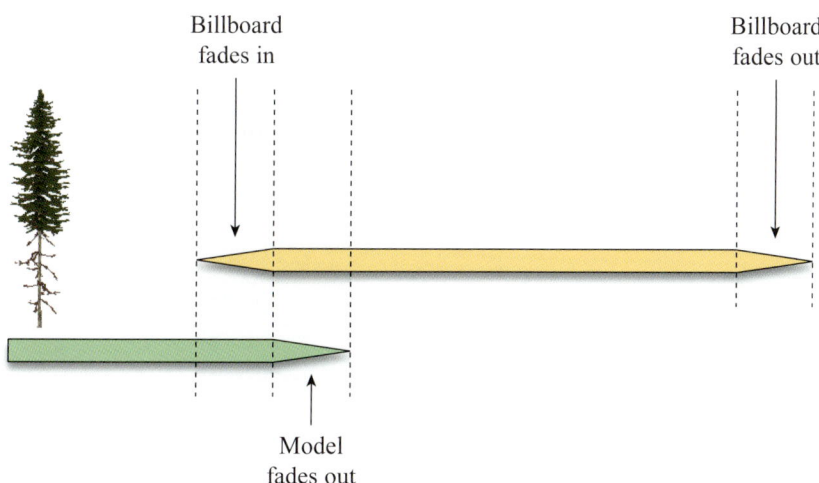

Figure 4.5. When an instance reaches a certain distance from the camera (positioned on the left), the billboard object begins to fade in using a dissolve effect. Once the billboard is completely visible, the model begins to fade out. This provides a smooth transition between LOD stages. The billboard also fades out as the maximum view range is reached.

As the distance from an instance reaches the billboard rendering distance, the billboard begins dissolving in. At the distance where the billboard is completely solid, the 3D model begins dissolving out. Finally, when the maximum view distance is reached, the billboard is dissolved out over a short distance. See Figure 4.5 for an illustration of these transitions.

The billboard orientation we used, combined with the dissolve effect for distance fading and billboard view blending, results in smooth transitions and accurate lighting that eliminate the "popping" artifacts observed in our previous vegetation system.

4.7 Physics

Leadwerks Game Engine uses the Newton Game Dynamics library to simulate physics. Newton was chosen due to its accuracy, stability, and ease of implementation. One of the useful features Newton provides is a mechanism for specifying a user-defined collision mesh. This works by invoking a user-defined callback function any time an object intersects a specified bounding box. The callback builds a mesh dynamically for all mesh faces within the volume that the colliding object occupies. This can be used for efficient collisions with height map terrain or voxel geometry. In our case, the system allowed us to provide vegetation collision data to the physics simulator without having to actually store all the 4×4 matrices for each vegetation instance in memory.

A function to get all vegetation instances in an arbitrary AABB was implemented as follows.

```
int VegetationLayer::GetInstancesInAABB(const AABB& aabb,
      std::vector<Mat4>& instances, const float padding)
{
   int count = 0;
   iVec2 gridmin;
   iVec2 gridmax;
   float r = 0.0;
   Mat4 mat, identity;
   Vec3 scale;
   Vec3 center;
   AABB instanceaabb;

   if (model)
   {
      r = Vec2(model->recursiveaabb.size.x,
         model->recursiveaabb.size.z).Length() +
         Vec2(model->recursiveaabb.center.x,
         model->recursiveaabb.center.z).Length();
   }

   gridmin.x = floor((aabb.min.x - scalerange[1] * r) / density - 0.5);
   gridmin.y = floor((aabb.min.z - scalerange[1] * r) / density - 0.5);
   gridmax.x = ceil((aabb.max.x + scalerange[1] * r) / density + 0.5);
   gridmax.y = ceil((aabb.max.z + scalerange[1] * r) / density + 0.5);

   for (int x = gridmin.x; x <= gridmax.x; x++)
   {
      for (int y = gridmin.y; y <= gridmax.y; y++)
      {
         mat = GetInstanceMatrix(x, y);
         instanceaabb = Transform::AABB(model->recursiveaabb, mat,
               identity, false);
```

4.7 Physics

```
            if (instanceaabb.IntersectsAABB(aabb, padding))
            {
                instanceaabb = Transform::AABB(model->recursiveaabb, mat,
                    identity, true);

                if (instanceaabb.IntersectsAABB(aabb, padding))
                {
                    count++;
                    instances.push_back(mat);
                }
            }
        }
    }

    return count;
}
```

The same function that retrieves an instance matrix in GLSL was implemented in C++ as follows.

```
Mat4 VegetationLayer::GetInstanceMatrix(const int x, const int z)
{
    Mat4    mat;

    int ix = Math::Mod(x, variationmapresolution);
    int iz = Math::Mod(z + variationmapresolution / 2,
            variationmapresolution);
    int offset = (iz * variationmapresolution + ix) * 16;

    if (variationmatrices.size() == 0)
    {
        BuildVariationMatrices();
    }

    mat[0][0] = variationmatrices[offset + 0];
    mat[0][1] = variationmatrices[offset + 1];
    mat[0][2] = variationmatrices[offset + 2];
    mat[0][3] = 0.0;
```

```
    mat[1][0] = variationmatrices[offset + 4];
    mat[1][1] = variationmatrices[offset + 5];
    mat[1][2] = variationmatrices[offset + 6];
    mat[1][3] = 0.0;

    mat[2][0] = variationmatrices[offset + 8];
    mat[2][1] = variationmatrices[offset + 9];
    mat[2][2] = variationmatrices[offset + 10];
    mat[2][3] = 0.0;

    mat[3][0] = variationmatrices[offset + 12] + x * density;
    mat[3][2] = variationmatrices[offset + 14] + z * density;
    mat[3][1] = terrain->GetElevation(mat[3][0], mat[3][2]);
    mat[3][3] = 1.0;

    float scale = scalerange.x + variationmatrices[offset + 15] *
           (scalerange.y - scalerange.x);
    mat[0] *= scale;
    mat[1] *= scale;
    mat[2] *= scale;
    return mat;
}
```

In the Newton collision callback function, all the intersecting instances are retrieved. Their vertex positions and normals are transformed to global space and added to arrays that are returned to the physics simulator. The `FastMath` class functions are optimized inline functions designed for demanding real-time operations like the following.

```
int count = layer->GetInstancesInAABB(aabb,
        layer->instances[threadNumber]);

// Merge all intersecting instances into vertex / indice arrays
for (int n = 0; n < count; n++)
{
    for (int p = 0; p < vert_count; p++)
    {
        offset = p * 3;
```

```cpp
        pos.x = layer->vertexpositions[offset + 0];
        pos.y = layer->vertexpositions[offset + 1];
        pos.z = layer->vertexpositions[offset + 2];

        FastMath::Mat4MultiplyVec3(layer->instances[threadNumber][n],
            pos, result);

        offset = ((n * (vert_count + tris_count)) + p) * 3;
        layer->collisionsurfacevertices[threadNumber][offset + 0]
            = result.x;
        layer->collisionsurfacevertices[threadNumber][offset + 1]
            = result.y;
        layer->collisionsurfacevertices[threadNumber][offset + 2]
            = result.z;
    }

    for (int p = 0; p < tris_count; p++)
    {
        offset = p * 3;
        pos.x = layer->facenormals[offset + 0];
        pos.y = layer->facenormals[offset + 1];
        pos.z = layer->facenormals[offset + 2];

        FastMath::Mat3MultiplyVec3(Mat3(layer->instances[threadNumber][n]),
            pos, result);

        float m = 1.0F / result.Length();
        offset = ((n * (vert_count + tris_count)) + vert_count + p) * 3;
        layer->collisionsurfacevertices[threadNumber][offset + 0]
            = result.x * m;
        layer->collisionsurfacevertices[threadNumber][offset + 1]
            = result.y * m;
        layer->collisionsurfacevertices[threadNumber][offset + 2]
            = result.z * m;
    }

    // Add indices
    memcpy(&layer->collisionsurfaceindices[threadNumber]
        [n * layer->indices.size()], &layer->indices[0],
        layer->indices.size() * sizeof(int));
```

```
// Offset indices
index_offset = n * (collisionsurface->CountVertices() +
        collisionsurface->CountTriangles());

for (int p = 0; p < tris_count; p++)
{
    offset = n * layer->indices.size() + p * 9;

    layer->collisionsurfaceindices[threadNumber][offset + 0]
            += index_offset;
    layer->collisionsurfaceindices[threadNumber][offset + 1]
            += index_offset;
    layer->collisionsurfaceindices[threadNumber][offset + 2]
            += index_offset;
    layer->collisionsurfaceindices[threadNumber][offset + 4]
            += index_offset;
    layer->collisionsurfaceindices[threadNumber][offset + 5]
            += index_offset;
    layer->collisionsurfaceindices[threadNumber][offset + 6]
            += index_offset;
    layer->collisionsurfaceindices[threadNumber][offset + 7]
            += index_offset;
}
}
```

Although iterating through and transforming vertices is not an optimal design, in practice it has proven to be fast enough for production use. In the future, a new collision type could be implemented in Newton that retrieves an array of 4×4 matrices of all intersecting instances.

With this step complete, we finally have a system with parity between the instance orientations generated on both the CPU and GPU without actually having to store the data for each individual instance. Although it is not present in this implementation, a filter map can easily be added to discard instances at specific grid positions and allow dynamic insertion and deletion of instances.

4.8 Future Development

Because Leadwerks Game Engine 4 is a commercial product already on the market, system requirements are locked on OpenGL 4.0 hardware. In the future, an implementation using atomic counters could eliminate CPU/GPU synchronization when OpenGL 4.3-compliant drivers are detected.

Implementation of an "instance cloud" collision type in Newton Game Dynamics would provide better performance than dynamically constructing a mesh from transformed vertices.

Although this system does an excellent job of producing natural spacing among vegetation instances, different vegetation layers have no communication of the spaces they occupy. Multiple dense layers can easily appear on top of one another in unnatural arrangements, like a tree in the middle of a rock. As our worlds get bigger, the need for intelligent placement of instances will become more important.

Our culling algorithm only performs simple frustum culling on vegetation instances, which loses the advantages of the hierarchical occlusion system our standard object management system uses. In the future, nearby occluding volumes could be sent to the culling shader and used to discard occluded vegetation instances.

Our system is suited for geometry that is generally arranged on a 2D surface, but it could be adapted to 3D to handle things like a dense procedurally generated asteroid field.

References

[Rákos 2010] Daniel Rákos. "Instance Culling Using Geometry Shaders". RasterGrid Blog, 2010. Available at http://rastergrid.com/blog/2010/02/instance-culling-using-geometry-shaders/

[Shopf et al. 2008] Jemery Shopf, Joshua Barczak, Christopher Oat, and Natalya Tatarchuk. "March of the Froblins: Simulation and Rendering Massive Crowds of Intelligent and Detailed Creatures on GPU". *ACM SIGGRAPH 2008: Proceedings of the conference course notes, Advances in Real-Time Rendering in 3D Graphics and Games*, pp. 52–101.

5

Smooth Horizon Mapping

Eric Lengyel
Terathon Software

5.1 Introduction

Normal mapping has been a staple of real-time rendering ever since the first graphics processors with programmable fragment pipelines became available. The technique varies the normal direction at each texel to make it appear that a smooth surface actually has a more complex geometric shape. Because the normal direction changes, the intensities of the diffuse and specular reflections also change, and this produces an effective illusion. But it is an illusion that could be taken further by accounting for the fact that some of the incoming light would be occluded if the more complex geometry really existed.

Horizon mapping is a technique, first proposed by [Max 1988] for offline rendering, that uses an additional texture map to store information about the height of the normal-mapped geometry in several directions within a neighborhood around each texel. Given the direction to the light source at each texel, the information in the horizon map can be used to cast convincing dynamic shadows for the high-resolution geometric detail encoded in the normal map.

This chapter describes the process of creating a horizon map and provides the details for a highly efficient real-time rendering method that adds soft shadows to normal-mapped surfaces. The rendering method works in tangent space and thus fits well into existing normal mapping shaders. Furthermore, it does not require newer hardware features, so it can be used across a wide range of GPUs.

An example application of horizon mapping on a stone wall is shown in Figure 5.1. A conventional diffuse color map and normal map are used to render a cube having flat sides in Figure 5.1(e). A four-channel horizon map with two layers encodes horizon information for eight light directions, and this horizon map is used to render shadows on the same cube in Figure 5.1(f).

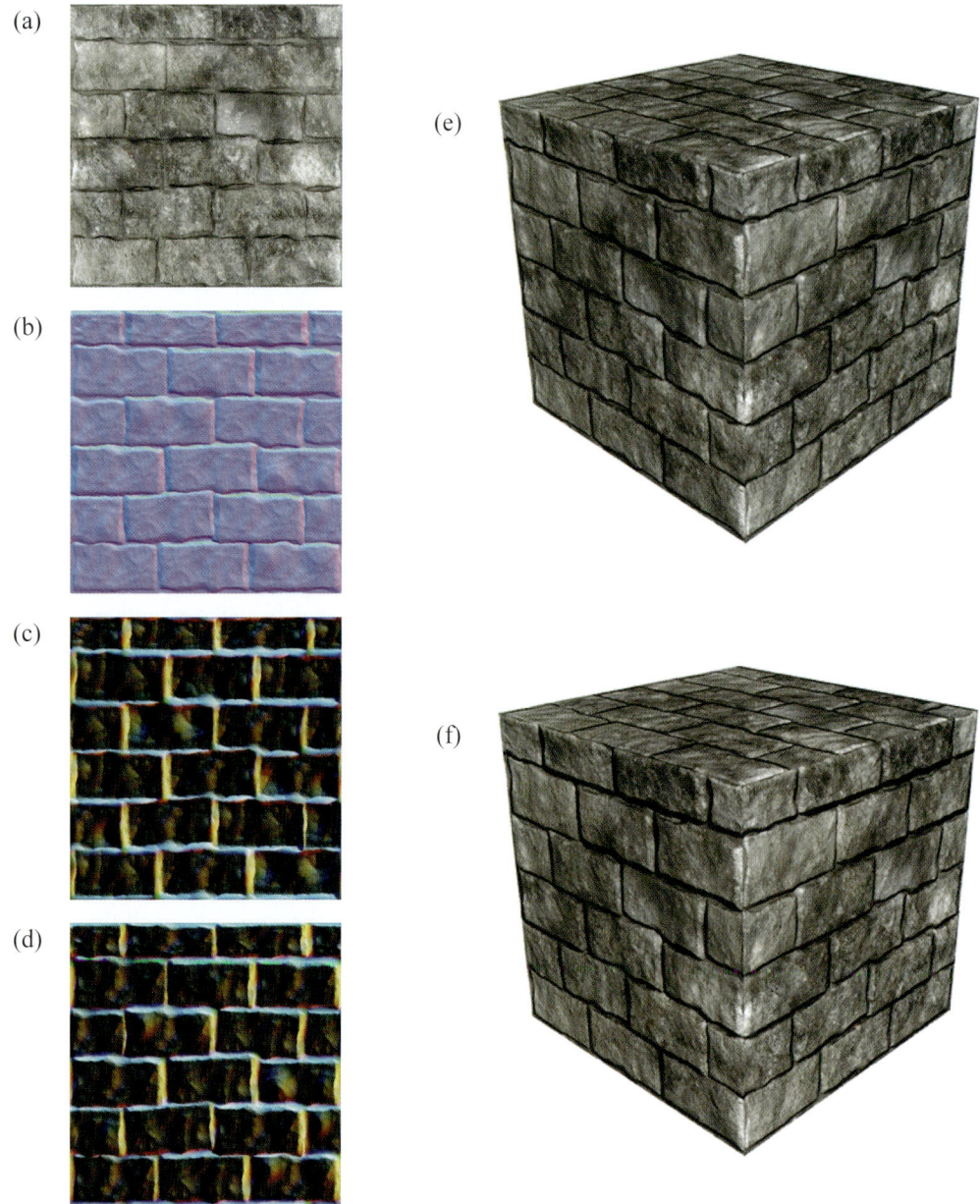

Figure 5.1. The conventional diffuse color map (a) and normal map (b) are augmented by eight channels of horizon mapping information in (c) and (d). A cube rendered only with ordinary normal mapping is shown in (e). Horizon mapping has been applied in (f).

A variety of materials rendered with and without shadows generated by horizon maps are shown in Figure 5.2. The shadows make a significant contribution to the illusion that the surfaces are anything but flat. This is especially true if the light source is in motion and the shadows are changing dynamically. Even though the horizon map contains height information for only eight distinct tangent directions (every 45 degrees about the normal), linearly interpolating that information for other directions is quite sufficient for rendering convincing shadows. In Figure 5.3, the same material is rendered nine times as the direction to the light source rotates about the surface normal by 15-degree increments.

5.2 Horizon Map Generation

A horizon map contains eight channels of information, each corresponding to a tangent direction beginning with the positive x axis of the normal map and continuing at 45-degree increments counterclockwise. (In Figure 5.1, the alpha channels of the two layers of the horizon map are not visible, so a total of six channels can be seen as RGB color.) The intensity value in each channel is equal to the sine of the maximum angle made with the tangent plane for which a light source would be occluded in the direction corresponding to that channel. This is the horizon. As illustrated in Figure 5.4, a light source is unoccluded precisely when the direction to the light makes an angle having a larger sine. Otherwise, the pixel being shaded with the particular texel from the horizon map is in shadow. Given the tangent-space unit-length direction vector **L** to the light source in a shader, determining whether a pixel is in shadow is simply a matter of comparing L_z to the value in the horizon map. The details about calculating this value for any light direction are discussed in the next section.

To construct a horizon map, we must calculate appropriate sine values for the horizon in eight directions. If the graphics hardware supports array textures, then the horizon map can be stored as a 2D texture image array with two layers. Otherwise, the horizon map must be stored as two separate 2D texture images at the tiny expense of needing to bind an additional texture map when rendering. In both cases, the texture images contain RGBA data with 8-bit channels. When the texture maps are sampled, the data is returned by the hardware as floating-point values in the range [0,1], which is a perfect match for the range of sine values that we need to store.

Using the raw height map as input, there are many valid ways of generating a horizon map. What follows is a description of the method used in the source code accompanying this chapter on the book's website. For each texel in the output

Figure 5.2. A variety of horizon mapping examples. In the left column, only ordinary normal mapping is applied. In the right column, shadows are added by horizon mapping.

5.2 Horizon Map Generation

Figure 5.3. This flat disk is illuminated from nine different angles ranging from −60° to +60° in 15-degree increments. Shadows are dynamically rendered using information stored in the eight channels of the horizon map.

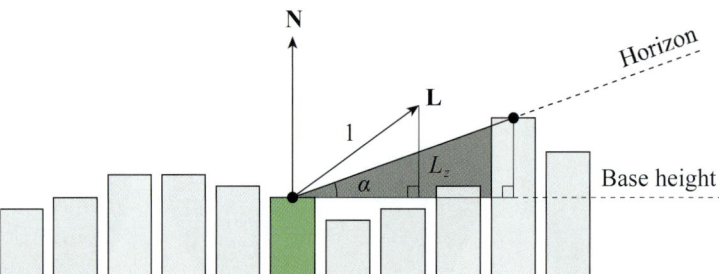

Figure 5.4. The horizon information for the central texel (green) in the direction to the right is given by the maximum angle α determined by the heights of other texels in a local neighborhood. The value stored in the horizon map is $\sin\alpha$, and this is compared against L_z when rendering to determine whether the pixel being shaded is illuminated. If $L_z > \sin\alpha$, then light reaches the pixel; otherwise, the pixel is in shadow.

horizon map, we examine a neighborhood having a 16-texel radius in the height map and look for heights larger than that of the central texel under consideration. Each time a larger height is found, we calculate the squared tangent of the angle α made with the central texel as

$$\tan^2\alpha = \frac{(h-h_0)^2}{(x-x_0)^2+(y-y_0)^2}, \tag{5.1}$$

where h is the height of the texel found at the location (x,y) in the height map, and h_0 is the height of the central texel at the location (x_0, y_0).

The maximum squared tangent is recorded for a array of 32 directions around the central texel, and after all of the texels in the neighborhood have been processed, the sine value for each direction is computed with

$$\sin\alpha = \frac{1}{\sqrt{\dfrac{1}{\tan^2\alpha}+1}}. \tag{5.2}$$

The affected directions in the array are determined by the position of the texel and its angular size relative to the central texel. It is possible for texels near the center to affect multiple entries in the array due to their larger angular sizes.

For each of the eight directions for which sine values are stored in the horizon map, the nearest five sine values in the array of 32 directions are simply averaged together. The sine values corresponding to the directions making angles

0°, 45°, 90°, and 135° with the x axis are stored in the red, green, blue, and alpha channels of the first layer of the horizon map, respectively. The sine values corresponding to the angles 180°, 225°, 270°, and 315° are stored in the red, green, blue, and alpha channels of the second layer.

Because the calculations are independent for each texel, the horizon map generation process is highly parallelizable. The horizon map can be sliced into subrectangles that are processed by different threads on the CPU, or each texel can be assigned to a thread to be processed by a GPU compute shader.

5.3 Rendering with Horizon Maps

Horizon mapping is applied in a shader by first calculating the color due to the contribution of a light source in the ordinary manner and then multiplying this color by an illumination factor derived from the information in the horizon map. The illumination factor is a value that is zero for pixels that are in shadow and one for pixels that are fully illuminated. We use a small trick to make the illumination factor change smoothly near the edge of the shadow to give it a soft appearance.

The horizon map stores the sine value corresponding to the horizon angle in eight tangent directions. For an arbitrary tangent-space direction vector $\mathbf{L}$ to the light source, we interpolate between the horizon map's sine values for the two tangent directions nearest the projected light direction (L_x, L_y) and compare the interpolated value to L_z in order to determine whether a pixel is in shadow.

It would be expensive to decide which channels of the horizon map contribute to the sine value and to calculate the interpolation factors in the fragment shader. However, it is possible and quite convenient to store the interpolation factors for all eight channels of the horizon map in a special cube texture map that is accessed directly with the vector $\mathbf{L}$. We can encode factors for eight directions in a four-channel cube map by taking advantage of the fact that if a factor is nonzero for one direction, then it must be zero for the opposite direction. This allows us to use positive factors when referring to channels in the first layer of the horizon map and negative factors when referring to channels in the second layer. (We remap factors in the $[-1,1]$ range to $[0,255]$ when constructing the cube map so that we can use ordinary 8-bit RGBA color.) For a value $\mathbf{f}$ sampled from the cube map with four components returned by the hardware in the range $[0,1]$, we can compute the horizon sine value s as

$$s = \max(2\mathbf{f}-1,0) \cdot \mathbf{h}_0 + \max(-2\mathbf{f}+1,0) \cdot \mathbf{h}_1, \qquad (5.3)$$

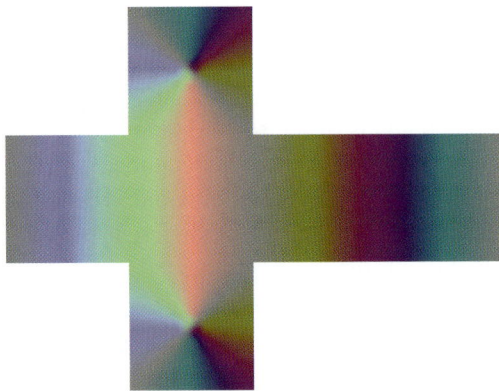

Figure 5.5. When sampled with coordinates given by the tangent-space direction to light vector, this cube texture map returns the channel factors to be applied to the information stored in the horizon map.

where $\mathbf{h}_0$ and $\mathbf{h}_1$ are the four-channel sine values read from layers 0 and 1 of the horizon map, and the max function is applied componentwise.

The cube texture map containing the channel factors has the appearance shown in Figure 5.5. This texture is included in the materials accompanying this chapter on the book's website along with code for generating it. We have found that a cube texture having a resolution of only 16×16 texels per side is sufficient, and it requires a mere six kilobytes of storage.

Once the interpolated sine value s has been calculated with Equation (5.3) using the information sampled from the horizon map, we can compare it to the sine of the angle that the direction to light $\mathbf{L}$ makes with the tangent plane, which is simply given by L_z when $\mathbf{L}$ is normalized. If $L_z \geq s$, then the light source is above the horizon, and the pixel being shaded is therefore illuminated. If we were to compute an illumination factor F that is one when $L_z \geq s$ and zero otherwise, then the shadow would be correct, but the shadow's edge would be hard and jagged as shown in Figure 5.6(a). We would instead like to have F smoothly transition from one to zero at the shadow's edge to produce the soft appearance shown in Figure 5.6(b). This can be accomplished by calculating

$$F = k(L_z - s) + 1 \tag{5.4}$$

and clamping it to the range $[0,1]$. The value of F is always one, corresponding to a fully illuminated pixel, when $L_z \geq s$. The value of F is always zero, corresponding to a fully shadowed pixel, when $L_z \leq s - 1/k$. The constant k is a positive

5.3 Rendering with Horizon Maps

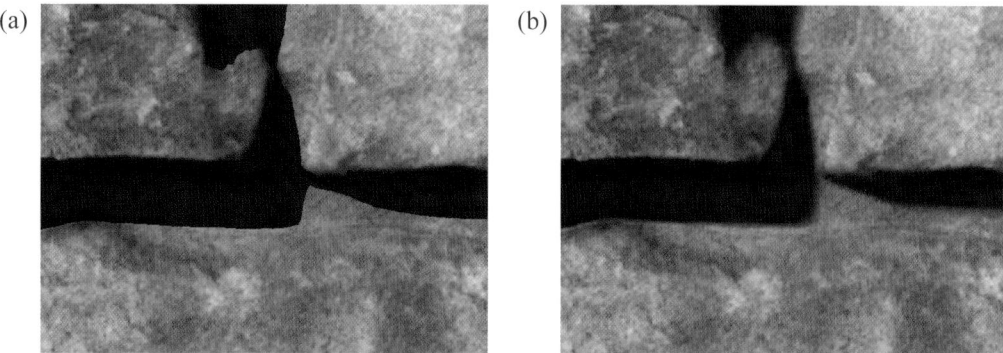

Figure 5.6. This close-up comparison shows the difference between a hard shadow and a soft shadow for a stone wall. (a) The illumination factor F is exactly one or zero, depending on whether $L_z \geq s$. (b) The illumination factor F is given by Equation (5.4) with $k = 8.0$.

number that determines how gradual the transition from light to shadow is. The transition takes place over a sine value range of $1/k$, so smaller values of k produce softer shadows.

The fragment shader code in Listing 5.1 implements the horizon mapping technique described in this chapter. It assumes that the shading contribution from a particular light source has already been computed, possibly with larger-scale shadowing applied, and stored in the variable `color`. The code calculates the interpolated sine value for the horizon using Equation (5.3) and multiplies the RGB components of `color` by the illumination factor F given by Equation (5.4). (Instead of using the max function that appears in Equation (5.3), the code clamps to the range $[0,1]$ because many GPUs are able to saturate the result of multiply and multiply-add operations at no additional cost.) An ambient contribution would typically be added to `color` before it is output by the shader.

Listing 5.1. This GLSL fragment shader code implements the horizon mapping technique. The texture `horizonMap` is a two-layer 2D array texture map that contains the eight channels of the horizon map. The texture `factorCube` is the special cube texture map that contains the channel factors for every light direction **L**. The interpolant `texcoord` contains the ordinary 2D texture coordinates used to sample the diffuse color map, normal map, etc. The interpolant `ldir` contains the tangent-space direction to the light source, which needs to be normalized before its z component can be used in Equation (5.4).

```glsl
const float kShadowHardness = 8.0;

uniform sampler2DArray horizonMap;
uniform samplerCube factorCube;

in vec2 texcoord;    // 2D texture coordinates.
in vec3 ldir;        // Tangent-space direction to light.

void main()
{
    // The direction to light must be normalized.
    vec3 L = normalize(ldir);

    vec4 color = ...;    // Shading contribution from light source.

    // Read horizon channel factors from cube map.
    float4 factors = texture(factorCube, L);

    // Extract positive factors for horizon map layer 0.
    float4 f0 = clamp(factors * 2.0 - 1.0, 0.0, 1.0);

    // Extract negative factors for horizon map layer 1.
    float4 f1 = clamp(factors * -2.0 + 1.0, 0.0, 1.0);

    // Sample the horizon map and multiply by the factors for each layer.
    float s0 = dot(texture(horizonMap, vec3(texcoord, 0.0)), f0);
    float s1 = dot(texture(horizonMap, vec3(texcoord, 1.0)), f1);

    // Finally, multiply color by the illumination factor based on the
    // difference between Lz and the value derived from the horizon map.
    color.xyz *= clamp((L.z - (s0 + s1)) * kShadowHardness + 1.0, 0.0, 1.0);
}
```

References

[Max 1988] Nelson L. Max. "Horizon mapping: shadows for bump-mapped surfaces". *The Visual Computer*, Vol. 4, No. 2 (March 1988), pp. 109–117.

6

Buffer-Free Generation of Triangle Strip Cube Vertices

Don Williamson
Celtoys

6.1 Introduction

Buffer-free rendering can be used to simplify interaction between the CPU and GPU or improve performance where reading from source data buffers becomes a bottleneck. A common example is generating a quad in the vertex shader without any inputs beyond the vertex ID, as shown in the following code.

```
float4 QuadPosition(uint vertex_id)
{
   // Triangle strip screen-space quad.
   float x = (vertex_id & 1) ? -1 : 1;
   float y = (vertex_id & 2) ? 1 : -1;
   return float4(x, y, 0, 1);
}
```

No data buffers are required, making the shader simpler to setup, call, and reuse. There are no branches, and the required constants can be encoded directly in the shader's load operations, thus requiring no trips through the data pipeline. This code can be instanced and used everywhere from full-screen quad generation to particle quad expansion.

If your mesh can be encoded as a single strip with no restarts and no vertex reuse, like the simple case here, then there is no benefit to indexing the data in an attempt to take advantage of the post-transform cache. The GPU will only call the vertex shader once for each vertex.

6.2 Generating Cube Vertices

Consider a cube with the vertex index layout shown in Figure 6.1. The origin-centered positions of the cube can be quickly generated with the following code.

```
float3 CubePosition(uint vertex_id)
{
    float x = (vertex_id & 1) ? 1 : -1;
    float y = (vertex_id & 2) ? 1 : -1;
    float z = (vertex_id & 4) ? 1 : -1;
    return float3(x, y, z);
}
```

If an index buffer is being used, then this code immediately eliminates the need to store vertex positions in the vertex buffer, reducing the amount of data that needs to be loaded. In the case that no other per-vertex attributes are present, then the vertex buffer can be completely eliminated.

Geometry shaders are limited by the number of vertices they are allowed to create. When generating cubes from such shaders it helps to emit cube vertices in the smallest representation possible. An unwrapped cube can be triangle-stripped such that only 14 vertices are created rather than 36 for a triangle list, as shown in Figure 6.2.

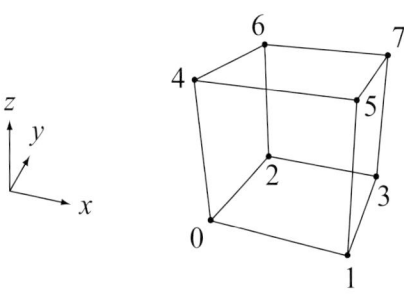

Vertex Index	Vertex Position		
	x	y	z
0	−1	−1	−1
1	+1	−1	−1
2	−1	+1	−1
3	+1	+1	−1
4	−1	−1	+1
5	+1	−1	+1
6	−1	+1	+1
7	+1	+1	+1

Figure 6.1. The numbering used for the cube vertices and the associated vertex positions.

6.2 Generating Cube Vertices

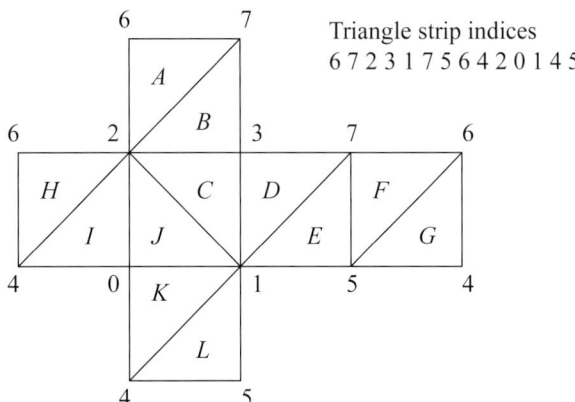

Figure 6.2. The 14 vertex indices used to generate a triangle strip for a cube.

The cube can be rendered in a single triangle strip draw call using the provided indices. After placing the cube origin at $(0.5, 0.5, 0.5)$ and making the sides length 1.0, the vertex positions for a triangle-stripped cube are shown in Table 6.1.

Index	x	y	z
6	0	1	1
7	1	1	1
2	0	1	0
3	1	1	0
1	1	0	0
7	1	1	1
5	1	0	1
6	0	1	1
4	0	0	1
2	0	1	0
0	0	0	0
1	1	0	0
4	0	0	1
5	1	0	1

Table 6.1. The vertex positions for the triangle-stripped cube shown in Figure 6.2.

After looking at the data in this form it's immediately obvious that there are three lookup tables with 1-bit entries that are entirely representable in 16-bit integers:

```
X: b0010100001111010 = 0x287A
Y: b0000001010101111 = 0x02AF
Z: b0011000111100011 = 0x31E3
```

It's now simple to generate triangle-stripped cube positions in the shader using only the vertex ID, as shown in the following code.

```
float3 TriStripCubePosition(uint vertex_id)
{
    uint x = (0x287A >> vertex_id) & 1;
    uint y = (0x02AF >> vertex_id) & 1;
    uint z = (0x31E3 >> vertex_id) & 1;
    return float3(x, y, z);
}
```

The generated microcode for the GCN architecture, shown in the following listing, reveals that there are no trips through any kind of memory and that all of the constants are encoded in the instructions themselves.

```
; v0 = vertex_id
v_lshr_b32    v1, 0x287A, v0
v_lshr_b32    v2, 0x02AF, v0
v_lshr_b32    v0, 0x31E3, v0
v_and_b32     v1, 1, v1
v_and_b32     v2, 1, v2
v_and_b32     v0, 1, v0
; <x, y, z> = <v1, v2, v0>
```

While this shares most of the benefits of the original quad example, there are six vertices that are referenced more than once in the strip, making less efficient use of previously transformed vertices than indexed lists would. There are also GPUs, such as Nvidia's Kepler series, that demonstrably perform worse at variable shifts than others; a property that can be attributed to lack of a hardware barrel shifter. As with everything, it's best to measure first and make the call as to

6.3 Wireframe Cubes

whether the agility of this code outweighs any instances in which it might be slower.

6.3 Wireframe Cubes

Drawing a wireframe cube as a line strip requires retracing some lines. Tracing a line through a connected graph without retracing edges, starting and ending at the same vertex, is called an *Eulerian circuit*. This is only possible if all vertices in the graph have even degree, but a cube's vertices have degree 3.

Alternatively, we can just draw the cube as a line list with the following lookup tables:

```
X: b0011101110000000001111110 = 0x3B807E
Y: b1000111000000011111111000 = 0x8E07F8
Z: b1110001111100001111100000 = 0xE3E1E0
```

Each pair of bits represents start and end positions for a single line that can be indexed in a shader by vertex ID. Replacing the constants in the `TriStrip-CubePosition()` function is all that's needed. The larger size of the constants, however, may require more instructions on some architectures.

7

Edge-Preserving Smoothing Filter for Particle Based Rendering

Kin-Ming Wong
Tien-Tsin Wong

Shenzhen Research Institute
Department of Computer Science and Engineering
The Chinese University of Hong Kong

7.1 Introduction

The level of photorealism delivered by the latest game visuals is quickly matching what was once possible only with off-line rendering techniques. Particle based rendering effects like flint, smoke, and particle trails in most computer games still suffer from grainy artifacts caused by an insufficient number of particles, but this artifact can often be reliably suppressed by using edge-preserving filters such as the bilateral filter. Unfortunately, the bilateral filter is often too expensive for a real-time rendering pipeline. In this chapter, we introduce a highly efficient edge-preserving filter to the game development community.

7.2 Guided Image Filtering

Shown in Figure 7.1, *guided image filtering* is a technique introduced by computer vision researchers a few years ago and has quickly become a popular drop-in replacement for the bilateral filter. Best known for its efficient edge-preserving power, the guided image filter relies on integral images known as *summed area tables* [Crow 1984] for its unmatched performance, and this makes it a perfect candidate for modern real-time image processing pipelines because summed area tables have already been widely adopted for fast filtering purposes in games. This chapter demonstrates the guided image filter and discusses how it can be imple-

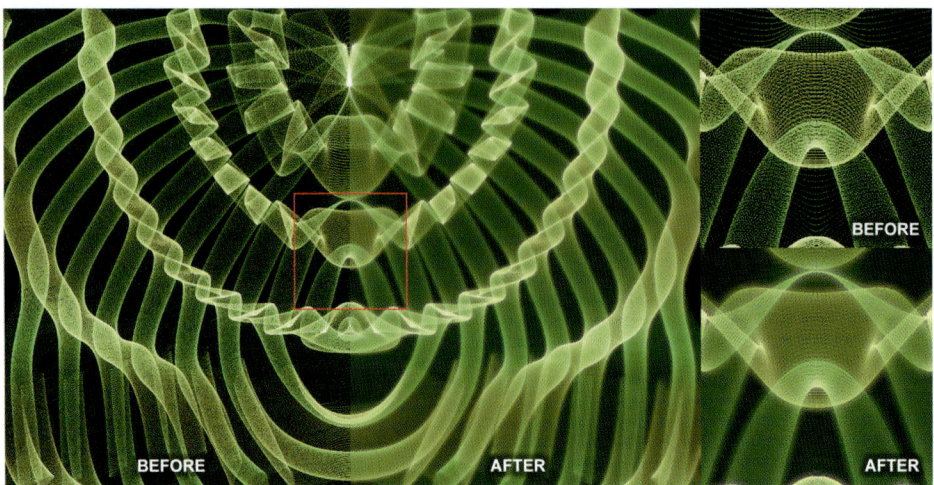

Figure 7.1. Before and after guided image filtering.

mented quickly in shading languages for summed-area-table-enabled image processing pipelines.

The guided image filter is designed to serve multiple purposes, and a detailed discussion of it is beyond the scope of this chapter. Interested readers may refer to the original paper [He et al. 2010] for a complete theoretical formulation and additional applications, which include refining a compositing matte and other interesting image processing uses.

In order to understand the guided image filter without going through its mathematics in detail, we explain the intuition of its design. As an edge-preserving filter, its main goal is to identify edges efficiently and preserve the intensity of the original pixels on the edge as much as possible. As illustrated in Figure 7.2, for any guided image filtered patch, we may consider the pixels inside as a linear blend of two components. The first component represents the *original* pixel values on the unfiltered patch, and the second component represents the *average* value of all pixels in the patch.

Based on the simple formula shown in Figure 7.2, it becomes easy to understand how the guided image filter preserves edges. It relies on a good estimation of the value of A. If an image patch covers an area with an edge, then the value of A in the above formula should be close to one. If the patch covers an area with no edge, then the value of A should be close to zero, and the whole patch should be smoothly filtered. We will now explain how the guided image filter uses a two-stage approach to estimate the value of A to achieve its edge-preserving filtering.

7.2 Guided Image Filtering

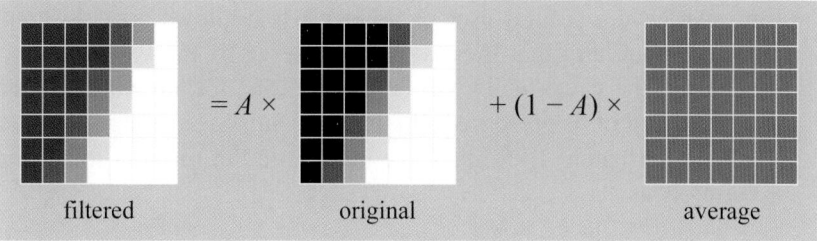

Filtered patch = A × original patch + $(1 − A)$ × patch's mean.

Figure 7.2. How guided image filter works for edge-preserving smoothing.

Per-patch variance evaluation

The first step of the guided image filter is to determine whether an edge exists in each patch within a given image. The size of a patch is given by the parameter ω defining the total number of pixels (often evaluated from a given width for convenience) on the patch in a local neighborhood around each pixel in the image. The filter identifies edges by measuring the statistical variance of the pixel intensity values I inside the patch. So for a patch of size ω centered on pixel k, this statistical variance σ_k is given by the following formula:

$$\sigma_k = \left(\frac{1}{\omega} \sum_{j \in \omega_k} I_j^2 \right) - \mu_k^2,$$

where ω_k is the set of pixels in the patch, I_j is the intensity of pixel j, and μ_k is the mean intensity inside the patch.

It is fairly obvious that for a patch containing an edge, the statistical variance of pixel intensity values will be high due to the polarized intensities of pixels that define the edge. In the case where there is no visual edge, the statistical variance of pixel intensity values should be low because intensity values should span a narrow range. Computation of this per-patch variance and mean can both be accelerated by using summed area tables for both the intensity and squared intensity values in the image.

Once the patch's variance is computed, the value of A, or more precisely, what we call the per-patch A_k, is given by the formula

$$A_k = \frac{\sigma_k}{\sigma_k + \varepsilon}.$$

Here, we have a second user parameter ε that allows users to control the minimum edge strength that they want to preserve. If the value of this parameter is very small, the value of A_k will be close to one for any value of variance, so the whole patch will be preserved. If ε is large, only strong edges will be preserved.

With per-patch A_k defined, we may write the formula for a filtered patch $\widehat{I_k}$ in formally as

$$\widehat{I_k} = A_k I_k + (1 - A_k)\mu_k$$

or $\widehat{I_k} = A_k I_k + B_k$, where $B_k = (1 - A_k)\mu_k$.

Per-pixel filtering

Our discussion so far focuses on individual image patches, but we have to be aware that each pixel is actually member of multiple image patches. As every patch includes ω pixels, it is not hard to see that each single pixel contributes to the same number of image patches. In order to obtain the final filtered value of a given pixel p_k, we take the average value of per-patch A_k and B_k of all image patches that include pixel p_k and then apply the formula

$$\widehat{p_k} = \overline{A_k} p_k + \overline{B_k}$$

$$\overline{A_k} = \frac{1}{|\Omega|} \sum_{i \in \Omega_k} A_i$$

$$\overline{B_k} = \frac{1}{|\Omega|} \sum_{i \in \Omega_k} B_i,$$

where Ω_k defines the set of patches that include the pixel p_k. Obviously, this final filtering step can be similarly accelerated by using summed area tables of per-patch A_k and B_k.

7.3 GLSL Implementation

As described in previous section, the guided image filtering operation is divided into two steps, and computation for pixel value variance and mean in both stages can be easily accelerated by using summed area tables. Once the image data has been transformed into summed area tables, computation of the rest of the filter is embarrassingly parallel, and this explains why we believe the guided image filter is a perfect edge-preserving smoothing filter for modern GPU based graphics pipeline.

7.3 GLSL Implementation

For illustration purposes, we implemented the filter as GLSL fragment shaders for an OpenGL pipeline (see Listings 7.1 and 7.2). We assume that summed area table code is readily available in the pipeline. The filter can be summarized as a simple two-stage process:

1. Per-patch computation. First compute summed area tables of intensity I and squared intensity I^2 of the input image. Then compute the per-patch A_k and B_k as shown in Listing 7.1.
2. Per-pixel computation. First compute summed area tables of per-patch A_k and B_k. Then compute the average of A_k and B_k for each pixel and the final filtered value as shown in Listing 7.2.

Listing 7.1. GLSL fragment shader for per-patch A_k and B_k computation.

```
#version 430 core

layout(binding = 0) uniform sampler2D sat_I2;
layout(binding = 1) uniform sampler2D sat_I;
layout(location = 0) out vec4 Ak;
layout(location = 1) out vec4 Bk;

uniform int r;
uniform float epsilon;

void main(void)
{
    vec2 s = 1.0 / textureSize(sat_I2, 0);
    vec2 coord = gl_FragCoord.xy;

    int r1 = -r - 1;
    vec2 P0 = s * (coord + vec2(r1, r1));
    vec2 P1 = s * (coord + vec2(r1,  r));
    vec2 P2 = s * (coord + vec2( r, r1));
    vec2 P3 = s * (coord + vec2( r,  r));

    float patchWidth = r + r + 1;
    float omega = 1.0 / (patchWidth * patchWidth);

    vec3   a, b, c, d;
```

```
        a = textureLod(sat_I2, P0, 0).rgb;
        b = textureLod(sat_I2, P1, 0).rgb;
        c = textureLod(sat_I2, P2, 0).rgb;
        d = textureLod(sat_I2, P3, 0).rgb;
        vec3 ui2 = vec3(omega) * (a - b - c + d);

        a = textureLod(sat_I, P0, 0).rgb;
        b = textureLod(sat_I, P1, 0).rgb;
        c = textureLod(sat_I, P2, 0).rgb;
        d = textureLod(sat_I, P3, 0).rgb;
        vec3 ui = vec3(omega) * (a - b - c + d);

        vec3 var = ui2 - (ui * ui);
        vec3 ak = var / (vec3(epsilon) + var);
        vec3 bk = ui * (vec3(1.0) - ak);

        Ak = vec4(ak.rgb, 1.0);
        Bk = vec4(bk.rgb, 1.0);
}
```

Listing 7.2. GLSL fragment shader for per-pixel computation.

```
#version 430 core

layout(binding = 0) uniform sampler2D input_image;
layout(binding = 1) uniform sampler2D Ak;
layout(binding = 2) uniform sampler2D Bk;
layout(location = 0) out vec4 color;

uniform int r;

void main(void)
{
    vec2 s = 1.0 / textureSize(input_image, 0);
    vec2 C = gl_FragCoord.xy;

    int r1 = -r - 1;
    vec2 P0 = s * (vec2(C) + vec2(r1, r1));
    vec2 P1 = s * (vec2(C) + vec2(r1, r));
```

```
    vec2 P2 = s * (vec2(C) + vec2( r, r1));
    vec2 P3 = s * (vec2(C) + vec2( r, r));

    float patchWidth = r + r + 1;
    float omega = 1.0 / (patchWidth * patchWidth);

    vec3  a, b, c, d;

    a = textureLod(Ak, P0, 0).rgb;
    b = textureLod(Ak, P1, 0).rgb;
    c = textureLod(Ak, P2, 0).rgb;
    d = textureLod(Ak, P3, 0).rgb;
    vec3 A = vec3(omega) * (a - b - c + d);

    a = textureLod(Bk, P0, 0).rgb;
    b = textureLod(Bk, P1, 0).rgb;
    c = textureLod(Bk, P2, 0).rgb;
    d = textureLod(Bk, P3, 0).rgb;
    vec3 B = vec3(omega) * (a - b - c + d);

    vec3 res = A * textureLod(input_image, C * s, 0).rgb + B;
    color = vec4(res.rgb, 1.0);
}
```

7.4 Results and Performance

We have benchmarked the performance of the filter fragment shaders on an Nvidia GTX 760 graphics card with an OpenGL 4.5 compatible driver on the Windows platform. A floating-point RGB image of size 1024 × 1024 was used in benchmarking and a summed area table compute shader published in [Sellers et al. 2013] was used in our pipeline.

Table 7.1 summarizes the results, and because the filter relies heavily on summed area table data structure for its performance, the overall speed is naturally determined by summed area table computation. The good thing about it is that any speed boost achieved by improved the summed area table component of the graphics pipeline can immediately benefit the guided image filter shader.

Figure 7.3 demonstrates the impact of patch size. As this parameter determines the size of the neighborhood for smoothing, we can see the smoothed halo effect is more spread out when the patch width is larger.

Shader	Per-call time (ms)	Number of calls	Total time (ms)
Squared intensity	0.61	1	0.63
Summed area table	2.46	4	9.84
Per-patch A_k and B_k	1.75	1	1.75
Per-pixel result	0.88	1	0.88
		TOTAL	13.1

Table 7.1. GPU timing result for an image of resolution 1024 × 1024.

Figure 7.4 shows the use of the edge strength control parameter ε. This parameter determines the minimum edge strength to be preserved, and we can see most edge-like features are better preserved when its value is relatively small.

Apart from being a GPU friendly edge-preserving filter, the guided image filter performs equally well on multicore architectures. We have seen fully multi-threaded and vectorized CPU implementation provide a satisfactory interactive rendering rate.

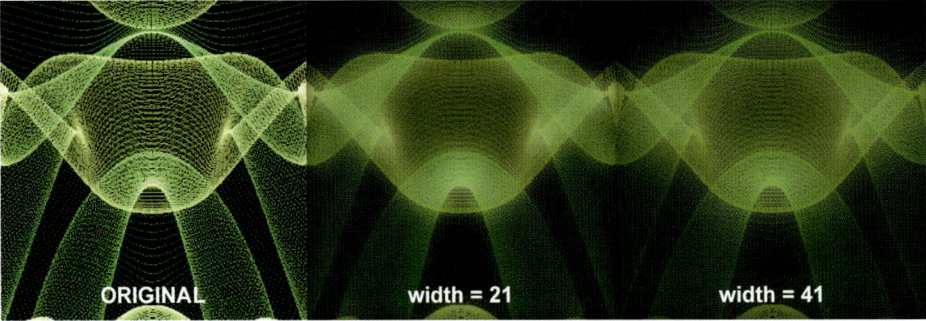

Figure 7.3. Using different patch width with same $\varepsilon = 0.25$.

Figure 7.4. Using different ε with same patch width = 21.

Acknowledgements

This work is partially supported by NSFC (Project No. 61272293) and the Research Grants Council of the Hong Kong Special Administrative Region under RGC General Research Fund (Project No. CUHK417913 and CUHK14200915).

References

[Crow 1984] Franklin C. Crow. "Summed-area tables for texture mapping". *Proceedings of the 11th annual conference on Computer graphics and interactive techniques*, 1984, pp. 207–212.

[He et al. 2010] Kaiming He, Jian Sun, and Xiaoou Tang. "Guided image filtering". *Proceedings of the 11th European conference on Computer Vision: Part I*, 2010, pp. 1–14.

[Sellers et al. 2013] Graham Sellers, Richard S. Wright Jr., and Nicholas Haemel. "Compute Shaders". *OpenGL SuperBible, 6th edition*, Addison-Wesley, 2013.

8

Variable Precision Pixel Shading for Improved Power Efficiency

Rahul P. Sathe
Intel

We propose a technique for selectively reducing the pixel shader precision for the purpose of efficient rendering in a low-power environment. Typically, pixel shading consumes the largest percentage of the power on GPUs [Pool 2012]. Modern APIs like Direct3D 11.1 allow users to reduce the shading precision to meet the low power requirements, but they don't allow doing so adaptively. Rendering at reduced precision can potentially produce artifacts in the rendered image. These artifacts are most noticeable where the user's attention is focused, which is typically at the center of the screen or, in the case of an eye tracking device, at the point provided as input by such a device. This chapter presents a scheme to render the scene at the highest precision where user's attention is focused and gradually reduce the precision at the points farther away from the focal point.

8.1 Introduction and Background

Image artifacts are more acceptable in some parts of the screen than others. Techniques proposed in the past like foveated 3D graphics [Guenter et al. 2012], coarse pixel shading [Vaidyanathan et al. 2014], and extending the graphics pipeline with adaptive, multirate shading [He et al. 2014] try to exploit this observation by reducing the sampling rate in less important parts of the screen. But none of these techniques propose reducing the shading precision. One can write a pixel shader that dynamically chooses the precision depending on the region of the screen that is being shaded. However, such a shader is less efficient because of the reduced SIMD usage due to the presence of dynamic control flow.

Forward shading refers to a technique where pixel shading is done immediately after rasterization (or after early and hierarchical Z/stencil testing, when applicable). Forward shading typically suffers from the issue of overdrawing the same pixel multiple times. Deferred shading overcomes the overdraw issue by decoupling the visibility determination and the shading. In the first pass, it writes out the pixel shader input (interpolated attribute values) into a buffer commonly called the *G-buffer* (Geometry buffer). In the second pass (a full-screen pass or a compute shader), it loads the G-buffer values and evaluates shading.

The key to lowering the pixel shader precision while shading certain parts of the screen is the ability to bind a lower precision shader while shading those pixels. With forward shading, one does not know where the polygons being shaded will land at the time that the pixel shader is bound. One can avoid shading regions that need different precision with the use of Z-buffer or stencil mask, but to shade the parts that require a different precision in a separate pass, the entire geometry processing stage needs to be done again. As a result, it is not efficient to use a specialized low-precision shader with the forward rendering. During the shading phase of the deferred shading process, one can bind a shader with a particular precision for shading the relevant portions of the screen. One can then repeat this with a different precision for different portions of the screen without processing the geometry multiple times. As a result, variable precision pixel shading fits well in the deferred rendering pipeline. We propose using our technique in conjunction with the tiled deferred renderer proposed by [Lauritzen 2010].

Texturing is one area that could be very sensitive to the precision. A small change in (u,v) values as a result of lowering the precision could mean vastly different looking texels. This is more likely to happen for large textures. Fortunately, texturing is typically done during the forward pass where we continue to use standard full-precision shading.

8.2 Algorithm

G-Buffer Generation

Just like in a normal deferred shading engine, our algorithm starts off by generating a G-buffer by writing out shading inputs at the pixel center. The G-buffer stores the derivatives of the view-space depth values in addition to the other surface data (position, normal, UVs, TBN basis, etc.) required for evaluating the BRDF during the shading pass. View-space depth derivatives are calculated by first multiplying the position with the camera-world-view matrix and evaluating

8.2 Algorithm

the `ddx_coarse()` and `ddy_coarse()` functions. We use spherical encoding to store the surface normal as a `float2` to save some G-buffer space and bandwidth. We pack the specular intensity and the specular power in the other two components to occupy a full `float4`. The G-buffer layout is given by the following structure.

```
struct GBuffer
{
    float4 normal_specular   : SV_Target0; // normal and specular params
    float4 albedo            : SV_Target1; // albedo
    float2 positionZGrad     : SV_Target3; // ddx, ddy of view-space depth
    float  positionZ         : SV_Target4; // view-space depth
};
```

Shading Passes

Normally, deferred shading has only one shading pass. But because we propose using different precisions while shading different parts of the screen, we have to perform multiple shading passes, one corresponding to each precision level. The compute shader is launched such that one thread group processes one region of the screen, henceforth referred to as a *tile*. Figure 8.1 shows how we statically mark the regions on the screen. Region A corresponds to the center region where image artifacts would be most noticeable. As a result, that needs to be shaded at the highest available precision. Regions B and C are further away from the center of the screen, so artifacts are progressively less noticeable in those regions.

Starting with DirectX 11.1 on Windows 8, new HLSL data types were introduced that allow applications to use lower precision, namely `min16float` and `min10float`. One can find out which types are supported on a given GPU by using the following snippet.

```
D3D11_FEATURE_DATA_SHADER_MIN_PRECISION_SUPPORT   minPrec;

hr = pd3dDevice->CheckFeatureSupport(
    D3D11_FEATURE_SHADER_MIN_PRECISION_SUPPORT, &minPrec, sizeof(minPrec));

if (FAILED(hr)) memset(&minPrec, 0, sizeof(minPrec));
```

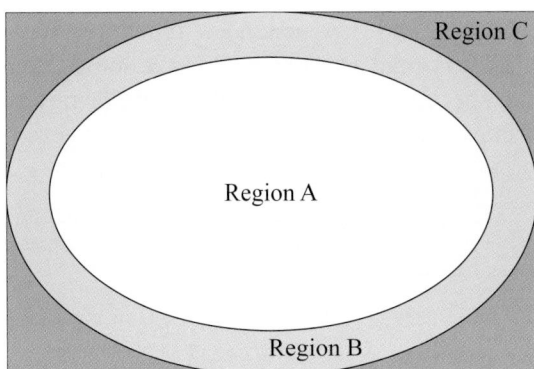

Figure 8.1. The screen is statically partitioned into the elliptical regions A, B, and C. Axis dimensions for region A are chosen arbitrarily and can be set to the desired values with the experimentation.

The value of `minPrec` in the above code tells the user what precisions are supported by the GPU for different shader types. If available, we compile three separate versions of the deferred shader, the one with the full precision for region A, the one with `min16float` precision for region B and the one with `min10float` precision for region C. If the `min10float` type is not supported, then we just use `min16float` for region C and full precision for regions A and B. The major and minor axes for elliptical regions corresponding to region A are a function of viewing distance. Since we use a compute shader for deferred shading, we do not mark these regions in the stencil buffer to selectively shade those regions. Instead, we check whether the tile on the screen is within the region of interest that is being shaded. We simply skip rendering if the tile is outside of region being shaded and free the corresponding hardware resources. Since the regions of interest are elliptical in shape, we use the following equation to test whether a point (x,y) is inside an ellipse centered at (h,k) with the major and minor axis lengths a and b.

$$\frac{(x-h)^2}{a^2} + \frac{(y-k)^2}{b^2} < 1$$

We perform the test at the each of the tile corners, and we shade all the pixels of the tile only if all the corners of the tile are within the region being shaded. If multisampling is enabled during the G-buffer generation pass, one should be careful to evaluate the above equation at the corners of the tile and not at the centers of the corner pixels. The reason for doing this is the fact that the sample locations can vary from one hardware vendor to another and only way to guarantee that all the samples in the tile are in a particular region is to do the in-out test at the tile corners. If multisampling is enabled during the G-buffer generation pass, one should use the technique discussed in [Lauritzen 2010] during the lighting pass in order to shade at the sample rate only when necessary.

After the in-out test for the entire tile, the compute shader is conceptually divided into the following phases:

1. Light tiling phase.
2. Analysis phases (if multisampling is enabled).
3. Pixel shading phase.
4. Sample shading phase (if multisampling is enabled).

At the end of each phase, the threads within the thread group synchronize. The details of the phases can be found in [Lauritzen 2010]. Listing 8.1 shows the pseudocode for the shading pass.

Listing 8.1. Pseudocode for the shading pass. It has four phases: the light tiling phase, the analysis phase, the pixel shading phase, and the sample shading phase. Phases are separated by a call to Groupsync().

```
#define GROUP_DIM 16
#define GROUP_SIZE (GROUP_DIM * GROUP_DIM)

groupshared uint sMinZ, sMaxZ; // Z-min and max for the tile.

// Light list for the tile.
groupshared uint sTileLightIndices[MAX_LIGHTS];
groupshared uint sTileNumLights;

[numthreads(GROUP_DIM, GROUP_DIM, 1)] // Coarse pixel is NxN.

void ComputeShaderTileCS(...)
{
    // Check to see if each of the corners of the tile lie within the
    // region being shaded. Proceed only if the tile lies inside.
    Groupsync();
```

```
// Load the surface data for all the pixels within NxN.
// Calculate the Z-bounds within the coarse pixel.
// Calculate min and max for the entire tile and store as sMinZ, sMaxZ.

// One thread processes one light.
for (lightIndex = groupIndex..totalLights)
{
    // If light intersects the tile append it to sTileLightIndices[].
}

Groupsync();

// Read the lights that touch this tile from the groupshared memory.
// Evaluate and accumulate lighting for every light for top left pixel.

// Check to see if per sample lighting is required.
bool perSampleShading = IsPerSampleShading(surfaceSamples);
if (perSampleShading)
{
    // Atomically increment sNumPerSamplePixels with the read back.
    // Append the pixel to the sPerSamplePixels[].
}
else
{
    // Store the results in the intermediate buffer in groupshared or
    // global memory OR if no per pixel component, splat the top-left
    // pixel's color to other pixels in NxN.
}

GroupSync();

uint globalSamples = sNumPerSamplePixels * (N * N - 1);
for (sample = groupIndex..globalSamples..sample += GROUP_SIZE)
{
    // Read the lights that touch this tile from the groupshared memory.
    // Accumulate the lighting for the sample.
    // Write out the results.
}

GroupSync();
```

```
}
```

8.3 Results

We measured the image quality on Intel Core i7-6700K 8M Skylake Quad-Core running at 4.0 GHz. Intel hardware does not support `min10float`, so our screen was divided in two regions. Regions A and B were shaded with the full-precision shader, and region C was shaded with the half-precision shader. We used the assets that we thought were representative of real game assets. We distributed 1024 lights in our scenes.

Figure 8.2 shows images produced at different shading precisions. The top row of the Figure 8.2 shows the images rendered at 1600×1200 resolution with a full-precision shader used for the rendering pass. The second row shows the same scenes rendered with the half-precision shader used for shading every pixel on the screen. The third row shows the images where region B was shaded with full precision and region C was shaded with half precision during the rendering pass. The last row shows scaled (100 times) image differences between screenshots with full precision and mixed precision (rows 1 and 3). The PSNR for the mixed precision with respect to full precision was 41.22 for the power plant scene and 38.02 for the Sponza scene.

8.4 Discussion

Following the trajectory of the evolving GPU languages, dynamic binding in the shaders is a real possibility in the near future. With dynamic shader binding, there won't be a need to bind a specialized shader prior to the draw or dispatch call. With this restriction removed, the technique could be used during forward shading as well, but one has to be mindful of texture sampling issues and SIMD efficiency when using such a technique with forward rendering.

Figure 8.2. Images in the top row were rendered entirely with the full-precision shader, and images in the second row were rendered entirely with the half-precision shader. The third row shows the images when screen was partitioned into regions B and C as per Figure 8.1, region B was shaded at full precision, and region C was shaded at half precision. The last row shows the differences between rows 1 and 3 scaled 100 times.

Acknowledgements

Thanks to Tomas Akenine-Möller and Karthik Vaidyanathan for their help with writing this chapter. Tomas Akenine-Möller is a Royal Swedish Academy of Sciences Research Fellow supported by a grant from the Knut and Allice Wallenberg foundation.

References

[Guenter et al. 2012] Brian Guenter, Mark Finch, Steven Drucker, Desney Tan, and John Snyder. "Foveated 3D Graphics". *ACM Transactions on Graphics*, Vol 31, No. 6 (November 2012), Article 164.

[Vaidyanathan et al. 2014] Karthik Vaidyanathan, Marco Salvi, Robert Toth, Tim Foley, Tomas Akenine-Möller, Jim Nilsson, Jacob Munkberg, Jon Hasselgren, Masamichi Sugihara, Petrik Clarberg, Tomasz Janczak, and Aaron Lefohn. "Coarse Pixel Shading". *High Performance Graphics*, 2014.

[Lauritzen 2010] Andrew Lauritzen. "Deferred Rendering for Current and Future Rendering Pipelines". Beyond Programmable Shading, Siggraph Course, 2010.

[Pool 2012] Jeff Pool. "Energy-Precision Tradeoffs in the Graphics Pipeline". PhD dissertation, 2012.

[He et al. 2014] Yong He, Yan Gu, and Kayvon Fatahalian. "Extending the graphics pipeline with adaptive, multi-rate shading". *ACM Transactions on Graphics*, Vol. 33, No. 4 (July 2014), Article 142.

9

A Fast and High-Quality Texture Atlasing Algorithm

Manny Ko
Activision Blizzard Inc.

We introduce a fast atlasing algorithm that is good at filling holes and can handle highly irregular shapes. It produces much tighter packing than the popular Tetris method. We also address the various issues stemming from texture filtering, including a means to filter across charts robustly. Our method has been implemented as a Maya plugin and used successfully in several Sony first-party games.

9.1 Introduction

Texture mapping requires (u,v) texture coordinates (UVs) to be assigned to vertices of a mesh. It is usually a three step process of segmentation, parameterization, and packing [Lévy et al. 2002]. In games, segmentation is usually a labor-intensive manual process of unwrapping, which involves unfolding the mesh at seams. The resulting disk-like pieces are what we call *charts*. The charts are packed into an atlas to optimize the use of texture memory and reduce the number of draw calls that would be necessary due to intervening state changes. Nvidia's white paper demonstrates the importance of batching in real-time rendering [Kwatra et al. 2004].

This chapter addresses the third step in the process, that of packing. We discuss an efficient algorithm that can generate high-quality atlases out of arbitrarily-shaped charts. The algorithm is also very simple to implement and does not involve complicated components like nonlinear solvers. The atlasing algorithm is very good at filling holes and can reserve borders around charts to handle the bilinear filtering kernels used in real-time rendering. To minimize the filtering artifacts, we also introduce a novel approach to blending texels across shared chart boundaries *before* they are moved by the atlasing code. The algorithm is inspired by Sibley's poster [Sibley and Taubin 2004], which uses rasterization to reconstruct the chart adjacencies. We instead use the chart's topology to reliably establish adjacency, which is critical for reliable filtering.

From the point of view of game production, the problem is even a little more general. We are trying to pack a given set of textures that the artists have applied to a set of models into a limited set of texture objects. The total size of the set of texture is limited by available texture memory, and the sizes are usually limited to powers of two and a very limited set of dimensions. Those limits are frequently associated with the game's texture management scheme. From an algorithmic point of view, this is the classic bin packing problem.

9.2 Background

When I was researching the packing problem a few years back, I was surprised to find very little relevant work in CG research. The problem has been well studied in operations research [Chen et al. 2003] and even in the fabric industry as the stock cutting problem. In graphics, Lévy's work on least-square conformal mapping (LSCM) [Lévy et al. 2002] is one of the few attempts at tackling all three phases of the problem, although the heart of their work concerns the parameterization step. For packing, they proposed a Tetris algorithm that is often used by other works.

There is a large and interesting body of work on parameterization. In game production, automatic unwrap and parameterization is seldom used because artists want exact control in order to optimize the precious texture memory. Atlas packing, on the other hand, is needed for the purely technical requirements of the real-time engine. As such, it is tedious and most appropriate for automation, especially when generating light maps.

Maya has a simple atlasing algorithm that seems to treat charts as rectangles and pack them using a variant of a descending first-fit heuristic. DirectX also has a UVAtlas tool that appears to produce tighter maps than Maya's but still leaves many holes that our algorithm can fill in.

The other well-known algorithm for atlasing is the Tetris algorithm by Lévy et al. [Lévy et al. 2002] as part of LSCM. Tetris tracks an irregular front and hence, can pack better than algorithms that model the canvas and shape as bounding rectangles. However, front tracking cannot capture many holes created during the course of packing. Hole-filling is a critical attribute of a good atlasing algorithm because holes can be created in the course of packing irregular shapes. In Figure 9.1, one can imagine the empty space surrounding the large circular chart

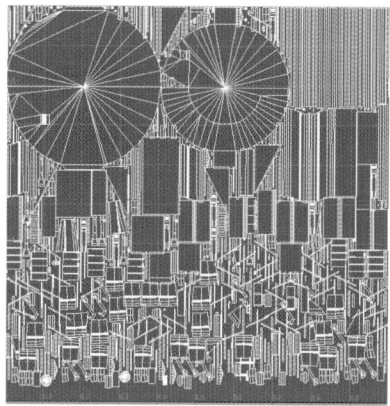 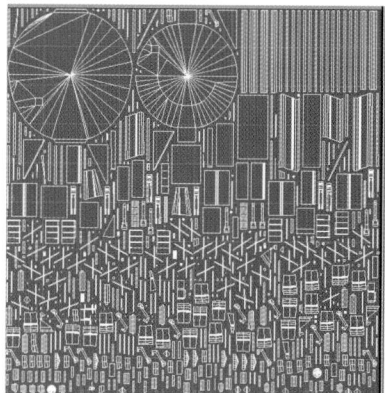

Figure 9.1. Output of the atlas packer. (a) No border pixels. (b) One-pixel borders.

after it has been placed in the atlas. If the atlasing algorithm only treats shapes as bounding rectangles, then all of that precious space is left empty. Our algorithm successfully packs a lot of thin shapes into that space.

9.3 Chart Segmentation

For segmentation, we followed the general idea of Lévy to break the mesh at creases. Creases are defined by angles across adjacent faces greater than a user defined tolerance. In addition, we also split charts based on shader/material and UV discontinuity. The rest is a standard application of a fast *equivalent class* algorithm. The best approach is to use *path compression*, which supports constant-time find and union queries. (The details are given in standard data structure books.) We do not attempt to trace crease lines as performed by Lévy et al., but instead we simply try to capture the unwrapped face connectivity that is already in the mesh.

Conceptually, each face is initially in its own set. Sets are joined when the IsSameChart() function in Listing 9.1 indicates they should be in the same chart. After one pass through the faces, path compression is applied to the PartitionSet object, during which each parent link is replaced by the root link. Both steps are $O(n)$ operations since Union() is a constant time operation. The final loop adds all the faces to the charts they belong to using the Find() operator, which is also an $O(n)$ operation since Find() is a constant time operation in a path-compressed partition set. The IsSameChart() function is typically implemented with a topology class using half-edges.

Listing 9.1. This code computes charts using path compression.

```
void GenerateTextureCharts(const Topology& topology)
{
    PartitionSet pset(numFaces);
    for (j = 0; j < numFaces; ++j)
    {
        const Face *tface = topology.GetFace(j);
        HalfEdge *firste = tface->FirstEdge(), *edgeiter = firste;
        do
        {
            const HalfEdge *pair = edgeiter->GetPair(); // Half-edge buddy.
            const Face *adjface = pair->GetFace(); // Neighboring face.
            if (adjface)
            {
                // Test for shared UVs and materials.
                if (IsSameChart(tface, adjface))
                {
                    pset.Union(j, adjface->m_faceId);  // Union is O(1).
                }
            }

            edgeiter = edgeiter->Next();   // Next edge for the face.
        } while (edgeiter != firste);
    }

    pset.CompressPath();    // Every parent is replaced by the bin #.
    for (j = 0; j < numFaces; ++j)
    {
        // Add faces to their charts.
        const Face *tface = topology.GetFace(j);
        if (tface->IsValid())
        {
            (*charts)[pset.Find(j)].AddFace(j);   // Find is O(1).
        }
    }
}
```

9.4 Atlas Packing

Our atlas packing algorithm separates the problem into three steps:

1. Generating candidate positions for a chart.
2. A quick check to see if the proposal is a valid one.
3. A goodness metric that measures how good the proposed position is.

This decomposition allows us to use many different heuristics in Step 1 and share the time-critical implementation in Step 2. We encode the metric in a strategy object for loose coupling. This enables great flexibility in accommodating the different needs of studios and games.

Canvas and Shapes

The heart of the algorithm is Step 2, and this is the most time consuming step. The key is to design an efficient representation for the canvas and the shapes. Our algorithm is based on rasterizing the UV-triangles into a bitmap at the resolution of the target texture. The bitmap is converted into a shape encoded in a bitset. The rasterization should be performed accurately to reproduce the addressing and coverage calculation of the target GPU. One can either directly use the target GPU to render these shapes or exactly reproduce the logic in software. The key data structure used by the packer is a canvas that is another 2D bitset mirroring the dimension of our texture. This representation enables us to very quickly determine whether a given position in the canvas is already occupied by a previously placed chart. The checks consist of simple boolean ANDs and bit counting. A chart only has to be rasterized once and can be quickly placed in many proposed points until we decide that we have to change the scale.

If we want to implement back-tracking, then removing a shape from the canvas is simple and efficient. We just have to clear all the bits occupied by the shape. The history can be compactly encoded as a pair of (x, y) offsets. We choose to store these offsets with the shapes since we only have one active position for each shape. If you need to store multiple candidate positions (e.g., in a genetic algorithm), then the offsets can easily be stored in separate arrays. These offsets are needed by the atlas-aware blending so that split charts can find each other's edges.

We do not need to track a complicated geometric relationship like the front in the Tetris algorithm. Front tracking also limits the ability of Tetris to handle holes. Our algorithm is much freer to explore the entire search space and can do it very efficiently.

Shape Dilation

If the user requests border pixels to be reserved, then we simply apply an image dilation operator to our shapes before attempting to place them onto the 2D canvas. The code shown in Listing 9.2 is a simple, nonrecursive implementation.

Listing 9.2. This code dilates a shape by identifying any pixels having the property that at least one of their eight neighbors belong to the original shape.

```
void ShapekBuilder::Dilate(ShapeMask *shape, int border)
{
    ShapeMask& shapemask = *shape;

    int origin[2];
    shape->m_rect.GetOrigin(origin);

    ShapeMask edges;
    edges.Init(origin[0], origin[1], shape->Width(), shape->Height());

    int x, y;

    // Grow region.
    for (int p = 0; p < border; p++)
    {
        shapemask.FirstFree(&x, &y);        // First empty pixel.
        while (!shapemask.IsEnd(x, y))
        {
            // Do we have an 8-connected neighbor that is set?

            if (shapemask.HasNeighbor8(x, y))
            {
                edges.Add(x, y);
            }

            shapemask.NextFree(&x, &y);     // Next empty pixel.
        }

        shapemask += edges;
    }
}
```

Canvas Packing

The canvas packing logic is straightforward, as shown in Listing 9.3. We encapsulate the heuristic for picking the next chart in an oracle. (We have implemented several oracles.) The classic descending first-fit, where we sort the shapes by height, works surprising well. We also experimented with versions that sort by area or by width with and without randomization.

For the goodness metric, after some experimentation, we found a very simple metric that works surprising well:

$$\text{utilization} = \frac{\text{number of occupied pixels}}{\text{bounding rect of shapes}}.$$

This simple greedy packing approach might feel like it is too obvious to discuss. Readers can compare its output with those of LSCM and the DirectX SDK's atlas packer and see that it outperforms them by a significant margin in most cases. Its ability to fill holes very effectively is seldom matched in other popular methods. See Figure 9.2 for an example of it in action.

Listing 9.3. This code implements canvas packing.

```
for (int c = 0; c < numCharts; c++)
{
    chart = charts[c];
    oracle->NextPosition(pos, 0);
    while (!packed && pos.IsValid())
    {
        MoveChart(chart, pos);
        if (canvas.Fits(chart))
        {
            canvas.Add(chart);
            packed = true;
        }
        else
        {
            oracle->NextPosition(pos, chart);
        }
    }
}
```

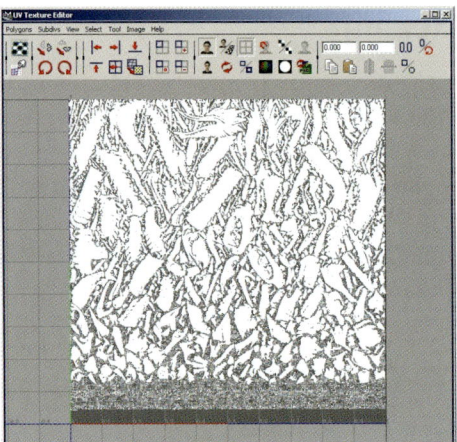

Figure 9.2. Output of the atlas packer for a dragon model.

The simple greedy method's main weakness shows up when it is presented with a few very large shapes or when the canvas (light map) is very small. If this is an important case for your game, you can add a simple annealing step to improve the solution when the degree of freedom available to the packer is small.

9.5 Atlas-Aware Filtering

Sibley's poster [Sibley and Taubin 2004] introduces an interesting idea of using *microedges* to perform Laplacian diffusion across chart boundaries. A microedge is a shared edge in the original UV map before segmentation and packing have been applied. When the texture filtering kernel is placed over that edge, its footprint includes pixels inside one chart as well as pixels in the empty space we have reserved for border pixels. If those border pixels are left as black, then the reconstructed color would be wrong. The desired result should be one where the filter is placed over the original unsplit map. That is clearly not possible because the other side of the chart's edge is likely to be far away in the texture. We do the next best thing, which is to blend the texels across the microedges to simulate the correct filtering result.

We directly build on top of their idea with one refinement. The original proposal uses rasterization and pixel classification to derive the microedges, for which it is not always easy to produce a consistent neighborhood structure. Instead, we obtain them directly from the topology data structure that we built for chart segmentation. In Laplacian and anisotropic diffusion, it is critical for

Figure 9.3. Output of atlas-aware diffusion.

neighbors to have a consistent neighborhood structure. If a pixel's neighbor fails to recognize the pixel as its neighbor, the energy flow becomes one-way, and serious artifacts are generated.

The microedges are stored in a list by the chart segmentation module. Next, we iterate through every texel in the canvas, checking to see if each texel is within the filter kernel that touches a border texel. These are the only texels we want to be involved in the blending. For texels that overlap the kernel, we find the nearest microedge using a 2D distance check, given in Listing 9.4. For the distance check, we use `PerpDot` [Hill 1994], which is an elegant and efficient way to compute the perpendicular distance to a line segment. Once we have located the nearest edge we compute the t value along the edge that is used for the linear interpolation needed to reconstruct the center pixel for the kernel. Please refer to [Sibley and Taubin 2004] for details. A sample output of the diffusion process is shown in Figure 9.3. One can build a search structure to accelerate this, but a carefully implemented linear search was good enough for an interactive Maya plugin.

Acknowledgements

The author would like to thank Peter Sibley for his helpful discussions and Naughty Dog for their support during this report.

Listing 9.4. This code calculates the 2D distance from the point p to the line passing through v0 and v1.

```
float Distance2Line(const Vec2& v0, const Vec2& v1, const Vec2& p)
{
    Vec2 a = v1 - v0;      // v0 + t * a
    return PerpDot(a, p - v0) / Length(a);
}
```

References

[Chen et al. 2003] Ping Chen, Zhaohui Fu, Andrew Lim, and Brian Rodrigues. "Two dimensional packing for irregular shaped objects". *Proceedings of the 36th Hawaii International Conference on System Sciences*, 2003.

[Degener and Klein 2007] Patrick Degener and Reinhard Klein. "Texture atlas generation for inconsistent meshes and point sets". *International Conference on Shape Modeling and Applications*, 2007.

[Hill 1994] F. S. Hill, Jr. "The Pleasures of 'Perp Dot' Products". *Graphics Gems IV*, edited by Paul S. Heckbert. Morgan Kaufmann, 1994.

[Kwatra et al. 2004] Vivek Kwatra, Irfan Essa, Aaron Bobick, and Nipun Kwatra. "Improving Batching Using Texture Atlases". Nvidia SDK Whitepaper, July 2004.

[Lévy et al. 2002] Bruno Lévy, Sylvain Petitjean, Nicolas Ray, and Jérome Maillot. "Least squares conformal maps for automatic texture atlas generation". *ACM Transactions on Graphics*, Vol. 21, No. 3 (July 2002).

[Ray and Lévy 2003] Nicolas Ray and Bruno Lévy. "Hierarchical least squares conformal map". *Proceedings of the 11th Pacific Conference on Computer Graphics and Applications*, 2003, p. 263.

[Sander et al. 2003] P. V. Sander, Z. J. Wood, S. J. Gortler, J. Snyder, and H. Hoppe. "Multi-chart geometry images". *Proceedings of the 2003 Eurographics/ACM SIGGRAPH symposium on Geometry processing*, pp. 146–155.

[Sibley and Taubin 2004] P.G. Sibley and Garbiel Taubin. "Atlas aware Laplacian smoothing". IEEE Visualization, Poster Session, 2004.

[Van Horn and Turk 2008] R. Brooks Van Horn III and Greg Turk. "Antialiasing procedural shaders with reduction maps". *IEEE Transactions on Visualization and Computer Graphics*, Vol. 14, No. 3 (2008), pp. 539–550.

Part II

Physics

10

Rotational Joint Limits in Quaternion Space

Gino van den Bergen
Dtecta

10.1 Introduction

The motions of an animated game character are generally controlled by a hierarchy of coordinate transformations. The coordinate transformations represent the skeletal bones. Except for the root bone, each bone is the child of exactly one parent bone. Game characters are animated by changing the relative placement of a child bone with respect to its parent bone over time. Character animation can be controlled manually by smoothly interpolating key frames, which are character poses at given instances of time. These key frames are either created by an animator or recorded using motion capture.

Characters can also be animated procedurally. The relative bone placements are then solved in real-time according to kinematic and dynamic rules (e.g., ragdoll physics). The rules describe restrictions on the relative motion of a child bone with respect to its parent, and the relative motions are determined by the joint type. A joint type defines one or more degrees of freedom (DOFs) between a child bone and its parent. The number of DOFs represent the number of parameters that are required for defining the configuration of a joint. Parameters often have a limited range. For example, door hinges have one DOF and usually have a range close to 180°.

The joints that connect the bones are in most practical cases idealized as purely rotational joints, but this is a simplification of reality. For example, a human knee combines a rotational movement with a slight translational movement. We can often get away with ignoring the translational component. It is safe to assume that for our character models, or organic models in general, all we need are rotational joints.

An unrestricted bone has three rotational DOFs. In mechanical devices, joints that have all three rotational DOFs are not very common. Examples are ball joints used for connecting the front wheel suspension of an automobile. In human or animal skeletons, ball joints, or rather ball-and-socket joints, are quite common. A human skeleton houses ball-and-socket joints in the shoulders and the hips.

Ball-and-socket joints have a limited range of admissible relative orientations. Enforcing joint limits in a ball-and-socket joint is tricky because of two reasons:

1. Parameterization of the three rotational DOFs is not intuitive and is prone to including singularities.
2. Human shoulder and hip range bounds are oddly shaped manifolds and are hard to represent in our chosen parameterization.

This chapter discusses how to define the joint limits for ball-and-socket joints and how to enforce them procedurally.

10.2 3D Rotations

Contrary to translations, the result of a sequence of rotations is order dependent. A series of translations can be executed in any order, and the resulting translation will always be the same. This is not the case for rotations. For example, a 90-degree rotation of a bunny over the Y axis followed by a 90-degree rotation over the Z axis gives a different orientation than a 90-degree rotation over the Z axis followed by a 90-degree rotation over the Y axis, as shown in Figure 10.1.

Nevertheless, independent of the number of consecutive rotations we apply to orient a 3D object, the resulting orientation can be reached by a single rotation from the initial orientation about a suitable 3D axis that is not necessarily one of the coordinate axes. This is known as *Euler's rotation theorem*. Consequently, we can, and often do, identify an orientation by a single rotation about a particular 3D axis.

A 3D coordinate system is defined by the position vector of its local origin plus three vectors that represent its basis. As a result, a 3D coordinate system has twelve degrees of freedom, three for the position and nine for the basis vectors. If we restrict ourselves to rigid body transformations, the three basis vectors have unit length and are mutually orthogonal. By imposing these restrictions, we lose

10.2 3D Rotations

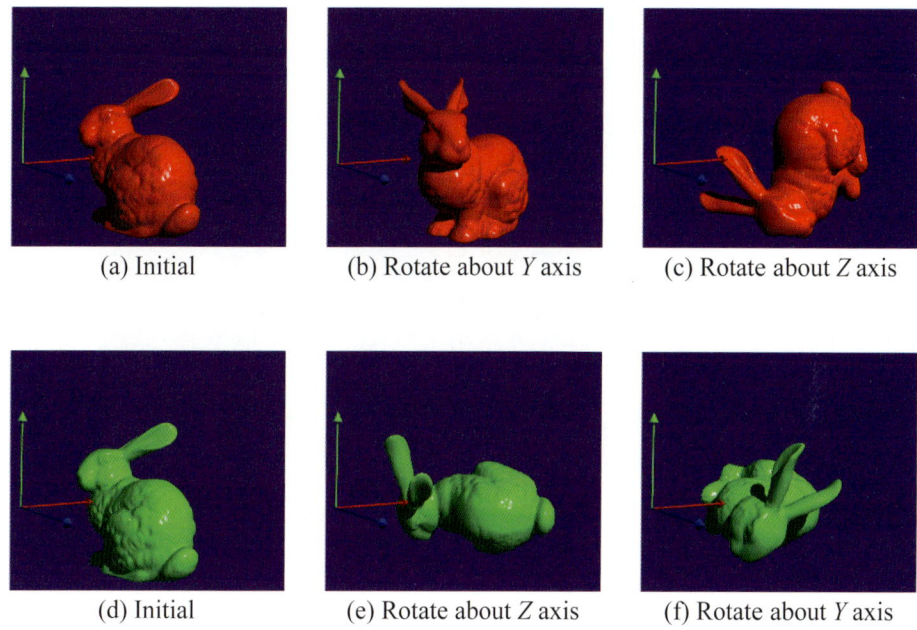

Figure 10.1. Consecutive rotations do not commute.

six degrees of freedom. A rigid body transformation has three rotational and three translational degrees of freedom. This means that we need at least three parameters to define a relative orientation in 3D.

So, how do we parameterize 3D rotations? A common choice is to define an orientation by a sequence of three rotations over predefined axes. Here, the parameters are the angles of rotation about the chosen axes, and they are referred to as *Euler angles*. The choice of axes is arbitrary, as long as no two consecutive axes in the sequence are the same. For example, *XYZ*, *ZYX*, *XZX*, *YXY*, etc., are proper sequences of axes. In fact, there are 12 possible sequences[1] of coordinate axes leading to 12 different Euler-angle parameterizations of the same orientation.

Orientations can be intuitively controlled by Euler angles, since they have a mechanical interpretation as three nested gimbals, as depicted in Figure 10.2. However, use of Euler-angle parameterization for limiting rotational movement

---

[1] Negative coordinate axes are excluded. We have three choices for the first axis, and two choices for the second and third axes.

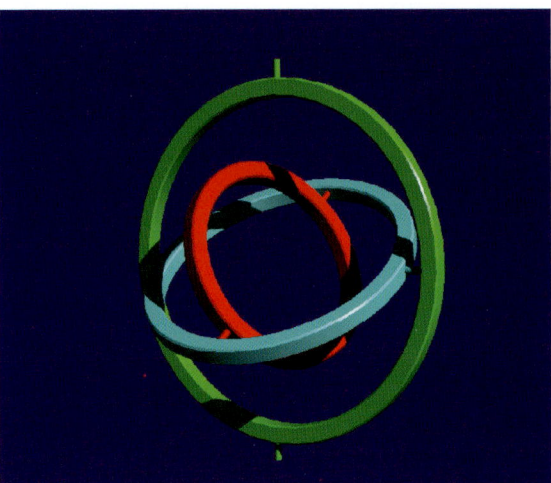

Figure 10.2. Euler angles are intuitively interpreted as three nested gimbals.

can be troublesome, notably when the underlying mechanics of the rotation is not a stack of gimbals, such as is the case for our ball-and-socket joint.

Limiting each of the three Euler angles independently is a bad idea for ball-and-socket joints. The manifold formed by the boundary of admissible angle triples often shows sharp corners. When clamping out-of-bounds angles to their allowed range under procedural animation, the bone can get temporarily stuck at a corner orientation. Furthermore, if the first and third axes are close to being aligned, the corresponding angles pretty much cancel each other out, resulting in a range of angle triples matching the same orientation. This singularity in the parameterization, better known as *gimbal lock*, may cause an orientation to be reachable only by following an implausible path through the volume of admissible angle triples.

There is a better parameterization of relative orientations that also uses three parameters. Euler's rotation theorem states that any orientation can be reached using a single rotation about a suitable axis. This rotation is usually expressed as an axis-angle pair, where the axis is a unit 3D vector representing the direction of the rotation axis, and the angle is the amount of rotation about that axis. Axis-angle pairs have a singularity for the zero orientation, since the zero orientation can be constructed from any direction and an angle that is a multiple of 2π radians (360°), including an angle of zero.

10.2 3D Rotations

We can get rid of the singularity for the zero angle by combining axis and angle into a single 3D vector that is the axis scaled by the angle. Given a normalized vector **u** and angle θ, we obtain a 3D vector **r** combining the two by setting

$$\mathbf{r} = \theta\mathbf{u}.$$

In this way, the zero orientation is uniquely identified by the zero vector. This parameterization as a 3D vector is called the *exponential-map* parameterization [Grassia 98].

The exponential-map parameterization still has a singularity for angles of $2k\pi$, where k is an integer not equal to zero. However, for our purpose, we can steer clear of this singularity by imposing that the vector length (angle of rotation) lies in the range $[0, 2\pi)$. We still have a double covering of the space of orientations, since for an axis **u** and angle θ we see that $\theta\mathbf{u}$ and $(2\pi - \theta)(-\mathbf{u})$ result in the same orientation. Further restriction of the maximum vector length to π clears us of the double covering except for rotations over an angle of π radians (180°) itself.

The exponential map offers a better parameterization for imposing rotational joint limits. It offers a singularity-free spherical subspace that encloses the range of all orientations generated by a ball-and-socket joint. The set of admissible orientations is defined by a volume inside the sphere. Identification of out-of-bounds orientations boils down to testing the exponential-map vector for containment inside that volume. Joint limits can be enforced by mapping out-of-bounds orientations to the closest admissible orientation in the volume. The Euclidean metric that we use for measuring the distance between points can also be used for measuring the distance between orientations. Using this metric to define the closest admissible orientation may not accurately give us the admissible orientation that requires the shortest angle of rotation to reach. However, in practical cases, the errors are small, and thus the Euclidean metric suffices to map an out-of-bounds orientation back to the admissible volume in a plausible manner.

What stops the exponential map from being our parameterization of choice when checking and enforcing joint limits is the fact that conversions between exponential-map vectors and matrices or quaternions is computationally expensive and susceptible to numerical error. Ideally, we would like to use the same parameterization for enforcing joint limits as we do for our other computations with rotations. The most promising candidate parameterization would be the space of unit quaternions.

10.3 Unit Quaternions

A lot has been written about quaternions, and yet their math remains somewhat elusive. Let's recap the basics and try to build some intuition for the math.

The quaternion number system extends the complex numbers by defining three imaginary units **i**, **j**, and **k** whose multiplication rules are given by the following table, where a unit from the left column is multiplied by a unit from the top row.

×	**i**	**j**	**k**
i	−1	**k**	−**j**
j	−**k**	−1	**i**
k	**j**	−**i**	−1

A quaternion is denoted as

$$\mathbf{q} = w + x\mathbf{i} + y\mathbf{j} + z\mathbf{k},$$

where w, x, y, and z are real numbers. w is the real or *scalar* part, and (x, y, z) is the imaginary or *vector* part. In scalar-vector notation, quaternion multiplication is given by

$$[w_1, \mathbf{v}_1][w_2, \mathbf{v}_2] = [w_1 w_2 - \mathbf{v}_1 \cdot \mathbf{v}_2, w_1 \mathbf{v}_2 + w_2 \mathbf{v}_1 + \mathbf{v}_1 \times \mathbf{v}_2],$$

giving us an expression in terms of the familiar and possibly more comfortable vector dot and cross products.

The conjugate of a complex number is straightforwardly extended to a quaternion. The conjugate of quaternion **q**, denoted by $\mathbf{q}^*$, is defined by

$$[w, \mathbf{v}]^* = [w, -\mathbf{v}].$$

Multiplication of a quaternion by its conjugate yields its squared magnitude:

$$\mathbf{q}\mathbf{q}^* = \mathbf{q}^*\mathbf{q} = w^2 + \mathbf{v} \cdot \mathbf{v} = w^2 + x^2 + y^2 + z^2.$$

Let's think of quaternions as points (w, x, y, z) in four-dimensional space. Then, the set of *unit quaternions*, i.e., quaternions having a magnitude of one, form a hypersphere. This hypersphere is a three-dimensional manifold, just as a sphere in 3D space is a two-dimensional manifold, and a circle in 2D is a one-dimensional manifold. Moreover, the multiplication of two unit quaternions always yields another unit quaternion. Unit quaternions form a multiplicative subgroup with 1 as the identity and the conjugate as the inverse.

Rotations map to unit quaternions and vice versa in a manner that is free of singularities. A rotation of θ radians about unit vector $\mathbf{u}$ is represented by the unit quaternion

$$\left[\cos\left(\frac{\theta}{2}\right), \sin\left(\frac{\theta}{2}\right)\mathbf{u}\right].$$

Many operations involving rotations can be executed directly in quaternion space using quaternion multiplication. For example, the image of a vector after rotation is computed using the so-called *sandwich product*,

$$\mathbf{v}' = \mathbf{q}\mathbf{v}\mathbf{q}^*.$$

Here, the vector $\mathbf{v}$ is regarded as a pure imaginary quaternion. We see that the conjugate indeed performs an inverse rotation.

However, 3D orientations and quaternions do not match one-to-one. We see that rotations of θ and $\theta + 2\pi$ result in the same orientation. However, they do not result in the same quaternion, but rather in two opposing quaternions. Our quaternion space is a double covering of orientation space, since for any quaternion $\mathbf{q}$, the negated quaternion $-\mathbf{q}$ represents the same orientation.

10.4 Quaternions vs. Exponential Map

Quaternion space is parameterized by four dependent parameters, where three should suffice. Moreover, the double covering of orientation space may complicate matters in defining and enforcing joint limits. However, let us not despair because things are not as bad as they appear.

Since we only consider unit quaternions, we can always find the fourth parameter less a sign, given the other three parameters. Given a vector part $\mathbf{v}$, we know that for the scalar part w the following must hold:

$$w = \pm\sqrt{1 - \mathbf{v}\cdot\mathbf{v}}.$$

Moreover, the full orientation space fits in the hemisphere of unit quaternions with nonnegative w. Indeed, any quaternion whose scalar part is negative can be negated to land it in the positive hemisphere without changing the orientation it represents. By restricting rotation angles to a maximum of π radians, we can still cover the full orientation space.

Any rotation with angle θ in the range $[-\pi, \pi]$ is mapped to a quaternion whose scalar part is nonnegative. Under the assumption that w is nonnegative, we can identify any orientation by the vector part only. This means that we have a parameterization of orientation space using three independent parameters. Any 3D vector whose length is at most one can be mapped to a 3D orientation. This parameterization is free of any singularities. However, double covering of orientations identified by 180° rotations exist. These orientations are represented by pairs of opposing vectors of length one.

The parameterization as unit-quaternion vector parts closely matches the exponential-map parameterization. Both parameterizations are given by a 3D ball. The quaternion-vector ball has radius one, whereas the exponential-map ball has radius π. Both parameterizations are singularity free and have double covering only for orientations represented by vectors on the surface of the ball. There is a one-to-one mapping from quaternion vectors to exponential-map vectors. For a quaternion vector $\mathbf{v}$, the corresponding exponential-map vector is

$$\frac{2\arcsin(\|\mathbf{v}\|)}{\|\mathbf{v}\|}\mathbf{v},$$

where $\|\mathbf{v}\|$ is the length of $\mathbf{v}$. The mapping changes only the length of the vector. The directions of the vectors are the same.

As can be seen in Figure 10.3, the arcsine mapping shows extreme warping towards the surface of the ball. This is something we need to take into account when imposing joint limits. Geometry close to the boundary requires prewarping to create a proper joint-limit manifold in rotation space. However, for rotation angles less than, say $\frac{2}{3}\pi$ radians (120°), we can pretty much regard the mapping as linear without introducing a huge error. In the next section, we examine a typical model for limiting ball and socket joints.

10.5 Swing-Twist Limits

In the swing-twist model, the relative rotation is decomposed into two rotations, and each component is limited independently. The twist component represents the rotation about the arm, and the swing component represents the rotation orthogonal to the arm. Assuming the arm is given by the local X axis, we decompose the rotation quaternion as a product of a rotation about the X axis and a rotation about an axis that lies in the local YZ plane. Optionally, when traversing from shoulder to elbow, we may choose to first apply the twist before applying the swing as depicted in Figure 10.4(a). However, in most practical cases the

10.5 Swing-Twist Limits

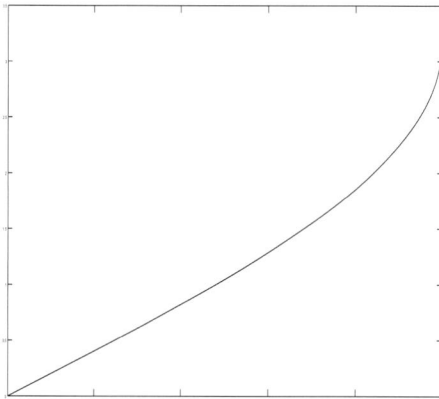

Figure 10.3. Lengths of quaternion vectors plotted against lengths of exponential map vectors.

twist follows the swing as depicted in Figure 10.4(b). Let $\mathbf{q} = w + x\mathbf{i} + y\mathbf{j} + z\mathbf{k}$ be our relative rotation (with $w \geq 0$). This rotation is decomposed into a swing and twist component as

$$\mathbf{q} = \mathbf{q}_{swing}\mathbf{q}_{twist}.$$

Here, $\mathbf{q}_{swing}$ has a zero $\mathbf{i}$ term and $\mathbf{q}_{twist}$ has zero $\mathbf{j}$ and $\mathbf{k}$ terms. Both are unit quaternions with nonnegative scalar parts. The unique decomposition is given by

$$\mathbf{q}_{swing} = s + \frac{wy - xz}{s}\mathbf{j} + \frac{wz + xy}{s}\mathbf{k}$$

and

$$\mathbf{q}_{twist} = \frac{w}{s} + \frac{x}{s}\mathbf{i},$$

where

$$s = \sqrt{w^2 + x^2},$$

as can be verified by writing out the multiplication.

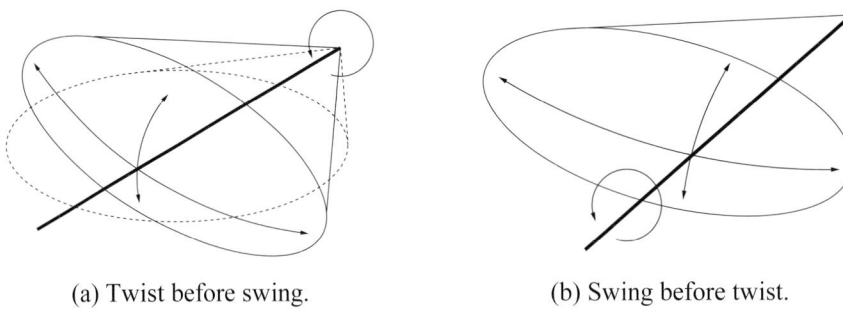

(a) Twist before swing.   (b) Swing before twist.

Figure 10.4. Two ways to decompose a rotation into a swing and twist component.

In the less common case, where twist is applied before swing,

$$\mathbf{q} = \mathbf{q}_{\text{twist}} \mathbf{q}_{\text{swing}}.$$

In this case, the decomposition results in the same twist component $\mathbf{q}_{\text{twist}}$. The swing component, however, differs from the previous case and is given by

$$\mathbf{q}_{\text{swing}} = s + \frac{wy + xz}{s}\mathbf{j} + \frac{wz - xy}{s}\mathbf{k}.$$

Notice the flipped addition and subtraction operations in the imaginary terms with respect to the swing-before-twist case.

The decomposition is unique except for the case where the rotation $\mathbf{q}$ is a pure swing rotation of π radians, in which case w and x, and therefore also s, are zero. In this case, the arm, or local X axis, is rotated 180° and aligns with the parent's negative X axis. This is a singularity, since any orientation that is the result of a full flip of the X axis can be obtained by flipping 180° over a different axis in the YZ plane and twisting the orientation into place. For the singularity case, we assume a twist angle of zero and take $\mathbf{q}_{\text{swing}}$ to be equal to $\mathbf{q}$.

Each component is limited by mapping the vector part to the desired range and then computing the scalar part accordingly. Limiting the twist component simply boils down to clamping the twist angle to the desired range. The twist angle, i.e., the angle of twist rotation about the local X axis, can be mapped straightforwardly to the twist vector part. Let $[\theta_{\min}, \theta_{\max}]$ be the angle range for the twist, where $-\pi \leq \theta_{\min} \leq \theta_{\max} \leq \pi$. Then, the vector part of the twist rotation is clamped to the range

10.5 Swing-Twist Limits

$$\left[\sin\left(\frac{\theta_{\min}}{2}\right), \sin\left(\frac{\theta_{\max}}{2}\right)\right].$$

Let $x\mathbf{i}$ be the result after clamping. Then, the twist scalar component w is simply $\sqrt{1-x^2}$.

2D Joint Limits

The swing component is a quaternion whose vector part lies in the *YZ* plane inside the unit disk. Basically, any shape contained by the unit disk can be used as joint limit for swing. For a proper behavior in procedural animation, smooth convex shapes seem to be the most useful, although concave star-shaped polygons have been applied [Wilhelms and Gelder 01].

Blow proposes convex polygons as the limiting shape [Blow 2002], allowing for a simple containment test while preserving maximum flexibility. Polygons often have sharp corners in which clamped orientations may get stuck temporarily, showing odd behavior in the simulation. In order to prevent this from happening, or at least to reduce the effect, we either need to increase the number of vertices in the polygon or use quadratic or higher-order shapes. Increasing the number of vertices negatively affects performance and makes tweaking the limits harder, so we'll opt for a simple quadratic shape.

In this chapter, we use an ellipse as limiting shape. Joint limits are enforced by clamping points outside the ellipse to their closest point on the ellipse. We define an ellipse in quaternion vector space. Note that due to the warped mapping of quaternion vectors to exponential-map vectors, an ellipse in quaternion space may not map to an ellipse in exponential-map space.

Figure 10.5 shows two ellipses in quaternion vector space. Figure 10.5(a) bounds the horizontal component to a 120° angle and the vertical component to a 60° angle. As can be seen, the mapping to exponential maps has some minor warping artifacts but otherwise pretty much resembles an ellipse. If we increase the horizontal component to the maximum angle of 180°, as shown in Figure 10.5(b), we see that the mapped curve in exponential map space no longer resembles a smooth ellipse. The curve has an eye shape due to the excessive warping of angles close to 180°, as we saw in Figure 10.3.

In cases where angular joint limits need to be an exact ellipse in exponential-map space, we have to transform to exponential-map vectors and back. However, in most practical cases, the shape obtained by mapping an ellipse in quaternion space suffices for representing the joint limits. Note that the ellipse is already an idealization of the limits obtained from human anatomy. A simple shape is chosen as a representation of a complex manifold such as a human shoulder or hip to

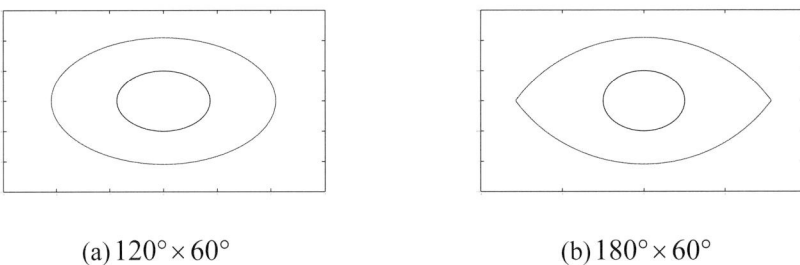

(a) $120° \times 60°$ (b) $180° \times 60°$

Figure 10.5. Ellipses mapped from quaternion vector space (inner curve) to exponential-map space (outer curve).

simplify the computational model. From that perspective, choosing an ellipse in quaternion vector space or in exponential-map space does not make a huge difference. Either way, in both cases we need to clamp a 2D point against an elliptical disk.

Clamping 2D Points to an Elliptical Disk

An axis-aligned elliptical disk is defined implicitly by the set of point (x, y) for which the function

$$f(x, y) = \left(\frac{x}{a}\right)^2 + \left(\frac{y}{b}\right)^2 - 1$$

is at most zero. Here, a and b are the maximum coordinates on the X and Y axes, respectively. Clamping a point to the disk boils down to computing the point on the disk closest to query point.

Let (x, y) be a point outside the disk. Then, necessarily $f(x, y) > 0$, and the line segment connecting the point to its closest point on the disk is normal to the ellipse, as is shown in Figure 10.6 and proven in [Eberly 2013].

The normal at point (x, y) is given by the partial derivatives of the implicit function

$$\left(\frac{\partial f}{\partial x}, \frac{\partial f}{\partial y}\right) = \left(\frac{2x}{a^2}, \frac{2y}{b^2}\right).$$

10.5 Swing-Twist Limits

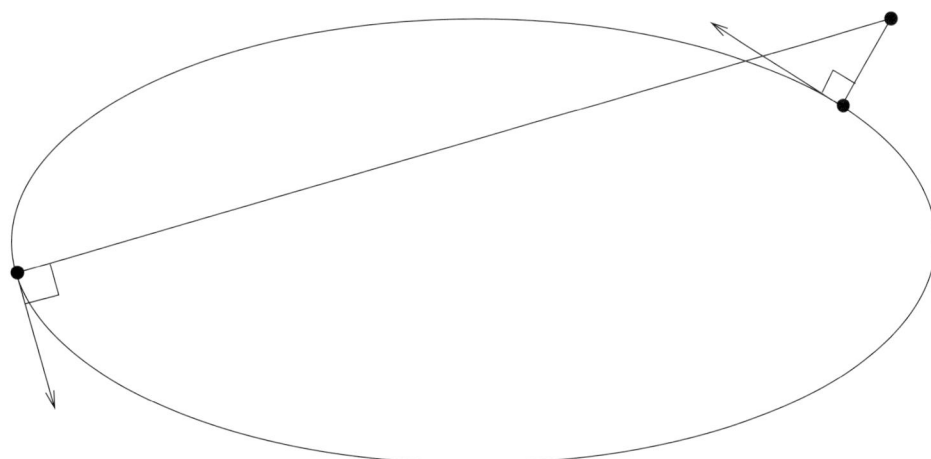

Figure 10.6. The line segment connecting the point on an ellipse closest to a point outside the ellipse is normal to the tangent at the closest point. The furthest point is the only other point on the ellipse for which this holds.

We are interested only in the direction of the normal, so we may remove the factor 2 in both components. The closest point can be defined as the point (x', y') on the ellipse (where $f(x', y') = 0$), such that

$$(x', y') + t\left(\frac{x'}{a^2}, \frac{y'}{b^2}\right) = (x, y)$$

for some parameter t. In other words, the line through the point along the point's normal has to pass through our query point for the closest point. As we saw in Figure 10.6, this is also the case for the furthest point, so we impose $t > 0$ to keep only the closest. After some rewriting, we find an explicit expression for (x', y') in the form of

$$(x', y') = \left(\frac{a^2 x}{t + a^2}, \frac{b^2 y}{t + b^2}\right).$$

The parameter t is the only unknown, and it can be found by requiring (x', y') to be a point on the ellipse. By substituting x' and y' into f, we obtain our generating function

$$g(t) = f(x', y') = \left(\frac{ax}{t+a^2}\right)^2 + \left(\frac{by}{t+b^2}\right)^2 - 1.$$

We need to solve for a t such that $g(t) = 0$. A closed-form solution requires us to solve a quartic (fourth order) polynomial function. Solving quadric polynomials is computationally expensive and sensitive to numerical error. Figure 10.7 shows a plot of $g(t)$. As the plot suggests, root finding for this function just screams for applying Newton's method.

The iteration step is given by

$$t_{n+1} = t_n - \frac{g(t_n)}{g'(t_n)}.$$

The function g is strictly convex on the domain $t \geq 0$. This means that for t' such that $g(t') = 0$, the inequality $0 \leq t_n \leq t_{n+1} \leq t'$ holds for any n. The first derivative $g'(t)$ is given by

$$g'(t) = -\frac{2a^2 x^2}{(t+a^2)^3} - \frac{2b^2 y^2}{(t+b^2)^3}.$$

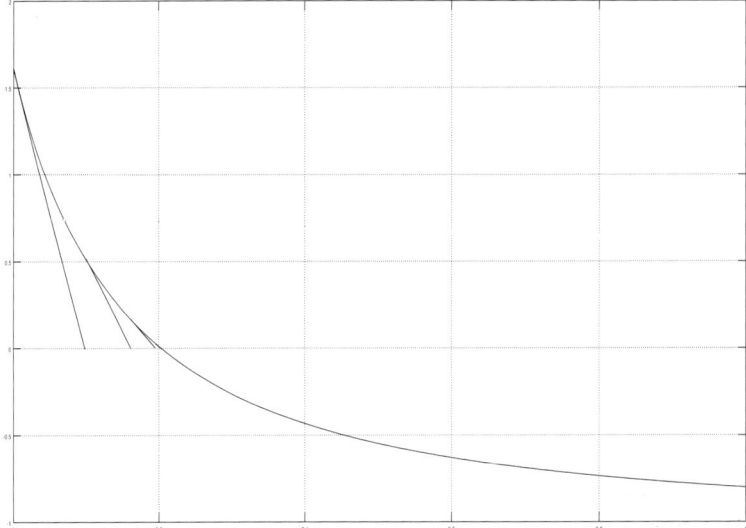

Figure 10.7. Root finding by Newton's method. Start with $t_0 = 0$ and iteratively compute each new t_{n+1} as the intersection of the tangent line at t_n and the X axis.

In the accompanying example code, the first derivative is not coded explicitly. Instead, the code applies a dual number trick to simultaneously compute $g(t)$ and $g'(t)$ [van den Bergen 2009].

10.6 Volumetric Limits

The swing-twist model is popular in physics and inverse kinematics due to its simple mechanical interpretation. However, as with the Euler-angle limits, the swing-twist model may not reflect to reality very well. For example, in a human shoulder, swing and twist are not independent. The amount of twist varies depending on the swing pose. This suggests that relative rotations should be constrained by a volume in quaternion vector space.

It turns out that the actual volume that models the full range of a human shoulder is not as nice of a shape as we would like it to be. Herda et al. propose modeling the volume by an implicit surface [Herda et al. 2003]. The proposed implicit surface that models the motion range is defined by a small number of spherical primitives.

Evaluation of the implicit function and its partial derivatives is computationally expensive. Often, we do not need this level of sophistication in modeling joint limits. A simple solution that generalizes from the elliptic swing-cone model is clamping of quaternion vectors to an ellipsoidal volume.

The solution is a straightforward generalization of the 2D case. We have an ellipsoid whose surface is the set of points (x,y,z) such that

$$f(x,y,z) = \left(\frac{x}{a}\right)^2 + \left(\frac{y}{b}\right)^2 + \left(\frac{z}{c}\right)^2 - 1$$

is at most zero, where a, b, and c are the maximum coordinates on the X, Y, and Z axes, respectively. Again, through the computation of the partial derivatives we find the clamped point (x',y',z') to be

$$(x,y,z) = (x',y',z') + t\left(\frac{x'}{a^2}, \frac{y'}{b^2}, \frac{z'}{c^2}\right),$$

solved for positive t such that $f(x',y',z') = 0$. This t is the positive root for

$$g(t) = f(x',y',z') = \left(\frac{ax}{t+a^2}\right)^2 + \left(\frac{by}{t+b^2}\right)^2 + \left(\frac{cz}{t+c^2}\right)^2 - 1.$$

Again, we apply Newton's method to approximate t for which $g(t) = 0$.

Another useful limiting shape is an elliptic cylinder. The component along the axis of the cylinder (usually the X axis) is clamped to the desired range, similar to the clamping after swing-twist decomposition. Only in this case, the X axis is generally not a pure rotation about the arm, nor is it a pure rotation about the parent's arm. The quaternion vector part is limited as a whole, and thus swing and twist are not independent. For a shoulder joint, we generally do not care about independence. Dropping the swing-twist decomposition and performing the clamping directly on the quaternion vector part saves us a few cycles and often shows acceptable results.

In the end, pretty much any smooth volume enclosed by the unit ball can be used as limiting shape. All that is required is an operation to test for point containment and for mapping points outside the volume to their closest point on the volume's surface. For convex shapes, we have the option of using GJK [Gilbert et al. 1988, van den Bergen 1999]. GJK is an iterative method for approximating the closest point of an arbitrary convex shape. It is mainly used for collision detection of convex shapes and has found its use in many modern physics libraries, so chances are you are already using it. GJK supports many convex shape types, such as convex polyhedra, cones, cylinders, ellipsoids. We do however give preference to the algorithm employing Newton's method for ellipsoids, as GJK is a somewhat heavier iterative method.

References

[Blow 2002] Jonathan Blow. "Inverse Kinematics with Joint Limits". *Game Developer*, Vol. 4, No. 12 (2002), pp. 16–18.

[Eberly 2013] David Eberly. "Distance from a Point to an Ellipse, an Ellipsoid, or a Hyperellipsoid". 2013. Available at http://www.geometrictools.com/ Documentation/DistancePointEllipseEllipsoid.pdf.

[Gilbert et al. 1988] E. G. Gilbert, D. W. Johnson, and S. S. Keerthi. "A Fast Procedure for Computing the Distance Between Complex Objects in Three-Dimensional Space". *IEEE Journal of Robotics and Automation*, Vol. 4, No. 2 (April 1988), pp. 193–203.

[Grassia 1998] F. Sebastian Grassia. "Practical parameterization of rotations using the exponential map". *Journal of Graphics Tools*, Vol. 3, No. 3 (March 1998), pp. 29–48.

[Herda et al. 2003] Lorna Herda, Raquel Urtasun, and Pascal Fua. "Automatic determination of shoulder joint limits using quaternion field boundaries". *International Journal of Robotics Research* Vol. 22, No. 6 (June 2003), pp. 419–438.

References

[van den Bergen 1999] Gino van den Bergen. "A Fast and Robust GJK Implementation for Collision Detection of Convex Objects". *Journal of Graphics Tools* Vol. 4, No. 2 (March 1999), pp. 7–25.

[van den Bergen 2009] Gino van den Bergen. "Dual Numbers: Simple Math, Easy C++ Coding, and Lots of Tricks". Game Developers Conference Europe, 2009.

[Wilhelms and Gelder 2001] Jane Wilhelms and Allen Van Gelder. "Fast and Easy Reach-cone Joint Limits". *Journal of Graphics Tools*, Vol. 6, No. 2 (2001), pp. 27–41.

11

Volumetric Hierarchical Approximate Convex Decomposition

Khaled Mamou
AMD

11.1 Introduction

Fast and precise collision detection is the cornerstone of realistic physics simulation in video games, virtual reality, and robotics. A rich literature has been dedicated to this topic [Weller 2013], and efficient algorithms have been devised especially for convex polyhedra [Gilbert et al. 1988, Mirtich 1998, van den Bergen 1999]. In order to leverage such algorithms, 3D models are usually approximated by a set of convex shapes such as ellipsoids, capsules, and convex hulls (see Figure 11.1). Manually computing such convex approximations is tedious and time consuming, and this makes automatic approximate convex decomposition algorithms highly desirable.

In this chapter, we propose an efficient fully-automatic algorithm that computes convex approximations of arbitrary 3D meshes. An open source implementation of the proposed algorithm, referred to as *volumetric hierarchical convex decomposition* (V-HACD), is publicly available[1] and has been already adopted by a wide range of game engines and physics simulation SDKs. In the first section of this chapter, we introduce the convex approximation problem and link it to the approximate convex decomposition research field. Next, we present the proposed convex approximation technique and evaluate its performance.

---

[1] https://code.google.com/p/v-hacd/

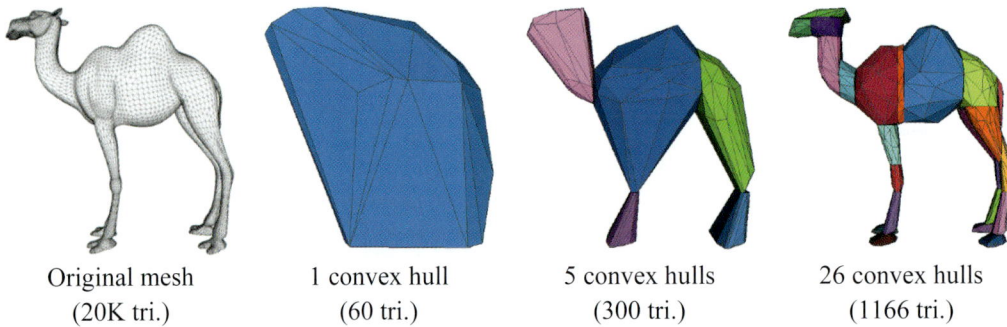

| Original mesh | 1 convex hull | 5 convex hulls | 26 convex hulls |
| (20K tri.) | (60 tri.) | (300 tri.) | (1166 tri.) |

Figure 11.1. Convex approximations with different accuracy and complexity levels.

11.2 Convex Approximation

Given an arbitrary polyhedron P, convex approximation algorithms aim at computing the smallest set of N convex polyhedra $\{C_i \mid i=0,\ldots,N-1\}$ such that the volume determined by the union $\bigcup_{i=0}^{N-1} C_i$ contains P and approximates it with a certain precision ε. Formally, the objective of convex approximation is to solve the minimization problem

$$\min_{P \subseteq C \text{ and } d(P,C) < \varepsilon} N, \tag{11.1}$$

where

- $C = \bigcup_{i=0}^{N-1} C_i$,
- $\{C_i \mid i=0,\ldots,N-1\}$ are convex polyhedra, and
- $d(P,C)$ is a distance measuring the approximation accuracy.

In this chapter, the distance $d(P,C)$ is defined as

$$d(P,C) = |C| - |P|, \tag{11.2}$$

where $|A|$ represents the volume of A.

As defined in Equation (11.1), the convex approximation problem is tightly related to the *exact convex decomposition* (ECD) problem [Chazelle 1984] and the *approximate convex decomposition* (ACD) problem [Lien and Amato 2004].

11.2 Convex Approximation

ECD aims at partitioning a polyhedron P into a minimum set of convex polyhedra. In [Chazelle 1984], the authors prove that ECD is NP-hard and discuss various heuristics to address it.

[Lien and Amato 2004] claim that ECD algorithms produce intractable convex decompositions with a high number of clusters (shown in Figure 11.2) and propose computing an *approximate* convex decomposition instead. The main idea is to relax the exact convexity constraint by allowing the clusters to be *almost* convex. More precisely, ACD aims at decomposing a polyhedron P into a minimum number of polyhedra $\{\Gamma_i \mid i=0,\ldots,N-1\}$ such that the concavity of each polyhedron Γ_i is lower than a predefined threshold ε. (The definition of concavity is discussed later.)

The convex approximation $\{C_i \mid i=0,\ldots,N-1\}$ associated with the convex decomposition $\{\Gamma_i \mid i=0,\ldots,N-1\}$ is defined as

$$C_i = CH(\Gamma_i), \tag{11.3}$$

where $CH(\Gamma_i)$ is the convex hull of Γ_i.

In order to avoid the higher computational complexity associated with volumetric representations, the convex decomposition algorithms described in [Chazelle 1984] and [Lien and Amato 2004] operate on the polyhedral surface S of P instead of computing a convex decomposition of the volume defined by P. Here, the surface S is decomposed into convex or near-convex patches $\{\Psi_i \mid i=0,\ldots,N-1\}$, as shown in Figure 11.2. The convex approximation $\{\Pi_i \mid i=0,\ldots,N-1\}$ associated with the approximate convex decomposition $\{\Psi_i\}$ of S is given by

$$\Pi_i = CH(\Psi_i), \tag{11.4}$$

where $CH(\Psi_i)$ is the convex hull of Ψ_i. Note that $\{\Pi_i\}$ is guaranteed to include the surface S (i.e., $S \subseteq \bigcup_{i=0}^{N-1} \Pi_i$) but not necessarily the entire volume of P, which is usually sufficient for collision detection purposes.

Several approximate convex decomposition algorithms have been recently proposed [Lien and Amato 2007, Ghosh et al. 2013, Attene et al. 2008, Kreavoy et al. 2007, Mamou 2010, Ren et al. 2011], and some implementations are publicly available.[2]

The hierarchical approximate convex decomposition (HACD) algorithm has been very popular and was adopted by various physics libraries (e.g., Bullet and PhysX) and game engines (e.g., Unreal Engine). As in [Lien and Amato 2004],

---

[2] http://sourceforge.net/projects/hacd/

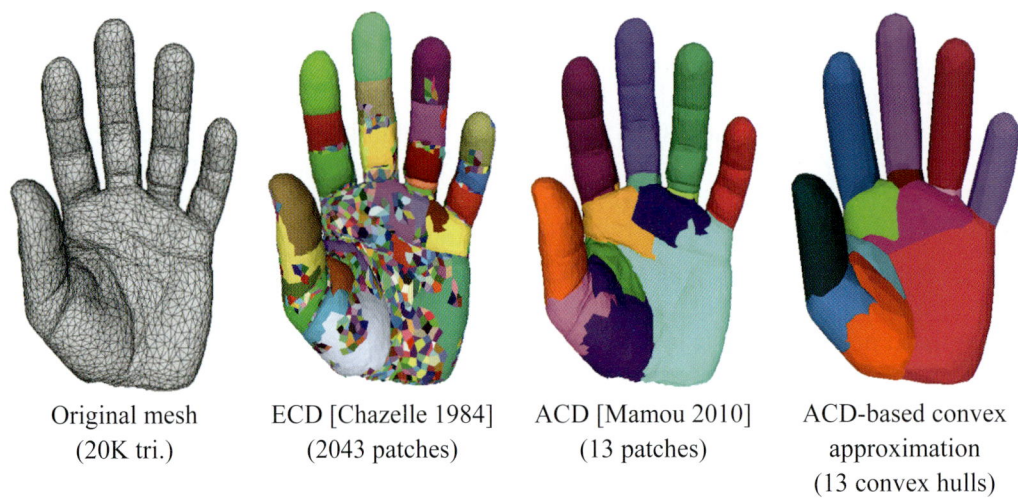

Figure 11.2. ECD, ACD, and ACD-based convex approximation.

Original mesh (20K tri.)   ECD [Chazelle 1984] (2043 patches)   ACD [Mamou 2010] (13 patches)   ACD-based convex approximation (13 convex hulls)

the HACD algorithm computes an approximate convex decomposition of the polyhedral surface S. HACD exploits a bottom-up greedy approach, which consists of successively merging the input mesh triangles based on concavity (i.e., distance between the surface patch and its convex hull) and aspect ratio criteria. The success of the HACD algorithm is mainly explained by its simplicity and generality in being able to handle open and closed manifold and non-manifold meshes of arbitrary genus.

However, HACD suffers from several limitations. First, HACD may generate intersecting convex hulls (visible in Figure 11.2), which makes the obtained convex approximations unsuitable for destruction effects. The computational complexity of the HACD algorithm may be prohibitive if applied to dense 3D meshes. In practice, a decimation process is applied to the input mesh before the decomposition stage, which may have a significant impact on the precision of the derived convex approximations. Finally, the HACD algorithm may also suffer from numerical instabilities when dealing with poorly sampled input meshes.

In order to overcome the HACD limitations, we propose a new convex decomposition algorithm, so-called V-HACD, that offers accurate convex decompositions while guaranteeing non-overlapping convex hulls. V-HACD overcomes the numerical instability issues related to the input mesh sampling and to the concavity distance criterion by operating on a voxelized or tetrahedralized version of the input mesh and by introducing a more stable volumetric concavity measure.

11.3 Volumetric Hierarchical Approximate Convex Decomposition

Figure 11.3 provides an overview of the proposed V-HACD algorithm. V-HACD takes as input the polyhedral surface S of the polyhedron P and computes an approximate convex decomposition of P. The algorithm proceeds as follows. First, a voxelization or tetrahedralization process is applied in order to approximate the volume defined by P with a set of either voxels or tetrahedra. The computed primitives (i.e., voxels or tetrahedra) are then recursively split according to a top-down hierarchical approach. This splitting process is successively applied to the generated subparts until a concavity threshold is reached. In order to guarantee

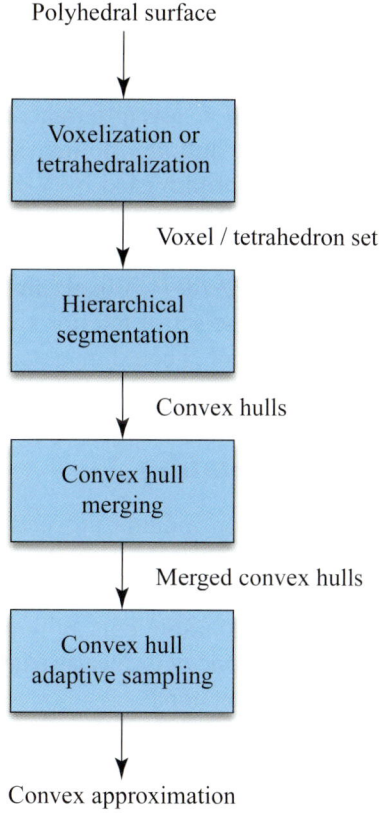

Figure 11.3. Overview of the proposed V-HACD algorithm.

non-overlapping convex hulls, V-HACD splits the object according to a set of clipping planes based on concavity, balance, and symmetry criteria. V-HACD leverages a greedy, highly parallelizable algorithm in order to determine the best clipping plane at each stage. This process could be efficiently accelerated by leveraging both CPU and GPU multithreading. Because of its greedy nature, the splitting process may produce over-segmentation. An optional post processing step may be applied in order to successively merge the generated convex hulls under a maximum concavity criterion. Finally, the obtained convex hulls are resampled in order to minimize their complexity (i.e., the number of triangles they are made of) while preserving the approximation accuracy.

Voxelization and Tetrahedralization

The V-HACD algorithm is independent from the voxelization or tetrahedralization algorithm (e.g., [Huang et al. 1998] or [Si 2015]) used to generate the volumetric representation of the input polyhedron P. The user can either apply his custom voxelization or tetrahedralization algorithm to the polyhedral surface S and directly feed the obtained voxels or tetrahedra into the hierarchical segmentation stage or leverage the default algorithms shipped with the V-HACD library. The default voxelization algorithm used by V-HACD proceeds as follows. First, the bounding box of the model is computed and uniformly split according to a regular grid of voxels. The voxels intersecting the surface S are then marked as belonging to the boundary B of P. Voxels inside the volume bound by B are marked as interior voxels. The set of interior voxels is denoted by I. An approximate tetrahedralized version of P could be obtained by splitting each voxel into a set of tetrahedra.

Hierarchical Segmentation

The hierarchical segmentation module proceeds according to the algorithm described in Listing 11.1. The input primitive set generated by the voxelization or tetrahedralization stage is recursively split until the concavity of each subpart is lower than a user-defined maximum concavity parameter ε or a maximum recursion depth is reached. The concavity measure and clipping plane strategy are described in the following subsections.

Concavity Measure

Unlike other measures such as volume and area, the concavity of a polyhedron does not have a standard definition, but various concavity measures have been

11.3 Volumetric Hierarchical Approximate Convex Decomposition

Listing 11.1. Hierarchical segmentation algorithm.

```
// Input: Primitive set inputPSet
// Output: Vector of primitive sets output
// Parameters:
//      * Maximum recursion depth maxDepth
//      * Maximum allowed concavity ϵ
//      * Clipping cost parameters α and β

vector<PrimitiveSet *> output;
vector<PrimitiveSet *> toProcess;
vector<PrimitiveSet *> processed;

int sub = 0;
double volumeCH0 = inputPSet->ComputeConvexHullVolume();
toProcess.push_back(inputPSet);

while (sub++ < maxDepth && toProcess.size() > 0)
{
    for (size_t p = 0; p < toProcess.size(); ++p)
    {
        PrimitiveSet *pset = inputParts[p];
        double concavity = ComputeConcavity(pset) / volumeCH0;
        if (concavity > ϵ)
        {
            Plane bestClipPlane = ComputeBestClippingPlane(pset, α, β);
            PrimitiveSet *bestLeftPSet;
            PrimitiveSet *bestLeftPSet;
            pset->Clip(bestClipPlane, bestLeftPSet, bestRightPSet);
            processed.push_back(bestLeftPSet);
            processed.push_back(bestRightPSet);
        }
        else
        {
            output.push_back(pset);
        }
    }

    toProcess = processed;
    processed.clear();
}
```

proposed in the literature. In [Lien and Amato 2004], the authors define the concavity of a polyhedron P as the maximum concavity of the points located on its polyhedral surface S. The concavity of a point **M** of S is defined as the length of the path travelled by **M** during the process of balloon inflation of the polyhedron P until it assumes the shape of its convex hull $CH(P)$. This is shown in Figure 11.4.

Inspired by [Lien and Amato 2004], the authors in [Mamou 2010] define the concavity of a point **M** by the Euclidian distance $\|\mathbf{M} - \wp(\mathbf{M})\|_2$ between **M** and its projection onto the polyhedral surface of $CH(P)$, with respect to the ray having origin **M** and direction normal to S at **M**. While this later concavity measure is able to capture the important features of P well, it suffers from numerical instabilities especially in the case of degenerate or poorly sampled surfaces.

In this chapter, we propose using the difference between the volume of a primitive set and its convex hull as a concavity measure, which corresponds to an approximated version of accuracy measure described in Equation (11.2). The volume of the primitive set is computed by summing the volumes of all the primitives. The volume of the convex hull is computed by using the algorithm described in [Allgower and Schmidt 1986]. In practice, this new volume-based concavity measure offers a more numerically stable alternative to the concavity measure defined in [Mamou 2010].

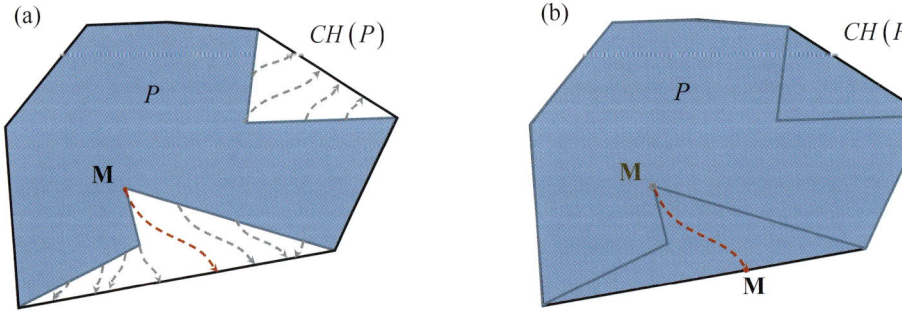

Figure 11.4. Concavity of a point **M** measured as the length of the path travelled during the process of balloon inflation. (a) Initial non-convex polyhedron P. During the inflation process, the points of the polyhedral surface S are pushed toward $CH(P)$. (b) P after inflation.

Clipping Plane Selection Strategy

Let K be the primitive set to be clipped and let K_{left} and K_{right} be the left and right subparts generated after clipping against a plane **p**. The V-HACD algorithm aims at finding, for each splitting stage, the best clipping plane by solving the minimization problem

$$\mathbf{p}^* = \arg\min_{\mathbf{p} \in \mathcal{H}(\mathbb{R}^3)} E(K, \mathbf{p}), \tag{11.5}$$

where

- $\mathcal{H}(\mathbb{R}^3)$ is the linear space of the planes of $\mathbb{R}^3$, and
- $E(K, \mathbf{p})$ is an energy function measuring the concavity, the balance and the symmetry of K_{left} and K_{right}.

More formally, the energy $E(K, \mathbf{p})$ is defined as follows:

$$E(K, \mathbf{p}) = E_{\text{con}}(K, \mathbf{p}) + \alpha E_{\text{bal}}(K, \mathbf{p}) + \beta E_{\text{sym}}(K, \mathbf{p}), \tag{11.6}$$

where

- E_{con}, E_{bal}, and E_{sym} are the connectivity, balance, and symmetry components of E, and
- α and β are the weighting coefficients associated with E_{bal} and E_{sym}, respectively.

E_{con} is given by the normalized sum of the concavities of K_{left} and K_{right}:

$$E_{\text{con}}(K, \mathbf{p}) = \frac{d(K_{\text{left}}, CH(K_{\text{left}})) + d(K_{\text{right}}, CH(K_{\text{right}}))}{V_0}, \tag{11.7}$$

where

- $V_0 = |CH(S)|$ is the volume of the convex hull of S, and
- $d(\cdot, \cdot)$ is the accuracy measure described in Equation (11.2).

The energy component E_{bal} favors the clipping planes that result in balanced subparts where K_{left} and K_{right} have comparable volumes. E_{bal} is defined as

$$E_{\text{bal}}(K,\mathbf{p}) = \frac{\text{abs}(|K_{\text{left}}| - |K_{\text{right}}|)}{V_0}, \tag{11.8}$$

where abs(x) is the absolute value of x and $|K|$ is the volume of the primitive set K.

E_{sym} is introduced in order to penalize clipping planes orthogonal or *almost* orthogonal to a potential revolution axis $\boldsymbol{\delta}$. E_{sym} is given by

$$E_{\text{sym}}(K,\mathbf{p}) = w(\boldsymbol{\delta} \cdot \mathbf{p}), \tag{11.9}$$

where $\boldsymbol{\delta}$ is a potential revolution axis, and w is a weighting coefficient describing how close $\boldsymbol{\delta}$ is to an actual revolution axis.

In order to determine $\boldsymbol{\delta}$ and w, the V-HACD algorithm proceeds as follows. First, the primitive set is centered around its barycenter and a singular value decomposition is applied to its covariance matrix in order to extract both the eigenvectors $\{\mathbf{e}_x, \mathbf{e}_y, \mathbf{e}_z\}$ and their associated eigenvalues $\{\lambda_x, \lambda_y, \lambda_z\}$. The potential revolution axis is determined by looking for the two closest eigenvalues. For instance, if $|\lambda_y - \lambda_z| < |\lambda_x - \lambda_z|$ and $|\lambda_y - \lambda_z| < |\lambda_x - \lambda_y|$, then $\mathbf{e}_x$ is considered as the potential revolution axis $\boldsymbol{\delta}$. In this case, the weighting coefficient w is given by

$$w = 1 - \frac{(\lambda_y - \lambda_z)^2}{(|\lambda_y| + |\lambda_z|)^2}. \tag{11.10}$$

Note that if $\lambda_y = \lambda_z$, which corresponds to the case of a perfect revolution axis, then w reaches its maximum value of 1. The more λ_y and λ_z are different (i.e., $\boldsymbol{\delta}$ is far from being a revolution axis), the smaller w is, and the smaller the contribution of E_{sym} is to the overall energy E.

In order to solve the nonlinear minimization problem described in Equation (11.5), the V-HACD restricts the search space $\mathcal{H}(\mathbb{R}^3)$ to the discrete subset $\mathcal{H}_{\text{res}}(\mathbb{R}^3)$ of axis-aligned planes passing through the centers of the primitives composing the set K. Moreover, a hierarchical search strategy is applied in order to further reduce the computational complexity. The idea is to apply first a coarse search by computing the energy E for a subset of $\mathcal{H}_{\text{res}}(\mathbb{R}^3)$ in order to determine the best clipping plane $\hat{\boldsymbol{\delta}}$ (i.e., the one with the lowest energy E). This coarse solution is then refined by applying a second search while considering the neighbors of $\hat{\boldsymbol{\delta}}$ in $\mathcal{H}_{\text{res}}(\mathbb{R}^3)$ located within a predefined distance.

Merging Convex Hulls

The objective of the convex hulls merging module is to eliminate potential oversegmentations generated by the hierarchical segmentation stage. The algorithm

11.3 Volumetric Hierarchical Approximate Convex Decomposition

consists of successively merging convex hulls under a maximum concavity constraint. At each iteration, two convex hulls H_1 and H_2 are selected, and the concavity $\eta(H)$ of their union $H = H_1 \cup H_2$ is computed as

$$\eta(H) = \frac{d(H, CH(H))}{V_0}. \quad (11.11)$$

If $\eta(H)$ is lower than a user-defined parameter γ, then H_1 and H_2 are merged. This process is iterated until no more convex hulls can be merged.

Adaptive Convex Hull Resampling

The convex hulls generated so far could exhibit an arbitrary number of triangles and vertices, which may unnecessarily increase the computational complexity of collision detection queries. The V-HACD library addresses this issue by applying an optional postprocessing stage during which the convex hulls are resampled in order to generate a lower number of triangles and vertices while preserving their shapes. More precisely, a slightly modified version of the iterative convex hull algorithm described in [Clarkson and Shor 1989] is applied.

The algorithm proceeds as follows. First, four non-coplanar vertices of the initial convex hull CH are selected in order to construct a tetrahedron T. T is considered as the first approximation A_0 of CH. A_0 is then iteratively refined by successively including the remaining vertices. At each stage, a new vertex v_i is included. The associated approximation A_i is computed by generating the convex hull of $A_{i-1} \cup v_i$. In [Clarkson and Shor 1989], the vertices $\{v_i\}$ are introduced in an arbitrary order. The V-HACD algorithm introduces, at each stage, the vertex v_i^* that results in the approximation A_i^* with the largest volume. This process is applied until the volume difference between A_i^* and A_{i-1}^* is lower than a user-defined threshold ζ or the number of vertices and triangles of A_i^* is higher than a user-defined parameter τ. Figure 11.5 shows various ACDs generated for different values of ζ and τ.

Implementation Optimizations

The computation times of the V-HACD are mainly dominated (more than 95% of the total time) by the hierarchical segmentation stage, and more precisely by the `ComputeBestClippingPlane()` function in Listing 11.1. By parallelizing this process on both CPU and GPU, the V-HACD computation times can be significantly reduced (see Table 11.1). The main idea is to exploit multiple CPU threads to compute the energy E of the potential clipping planes in parallel and find a

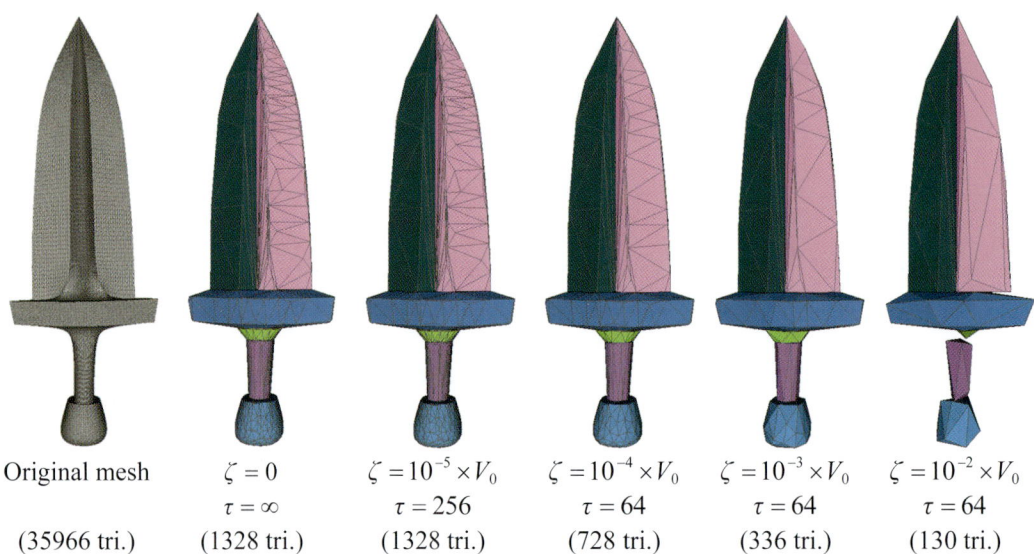

Figure 11.5. Impact of the threshold ζ on the adaptive convex hulls resampling process.

Model	Single threaded	Multithreaded (CPU only)	Multithreaded (CPU and GPU)
Block	199 s	71 s	49 s
Camel	383 s	129 s	77 s
Chair	389 s	124 s	84 s
Elephant	390 s	122 s	86 s
Feline	477 s	157 s	113 s
Sword	359 s	124 s	75 s

Table 11.1. Impact of CPU and GPU multithreading on the V-HACD computation times. Results generated on a MacBook Pro equipped with 2.5 GHz Intel Core i7, 16 GB 1600 MHz DDR3 RAM and AMD Radeon R9 M370X 2048 MB.

11.3 Volumetric Hierarchical Approximate Convex Decomposition

minimal energy plane $\mathbf{p}^*$ solution of the minimization problem described in Equation (11.5). Computing the energy of each potential clipping plane $\mathbf{p}$ requires computing

- the volumes $|K_{\text{left}}|$ and $|K_{\text{right}}|$ of the two subparts generated after clipping, and
- their associated convex hulls $CH(K_{\text{left}})$ and $CH(K_{\text{right}})$.

In the case of a voxel-based representation, the volumes $|K_{\text{left}}|$ and $|K_{\text{right}}|$ require computing the number of voxels on the left and right sides of the clipping plane. This process can be GPU-accelerated by leveraging a reduction-based approach.

Computing the convex hulls $CH(K_{\text{left}})$ and $CH(K_{\text{right}})$ is accelerated by considering only the primitives located on the boundary of the object, as illustrated in Figure 11.6. In practice, the V-HACD algorithm keeps track of the interior and boundary primitives during the clipping process.

The complexity of computing $CH(K_{\text{left}})$ and $CH(K_{\text{right}})$ can be further reduced by considering only a subset of the boundary primitives as shown in Figure 11.6(c). More precisely, let $K_{\text{left}}^{\text{sub}}$ and $K_{\text{right}}^{\text{sub}}$ be subsampled versions of the

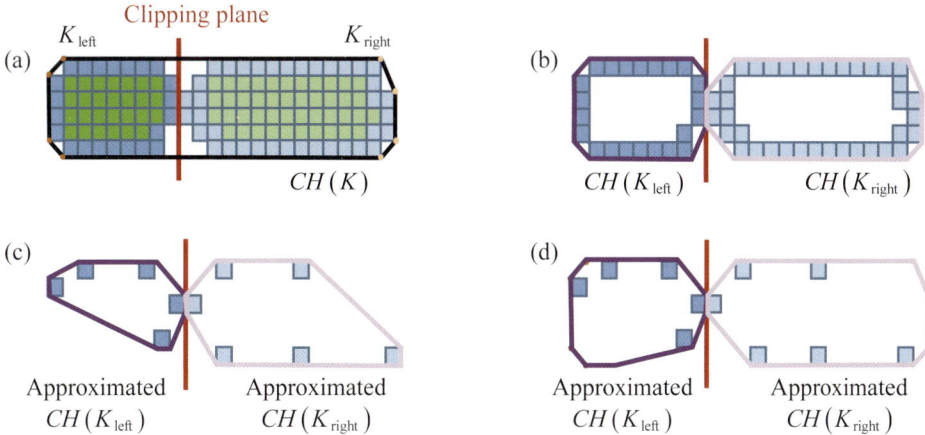

Figure 11.6. Computing the convex hulls $CH(K_{\text{left}})$ and $CH(K_{\text{right}})$. (a) The primitive set K, its convex hull $CH(K)$ (black), the vertices of $CH(K)$ (orange), the two subparts K_{left} (dark green/blue) and K_{right} (light green/blue), boundary primitives (blue), and interior primitives (green). (b) Computing the convex hulls $CH(K_{\text{left}})$ and $CH(K_{\text{right}})$ while considering only boundary primitives. (c) Computing an approximated version of $CH(K_{\text{left}})$ and $CH(K_{\text{right}})$ while considering a subset of the boundary primitives. (d) Improving the accuracy of (c) by considering the vertices of $CH(K)$.

boundary primitives of K_{left} and K_{right}. $CH(K_{\text{left}})$ and $CH(K_{\text{right}})$ are approximated by computing $CH(K_{\text{left}}^{\text{sub}})$ and $CH(K_{\text{right}}^{\text{sub}})$, which offers significant computation time reduction at the cost of potentially introducing approximation errors.

The approximation accuracy can be improved by considering the vertices of $CH(K)$ while computing $CH(K_{\text{left}}^{\text{sub}})$ and $CH(K_{\text{right}}^{\text{sub}})$, as shown in Figure 11.6(d). Here, the vertices of $CH(K)$ are first segmented into two sets K_{left}^{CH} and K_{right}^{CH} corresponding to the vertices located on the left and right sides of the clipping plane. $CH(K_{\text{left}})$ and $CH(K_{\text{right}})$ are then approximated by computing the convex hulls $CH(K_{\text{left}}^{\text{sub}} \cup K_{\text{left}}^{CH})$ and $CH(K_{\text{right}}^{\text{sub}} \cup K_{\text{right}}^{CH})$ instead of $CH(K_{\text{left}}^{\text{sub}})$ and $CH(K_{\text{right}}^{\text{sub}})$. Since $CH(K)$ usually has a limited number of vertices, this later approximation has almost the same computational complexity while providing more accurate results.

Experimental Evaluation

Figures 11.7 and 11.8 visually compare the ACDs generated by V-HACD to those obtained by the popular HACD technique. Note that the ACDs computed by V-HACD are able to better capture the models' symmetry and provide more accurate approximations with a lower or comparable number of convex hulls. HACD generates poor ACDs for some of the models in the figures, specifically those highlighted in red, due to numerical instability issues related to the concavity measure computation. V-HACD is able to overcome such issues and usually offers more consistent results.

11.3 Volumetric Hierarchical Approximate Convex Decomposition

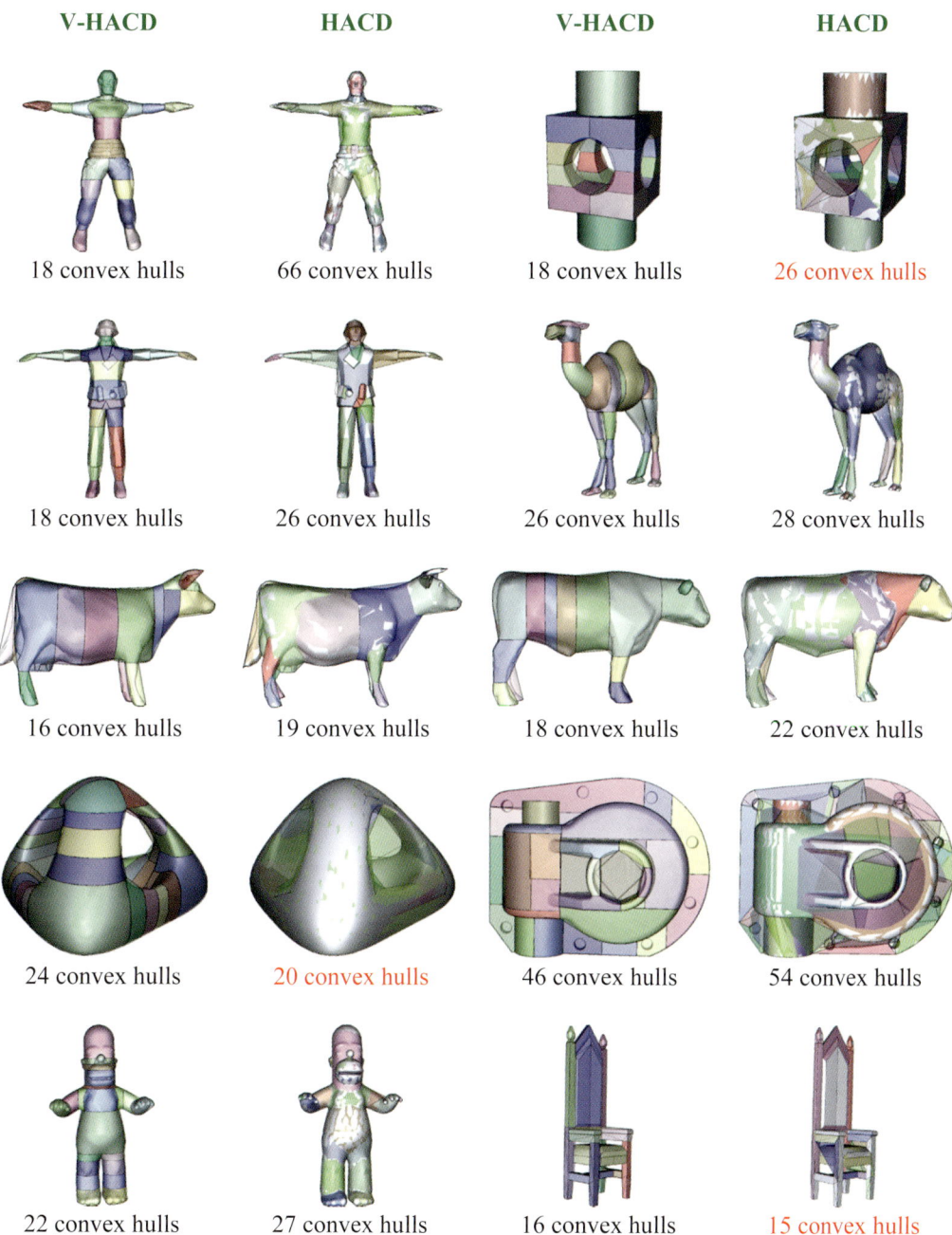

Figure 11.7. Experimental Evaluation: V-HACD vs. HACD (part 1).

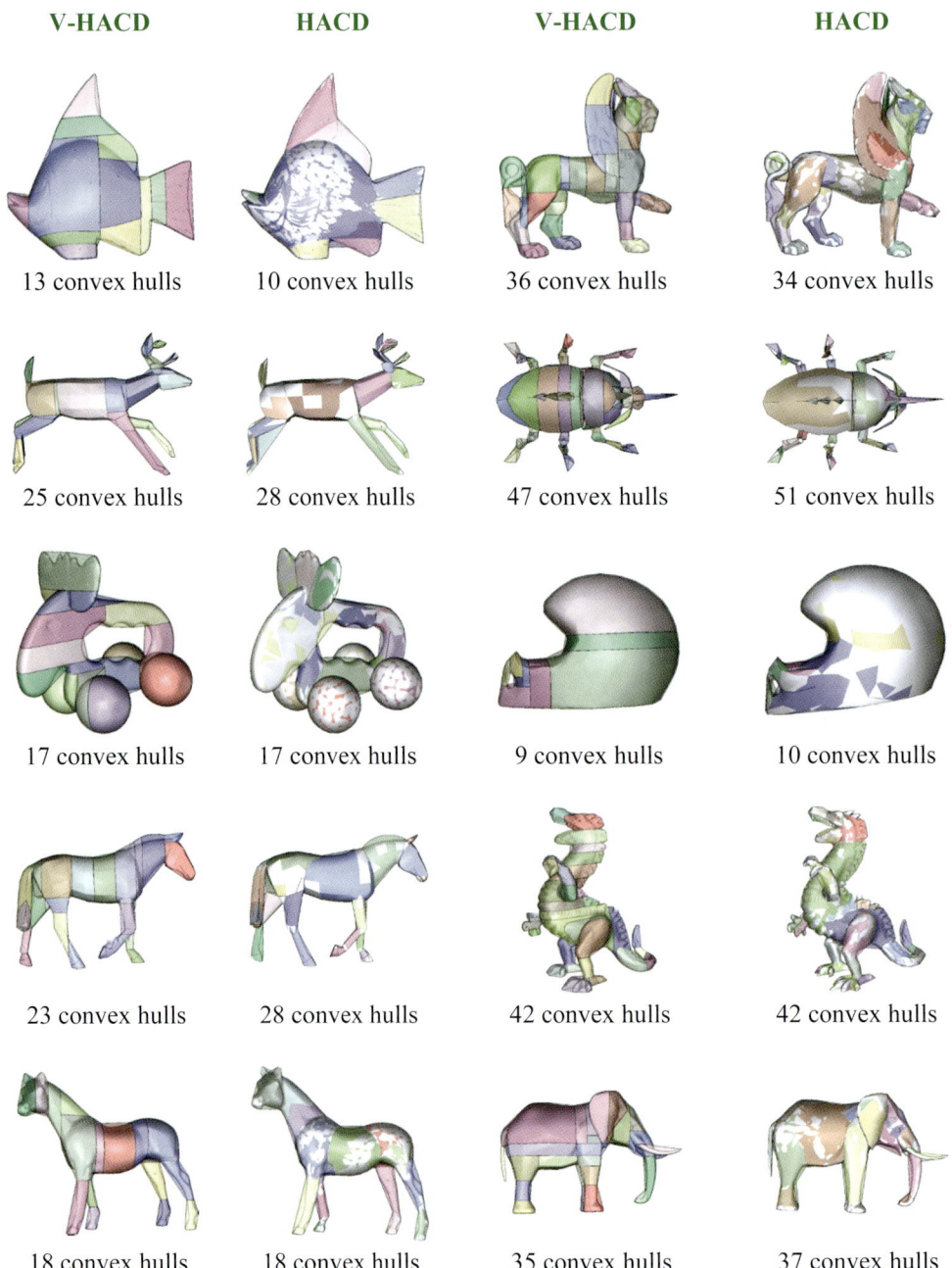

Figure 11.8. Experimental Evaluation: V-HACD vs. HACD (part 2).

References

[Allgower and Schmidt 1986] Eugene L. Allgower and Phillip H. Schmidt. "Computing Volumes of Polyhedra". *Mathematics of Computation*, Vol. 46, No. 173 (January 1986), pp. 171–174.

[Attene et al. 2008] Marco Attene, Michela Mortara, Michela Spagnuolo, and Bianca Falcidieno. "Hierarchical convex approximation of 3D shapes for fast region selection". *Proceedings of the Symposium on Geometry Processing*, 2008, pp. 1323-1332.

[Chazelle 1984] Bernard Chazelle. "Convex Partitions of Polyhedra: a Lower Bound and Worst-Case Optimal Algorithm". *SIAM Journal on Computing*, Vol. 13, No. 3 (1984), pp. 488–507.

[Clarkson and Shor 1989] Kenneth L.Clarkson and Peter W. Shor. "Applications of random sampling in computational geometry, II". *Discrete and Computational Geometry*, Vol. 4, No. 1 (October 1989), pp. 387–421.

[Ghosh et al. 2013] Mukulika Ghosh, Nancy M. Amato, Yanyan Lu, and Jyh-Ming Lien. "Fast Approximate Convex Decomposition Using Relative Concavity". *Computer-Aided Design*, Vol. 45, No. 2 (February 2013), pp. 494–504.

[Gilbert et al. 1988] E. G. Gilbert, D. W. Johnson, and S. S. Keerthi. "A fast procedure for computing the distance between complex objects in three-dimensional space". *IEEE Journal of Robotics and Automation*, Vol. 4, No. 2 (April 1988), pp. 193–203.

[Huang et al. 1998] Jian Huang, Roni Yagel, Vassily Filippov, and Yair Kurzion, "An Accurate Method for Voxelizing Polygon Meshes". *Proceedings of the 1998 IEEE symposium on Volume visualization*, pp. 119–126.

[Kreavoy et al. 2007] V. Kreavoy, D. Julius, A. Sheffer, "Model Composition from Interchangeable Components". *15th Pacific Conference on Computer Graphics and Applications*, 2007, pp. 129–138.

[Lien and Amato 2004] Jyh-Ming Lien and Nancy M. Amato. "Approximate Convex Decomposition". *ACM Symposium Computational Geometry*, 2004, pp. 457–458.

[Lien and Amato 2007] Jyh-Ming Lien and Nancy M. Amato. "Approximate Convex Decomposition of Polyhedra". *ACM Symposium on Solid and Physical Modeling*, 2007.

[Mamou 2010] Khaled Mamou. "Approximate Convex Decomposition for Real-Time Collision Detection". *Game Programming Gems 8*, edited by Adam Lake. Cengage Learning, 2010.

[Mirtich 1998] Brian Mirtich, "V-clip: fast and robust polyhedral collision detection". *ACM Transactions on Graphics*, Vol. 17, No. 3 (July 1998), pp. 177–208.

[Ren et al. 2011] Zhou Ren, Junsong Yuan, Chunyuan Li, and Wenyu Liu. "Minimum Near-Convex Decomposition for Robust Shape Representation". *2011 IEEE International Conference on Computer Vision*, pp. 303–310.

[Si 2015] Hang Si. "TetGen, A Delaunay-Based Quality Tetrahedral Mesh Generator". *ACM Transactions on Mathematical Software*, Vol. 41, No. 2 (January 2015), Article 11.

[van den Bergen 1999] Gino van den Bergen. "A fast and robust GJK implementation for collision detection of convex objects". *Journal of Graphics Tools*, Vol. 4, No. 2 (March 1999), pp. 7–25.

[Weller 2013] René Weller. "A Brief Overview of Collision Detection". *New Geometric Data Structures for Collision Detection and Haptics, Part I*. Springer, 2013.

12

Simulating Soft Bodies Using Strain Based Dynamics

Muhammad Mobeen Movania
DHA Suffa University

12.1 Introduction

Games and interactive simulation environments like surgical simulators require modeling of soft bodies. Over the years, several methods have been proposed to simulate such bodies in computer graphics [Nealen 2006]. These methods may be generally classified into physically based or nonphysically based methods. The physically based methods generate an approximate representation of the simulated object using finite element discretization. Then, forces and velocities are integrated for each finite element. The deformations estimated by these methods are accurate; however, significant processing time is required, making application of these methods challenging in a real-time environment.

On the contrary, nonphysically based methods like position based dynamics [Jakobsen 2001, Mathias 2007] produce physically plausible simulations by approximating deformations using constraints. This method compromises accuracy for speed, and therefore, it is extremely useful in games and interactive simulation scenarios. Most of the commercial physics engines like Havok, Nvidia PhysX, and Bullet use this method.

Strain based dynamics [Mathias 2014] is a recent extension of the position based dynamics model for simulating real-time soft bodies. Rather than solving each constraint individually, strain based dynamics projects constraints for each finite element. For example, in case of triangular meshes, rather than solving three separate distance constraints for the three edges of a given triangle, strain based dynamics solves a single triangle constraint. Similarly, for a tetrahedral element, a tetrahedral constraint is solved rather than solving separate distance and bending constraints.

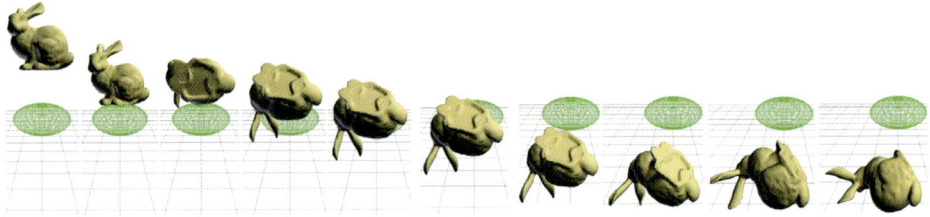

Figure 12.1. Real-time soft body simulation using strain based dynamics showing several frames from the deformation of the Stanford bunny dataset.

Stress and strain values are evaluated, and anisotropic behavior is introduced by augmenting additional stress and strain coefficients. This chapter provides a simple and straightforward implementation of strain based dynamics for both surface (cloth) and mesh models (tetrahedral mesh). A snapshot from an implementation of the technique described in this chapter is shown in Figure 12.1.

12.2 Position Based Dynamics

A general physically based simulation system simulates dynamics using a set of ordinary differential equations (ODEs). These ODEs are solved to obtain the new positions and velocities given the old positions and velocities. In position based dynamics (PBD), a number of constraints are introduced along with the ODEs. These constraints are projected one by one using a number of Gauss-Seidel iterations. The basic position based dynamics approach may be elaborated through the following algorithm. (Throughout this chapter, the subscript i refers to the time step index.)

Basic position based dynamics algorithm

1. Loop for N particles:
   a. Initialize initial positions $\mathbf{x}_i$ and velocities $\mathbf{v}_i$.
2. End loop.
3. Loop while simulation is running:
   a. Loop for N particles:
      i. Calculate $\mathbf{v}_i$ using explicit integration.
      ii. Apply dampening on $\mathbf{v}_i$.
      iii. Calculate projection positions $\mathbf{p}_i$ using $\mathbf{v}_i$.
   b. End loop.
   c. Generate M collision constraints.

d. Loop for K solver iterations:
   i. Loop over each constraint C_i:
      I. Solve C_i using $\mathbf{p}_i$.
   ii. End loop.
e. End loop.
f. Loop for N particles:
   i. Calculate $\mathbf{p}_i$ using $\mathbf{v}_i$ and $\mathbf{x}_i$.
   ii. Assign $\mathbf{p}_i$ to $\mathbf{x}_i$.
g. End Loop.
4. End loop.

The basic PBD algorithm first calculates the current velocity $\mathbf{v}_i$ using explicit Euler integration. Given the current time step Δt, the mass m_i, and external force $\mathbf{f}_i$, the in-place update of the current velocity $\mathbf{v}_i$ is given as

$$\mathbf{v}_i = \mathbf{v}_i + \Delta t \frac{\mathbf{f}_i}{m_i}.$$

Using the newly calculated velocity $\mathbf{v}_i$, the projected position $\mathbf{p}_i$ is obtained using semi-implicit Euler integration as

$$\mathbf{p}_i = \mathbf{x}_i + \Delta t\, \mathbf{v}_i.$$

A set of M constraints (for example, distance constraints or collision constraints) are then enforced on the projected positions $\mathbf{p}_i$ using K Gauss-Seidel iterations to obtain valid positions $\mathbf{p}'_i$. Finally, the constraint-relaxed positions $\mathbf{p}'_i$ are assigned to the new positions $\mathbf{x}_{i+1}$. These are also used to obtain the updated velocities $\mathbf{v}_{i+1}$ as follows:

$$\mathbf{v}_{i+1} = \frac{\mathbf{p}'_i - \mathbf{x}_i}{\Delta t}$$

$$\mathbf{x}_{i+1} = \mathbf{p}'_i$$

Mathias et al. [Mathias 2007] identify a set of constraints and their positional corrections $\Delta \mathbf{p}_i$. For example, the distance constraint C between two particles at positions $\mathbf{x}_1$ and $\mathbf{x}_2$ with a rest length d may be given as

$$C(\mathbf{x}_1, \mathbf{x}_2) = \|\mathbf{x}_1 - \mathbf{x}_2\| - d.$$

For this constraint, the positional corrections $\Delta \mathbf{p}_1$ and $\Delta \mathbf{p}_2$ are given as

$$\Delta \mathbf{p}_1 = \frac{-w_1}{w_1 + w_2}(\|\mathbf{p}_1 - \mathbf{p}_2\| - d)\frac{\mathbf{p}_1 - \mathbf{p}_2}{\|\mathbf{p}_1 - \mathbf{p}_2\|}$$

$$\Delta \mathbf{p}_2 = \frac{w_2}{w_1 + w_2}(\|\mathbf{p}_1 - \mathbf{p}_2\| - d)\frac{\mathbf{p}_1 - \mathbf{p}_2}{\|\mathbf{p}_1 - \mathbf{p}_2\|},$$

where w_1 and w_2 are the inverse masses of the particles.

The PBD algorithm uses explicit integration to get an estimate of the current positions and velocities. The new velocities are not blindly used to calculate the new positions. Instead, additional constraints are enforced using a number of Gauss-Seidel iterations on the new positions to ensure that they remain valid for the given configuration. Finally, once all constraints are satisfied, the projected positions are used to calculate the new velocities and positions.

12.3 Strain based Dynamics

The strain based dynamics approach uses the same basic framework of PBD. The difference from PBD is that instead of enforcing distance constraints on each edge of the mesh element, a single constraint is identified for each mesh element (tetrahedron for tetrahedral meshes and triangle for triangular meshes).

Tetrahedral Constraint Formulation

Given the projected positions $\{\mathbf{p}_0, \mathbf{p}_1, \mathbf{p}_2, \mathbf{p}_3\}$ and initial, nonsimulated positions $\{\mathbf{q}_0, \mathbf{q}_1, \mathbf{q}_2, \mathbf{q}_3\}$ of a tetrahedron, the current and initial positions may be given in new coordinate systems having $\mathbf{p}_0$ and $\mathbf{q}_0$ as their origins. Two 3×3 matrices $\mathbf{P}$ and $\mathbf{Q}$ are then constructed as

$$\mathbf{P} = [\mathbf{p}_1 - \mathbf{p}_0 \quad \mathbf{p}_2 - \mathbf{p}_0 \quad \mathbf{p}_3 - \mathbf{p}_0]$$
$$\mathbf{Q} = [\mathbf{q}_1 - \mathbf{q}_0 \quad \mathbf{q}_2 - \mathbf{q}_0 \quad \mathbf{q}_3 - \mathbf{q}_0].$$

The continuum mechanics formulation defines the deformation gradient $\mathbf{F}$ as

$$\mathbf{F} = \mathbf{P}\mathbf{Q}^{-1}.$$

Using the deformation gradient $\mathbf{F}$, the Green-St Venant strain tensor $\mathbf{G}$ may be given as

$$\mathbf{S} = \mathbf{F}^T\mathbf{F}$$
$$\mathbf{G} = \mathbf{S} - \mathbf{I}.$$

12.3 Strain based Dynamics

The matrix **G** is a 3×3 matrix, and **I** is the 3×3 identity matrix. The diagonal entries G_{ii} contain stretch values for the current tetrahedron, whereas the off-diagonal entries of **G** contain shear values. The stretch and shear constraints may be given as follows

$$C_{\text{stretch}}(\mathbf{p}_0, \mathbf{p}_1, \mathbf{p}_2, \mathbf{p}_3) = S_{ij} - s_i, \quad i, j \in \{0,1,2\} \text{ and } i = j;$$
$$C_{\text{shear}}(\mathbf{p}_0, \mathbf{p}_1, \mathbf{p}_2, \mathbf{p}_3) = S_{ij}, \quad i, j \in \{0,1,2\} \text{ and } i \neq j;$$

where s_i are rest stretches (typically one) that are additional input parameters to control initial deformation of the current tetrahedral element.

Triangular Constraint Formulation

For triangular constraints, the matrices **P** and **Q** are non-square, and hence, their inverses are undefined. The **Q** matrix (which stores the rest state of a triangle) is obtained using the 2D texture coordinates assigned to the triangle. The matrix **P** is given as

$$\mathbf{P} = [\mathbf{p}_1 - \mathbf{p}_0 \quad \mathbf{p}_2 - \mathbf{p}_0].$$

Let $\mathbf{u}_1, \mathbf{u}_2$, and $\mathbf{u}_3$ be the 2D texture coordinates of a triangle. The matrix **Q** may then be given in terms of these coordinates as

$$\mathbf{Q} = [\mathbf{u}_1 - \mathbf{u}_0 \quad \mathbf{u}_2 - \mathbf{u}_0].$$

A new matrix **T** containing two tangent vectors in world coordinates may then be given as

$$\mathbf{T} = \mathbf{P}\mathbf{Q}^{-1} = [\mathbf{p}_1 - \mathbf{p}_0 \quad \mathbf{p}_2 - \mathbf{p}_0][\mathbf{u}_1 - \mathbf{u}_0 \quad \mathbf{u}_2 - \mathbf{u}_0]^{-1}.$$

The matrix **T** is a 2×3 matrix. The two tangent vectors are converted to the local triangle frame by first normalizing the two tangent vectors and then multiplying them with the matrix **P** as follows:

$$\mathbf{N} = \left[\frac{\mathbf{T}_0}{\|\mathbf{T}_0\|}, \frac{\mathbf{T}_1}{\|\mathbf{T}_1\|} \right]$$

$$\mathbf{T}' = \mathbf{N}^T \mathbf{P}.$$

The matrix **T'** is used to transform positions from global coordinates to the triangle's material coordinates.

Bending Constraint Formulation

Additional constraints called bending constraints are identified for both triangular and tetrahedral mesh configurations. These constraints help maintain the initial shape of the mesh element and prevent it from collapsing onto itself. For each bending element, there are four positions: $\mathbf{p}_0$, $\mathbf{p}_1$, $\mathbf{p}_2$, $\mathbf{p}_3$. These are the four tetrahedral vertices for a tetrahedral mesh. For a triangular mesh, the four positions come from the two adjacent triangles $\{\mathbf{p}_0, \mathbf{p}_2, \mathbf{p}_3\}$ and $\{\mathbf{p}_1, \mathbf{p}_3, \mathbf{p}_2\}$. First, the two triangle normals $\mathbf{n}_1$ and $\mathbf{n}_2$ are obtained using the following set of equations

$$\mathbf{n}_1 = \frac{(\mathbf{p}_2 - \mathbf{p}_0) \times (\mathbf{p}_3 - \mathbf{p}_0)}{\|(\mathbf{p}_2 - \mathbf{p}_0) \times (\mathbf{p}_3 - \mathbf{p}_0)\|}$$

$$\mathbf{n}_2 = \frac{(\mathbf{p}_3 - \mathbf{p}_1) \times (\mathbf{p}_2 - \mathbf{p}_1)}{\|(\mathbf{p}_3 - \mathbf{p}_1) \times (\mathbf{p}_2 - \mathbf{p}_1)\|}.$$

The dihedral angle φ is then obtained by using the following equation

$$\varphi = \arccos(\mathbf{n}_1 \cdot \mathbf{n}_2).$$

The dihedral angles for all bending elements are precalculated at initialization. The spatial derivatives of dihedral angle with respect to each position are obtained through the following set of equations

$$\mathbf{e} = \mathbf{p}_3 - \mathbf{p}_2$$
$$\nabla_{\mathbf{p}_0} \varphi = \|\mathbf{e}\| \mathbf{n}_1$$
$$\nabla_{\mathbf{p}_1} \varphi = \|\mathbf{e}\| \mathbf{n}_2$$
$$\nabla_{\mathbf{p}_2} \varphi = \frac{(\mathbf{p}_0 - \mathbf{p}_3) \cdot \mathbf{e}}{\|\mathbf{e}\|} \mathbf{n}_1 + \frac{(\mathbf{p}_1 - \mathbf{p}_3) \cdot \mathbf{e}}{\|\mathbf{e}\|} \mathbf{n}_2$$
$$\nabla_{\mathbf{p}_3} \varphi = \frac{(\mathbf{p}_2 - \mathbf{p}_0) \cdot \mathbf{e}}{\|\mathbf{e}\|} \mathbf{n}_1 + \frac{(\mathbf{p}_2 - \mathbf{p}_1) \cdot \mathbf{e}}{\|\mathbf{e}\|} \mathbf{n}_2.$$

Finally, the spatial derivatives are used to obtain the positional corrections $\Delta \mathbf{p}_i$ as

$$\Delta \mathbf{p}_k = -\frac{w_k \sqrt{1 - d^2} (\arccos(d) - \varphi_0)}{\sum_j w_j |\mathbf{q}_j|^2} \mathbf{q}_k,$$

where w_k is the inverse mass of k-th particle, d is the dot product $\mathbf{n}_1 \cdot \mathbf{n}_2$ of the two normals for the current bending element, φ_0 is the dihedral angle of the current bending element, and $\mathbf{q}_k$ represents the material coordinates of the k-th particle. The corrected positions are then used to obtain the new position and velocity.

Volume/Area Conservation Constraint Formulation

Apart from the bending constraints, volume and area conservation constraints are also enforced for tetrahedral and triangular meshes, respectively, which ensure that the deforming element maintains its initial size. For a given tetrahedron, the volume conservation constraint is given as

$$C_{\text{volume}}(\mathbf{p}_0, \mathbf{p}_1, \mathbf{p}_2, \mathbf{p}_3, \mathbf{q}_0, \mathbf{q}_1, \mathbf{q}_2, \mathbf{q}_3) = \det \mathbf{P} - \det \mathbf{Q}.$$

The spatial derivatives of the volume constraint with respect to the element positions are obtained as follows:

$$\nabla_{\mathbf{p}_1} C_{\text{volume}} = (\mathbf{p}_2 - \mathbf{p}_0) \times (\mathbf{p}_3 - \mathbf{p}_0)$$
$$\nabla_{\mathbf{p}_2} C_{\text{volume}} = (\mathbf{p}_3 - \mathbf{p}_0) \times (\mathbf{p}_1 - \mathbf{p}_0)$$
$$\nabla_{\mathbf{p}_3} C_{\text{volume}} = (\mathbf{p}_1 - \mathbf{p}_0) \times (\mathbf{p}_2 - \mathbf{p}_0)$$
$$\nabla_{\mathbf{p}_0} C_{\text{volume}} = -(\nabla_{\mathbf{p}_1} C_{\text{volume}} + \nabla_{\mathbf{p}_2} C_{\text{volume}} + \nabla_{\mathbf{p}_3} C_{\text{volume}}).$$

For a triangular element, the area conservation constraint is given as follows:

$$C_{\text{area}}(\mathbf{p}_0, \mathbf{p}_1, \mathbf{p}_2, \mathbf{q}_0, \mathbf{q}_1, \mathbf{q}_2) = \|(\mathbf{p}_1 - \mathbf{p}_0) \times (\mathbf{p}_2 - \mathbf{p}_0)\|^2 - \|(\mathbf{q}_1 - \mathbf{q}_0) \times (\mathbf{q}_2 - \mathbf{q}_0)\|^2.$$

The spatial derivatives of area conservation constraints with respect to the element positions are obtained as follows:

$$\nabla_{\mathbf{p}_1} C_{\text{area}} = 2(\mathbf{p}_2 - \mathbf{p}_0) \times ((\mathbf{p}_1 - \mathbf{p}_0) \times (\mathbf{p}_2 - \mathbf{p}_0))$$
$$\nabla_{\mathbf{p}_2} C_{\text{area}} = 2(\mathbf{p}_1 - \mathbf{p}_0) \times ((\mathbf{p}_2 - \mathbf{p}_0) \times (\mathbf{p}_1 - \mathbf{p}_0))$$
$$\nabla_{\mathbf{p}_0} C_{\text{area}} = -(\nabla_{\mathbf{p}_1} C_{\text{area}} + \nabla_{\mathbf{p}_2} C_{\text{area}}).$$

For both volume and area conservation constraints, the particle projections for i-th particle are obtained using

$$\lambda = \frac{C_{\text{volume/area}}}{\sum_i w_i \|\nabla_{\mathbf{p}_i} C_{\text{volume/area}}\|^2}$$

$$\Delta \mathbf{p}_i = -\lambda w_i \nabla_{\mathbf{p}_i} C_{\text{volume/area}},$$

where, $i \in \{0,1,2\}$ for a triangular mesh and $i \in \{0,1,2,3\}$ for a tetrahedral mesh. The positional corrections $\Delta \mathbf{p}_i$ are then added to the current position to obtain the new positions. The new positions are then used to get the new velocities.

12.4 Implementation Details

The strain based dynamics is augmented in the PBD framework by applying additional constraints. The implementation details for modeling a cloth mesh and a tetrahedral mesh are discussed in this section. In the accompanying demo application, area and volume conservation constraints are not enforced, but adding these constraints should not be difficult.

In the demo framework provided with this chapter, a `StepPhysics()` function is defined, as shown in Listing 12.1. This function is called every frame to advance the real-time physics simulation, and it is given the elapsed time `dt` as a parameter. It first calculates all external forces, such as the gravitational force, wind forces, etc. Then, it performs the explicit Euler integration step. Next, a set of constraints that includes distance and bending constraints is satisfied, and positional corrections are obtained using a number of Gauss-Seidel iterations. Finally, the current velocities are integrated using the calculated positional corrections, and the new positions are obtained.

The `ComputeForces()` function is defined as shown in Listing 12.2. This function simply sums the gravitational force if the mass of the particle is greater than zero.

Listing 12.1. The `StepPhysics()` function definition.

```
void StepPhysics(float dt)
{
    ComputeForces();
    IntegrateExplicitWithDamping(dt);
    UpdateInternalConstraints();
    UpdateExternalConstraints();
    Integrate(dt);
}
```

12.4 Implementation Details

Listing 12.2. The `ComputeForces()` function definition.

```
void ComputeForces(void)
{
    for (size_t i = 0; i < total_points; i++)
    {
        F[i] = gravity * masses[i];
    }
}
```

The `IntegrateExplicitWithDamping()` function is defined as shown in Listing 12.3. This function first calculates the current velocity using an explicit Euler integration step and then dampens the current velocity. The previous position corrections `dp` are accumulated with the dampened velocities. Next, the dampened position corrections are subtracted from the current velocities. Finally, using the corrected velocities, the new positions are predicted.

Listing 12.3. The `IntegrateExplicitWithDamping()` function definition.

```
void IntegrateExplicitWithDamping(float deltaTime)
{
    float sumVN = 0.0F;

    for (size_t i = 0; i < total_points; i++)
    {
        V[i] = V[i] + (F[i] * deltaTime) * W[i];
        V[i] *= global_dampening;

        float lenDP = glm::length(dp[i]);
        if (lenDP > EPSILON)
        {
            sumVN = sumVN + glm::dot(V[i], dp[i] / lenDP);
        }
    }

    for (size_t i = 0; i < total_points; i++)
    {
        float lenDP = glm::length(dp[i]);
        if (lenDP > EPSILON)
```

```
            {
                V[i] = V[i] - kDamp * sumVN * dp[i] / lenDP;
            }
        }

        for (size_t i = 0; i < total_points; i++)
        {
            if (W[i] <= 0.0F)
            {
                tmp_X[i] = X[i];
            }
            else
            {
                tmp_X[i] = X[i] + V[i] * deltaTime;
            }
        }
    }
```

The `UpdateExternalConstraints()` function is responsible for updating the collision constraints such as the collision of a soft body with an object. In the demo application, the `UpdateExternalConstraints()` function is implemented as shown in Listing 12.4. This function checks each particle for collision, first against an oriented ellipsoid and then against the ground plane. If there is a collision, the particle is displaced to a position in which it is no longer in a colliding state.

Listing 12.4. The `UpdateExternalConstraints()` function definition.

```
void EllipsoidCollision(void)
{
    for (size_t i = 0; i < total_points; i++)
    {
        glm::vec4 X_0 = (inverse_ellipsoid * glm::vec4(tmp_X[i], 1));
        glm::vec3 delta0 = glm::vec3(X_0.x, X_0.y, X_0.z) - center;

        float distance = glm::length(delta0);
        if (distance < 1.0F)
        {
            delta0 = (radius - distance) * delta0 / distance;
```

```
            glm::vec3 delta = glm::vec3(ellipsoid * glm::vec4(delta0, 0));
            tmp_X[i] += delta;
            V[i] = glm::vec3(0);
        }
    }
}

void UpdateExternalConstraints(void)
{
    EllipsoidCollision();
    GroundCollision();
}
```

The `UpdateInternalConstraints()` function is responsible for updating the triangle constraint (for a cloth mesh) or tetrahedral constraint (for a tetrahedral mesh). It also updates the distance and bending constraints. The implementation of strain based dynamics for a cloth or tetrahedral mesh differs in how the `UpdateInternalConstraints()` function is implemented. The following sections detail how this function is implemented for each case individually.

12.5 Implementing Cloth Simulation

For cloth simulation, the `UpdateInternalConstraints()` function is implemented as shown in Listing 12.5. The function first loops through all triangle constraints and updates them. Next, it loops through all bending constraints and updates them.

Listing 12.5. The `UpdateInternalConstraints()` function definition for cloth simulation.

```
void UpdateInternalConstraints(void)
{
    memset(&dp[0].x, 0, sizeof(glm::vec3) * total_points);

    for (size_t si = 0; si < solver_iterations; ++si)
    {
        for (size_t i = 0; i < t_constraints.size(); ++i)
        {
            UpdateTriangleConstraint(i);
        }
```

```
            for (size_t i = 0; i < b_constraints.size(); i++)
            {
                UpdateBendingConstraint(i);
            }
        }
    }
```

In each update of the triangle constraint, the current shear and stress values are calculated. These are then used to obtain the positional correction dp for each triangle vertex. For space concerns, the definitions of `UpdateTriangleConstraint()` and `UpdateBendingConstraint()` functions have been omitted. The readers are referred to the `Cloth.cpp` file in the accompanying demo source code for details. For a cloth model, the triangle and bending constraints are generated at initialization as shown in Listing 12.6.

Listing 12.6. Code snippet showing generation of triangle and bending constraints.

```
void AddTriangleConstraint(int pa, int pb, int pc, float k)
{
    TriangleConstraint   c;

    c.p1 = pa; c.p2 = pb; c.p3 = pc;
    t_constraints.push_back(c);
}

void AddBendingConstraint(int pa, int pb, int pc, int pd, float k)
{
    BendingConstraint   c;

    c.p1 = pa; c.p2 = pb; c.p3 = pc; c.p4 = pd;
    c.k_prime = 1.0F - pow((1.0F - k), 1.0F / solver_iterations);
    if (c.k_prime > 1.0F)
    {
        c.k_prime = 1.0F;
    }

    b_constraints.push_back(c);
}
```

12.5 Implementing Cloth Simulation

```
for (size_t i = 0; i < indices.size(); i += 3)
{
    int i0 = indices[i];
    int i1 = indices[i + 1];
    int i2 = indices[i + 2];
    AddTriangleConstraint(i0, i1, i2, kStretch);
}

for (int i = 0; i < v - 1; ++i)
{
    for (int j = 0; j < u - 1; ++j)
    {
        int p1 = i * (numX+1) + j;
        int p2 = p1 + 1;
        int p3 = p1 + (numX+1);
        int p4 = p3 + 1;
        if ((j + i) & 1)
        {
            AddBendingConstraint(p3, p2, p1, p4, kBend);
        }
        else
        {
            AddBendingConstraint(p4, p1, p3, p2, kBend);
        }
    }
}
```

The inverse of the **Q** matrix is precalculated at initialization as shown in Listing 12.7.

Listing 12.7. Code snippet showing calculation of the **Q** inverse matrix.

```
for (size_t i = 0; i < indices.size(); i += 3)
{
    int i0 = indices[i];
    int i1 = indices[i + 1];
    int i2 = indices[i + 2];

    glm::vec3 x0 = X[i0];
```

```cpp
        glm::vec3 x1 = X[i1];
        glm::vec3 x2 = X[i2];
        glm::vec2 u0 = UV[i0];
        glm::vec2 u1 = UV[i1];
        glm::vec2 u2 = UV[i2];

        glm::mat2x3 P = glm::mat2x3(x1 - x0, x2 - x0);
        glm::mat2x2 U = glm::mat2x2(u1 - u0, u2 - u0);
        glm::mat2x2 Uinv = glm::inverse(U);

        glm::mat2x3 T = P * Uinv;
        glm::vec3 n1(T[0]);
        glm::vec3 n2(T[1]);
        n1 = glm::normalize(n1);
        n2 = glm::normalize(n2);

        glm::mat2x2 C = glm::transpose(glm::mat2x3(n1, n2)) * P;
        Qinv[count] = glm::inverse(C);
        count++;
    }
```

The cloth simulation calls the `StepPhysics()` function every frame and then passes the updated positions to the rendering function to display the deformed cloth.

12.6 Implementing Tetrahedral Mesh Simulation

For tetrahedral mesh simulation, the `UpdateInternalConstraints()` function is implemented as shown in Listing 12.8. The function first loops through all tetrahedral constraints and updates them. Next, it loops through all bending constraints and updates those. A set of tetrahedral constraints is generated at initialization as shown in Listing 12.9.

12.6 Implementing Tetrahedral Mesh Simulation

Listing 12.8. The `UpdateInternalConstraints()` function definition for the tetrahedral mesh simulation.

```
void UpdateInternalConstraints(void)
{
    memset(&dp[0].x, 0, sizeof(glm::vec3) * total_points);

    for (size_t si = 0; si < solver_iterations; ++si)
    {
        for (size_t i = 0; i < t_constraints.size(); ++i)
        {
            UpdateTetrahedralConstraint(i);
        }

        for (size_t i = 0; i < b_constraints.size(); i++)
        {
            UpdateBendingConstraint(i);
        }
    }
}
```

Listing 12.9. Code snippet showing generation of tetrahedral constraints.

```
for (size_t i = 0; i < tetraIndices.size(); i += 4)
{
    int i0 = tetraIndices[i];
    int i1 = tetraIndices[i + 1];
    int i2 = tetraIndices[i + 2];
    int i3 = tetraIndices[i + 3];

    glm::vec3 p0 = X[i0];
    glm::vec3 p1 = X[i1];
    glm::vec3 p2 = X[i2];
    glm::vec3 p3 = X[i3];

    glm::mat3 Q(p1 - p0, p2 - p0, p3 - p0);
    glm::mat3 Qinv = glm::inverse(Q);
    glm::vec3 c1(Qinv[0]);
    glm::vec3 c2(Qinv[1]);
    glm::vec3 c3(Qinv[2]);
```

```
    TetrahedralConstraint    t;

    t.c1 = c1; t.c2 = c2; t.c3 = c3;
    t.p0 = i0; t.p1 = i1; t.p2 = i2; t.p3 = i3;
    t_constraints.push_back(t);
}
```

For each tetrahedron, the barycentric coordinates are also obtained to find the nearest surface vertex so that the tetrahedral deformation can be transferred to the surface mesh. These are calculated in the `FindBarycentricMapping()` function as shown in Listing 12.10.

Listing 12.10. Code snippet showing generation of barycentric coordinates.

```
void FindBarycentricMapping(void)
{
    glm::vec3 *pVertices = mesh.GetPositionPointer();

    for (size_t j = 0; j < mesh.GetVerticesSize(); ++j)
    {
        TetraMap   tmap;

        float minDist = 0.0F;
        for (size_t i = 0; i < tetraIndices.size(); i += 4)
        {
            int i0 = tetraIndices[i];
            int i1 = tetraIndices[i + 1];
            int i2 = tetraIndices[i + 2];
            int i3 = tetraIndices[i + 3];

            glm::vec3 p0 = X[i0];
            glm::vec3 p1 = X[i1];
            glm::vec3 p2 = X[i2];
            glm::vec3 p3 = X[i3];
            glm::vec3 b = ComputeBarycentricCoordinates(pVertices[j],
                    p0, p1, p2, p3);

            if (b.x >= 0.0F && b.y >= 0.0F && b.z >= 0.0F &&
                    (b.x + b.y + b.z) <= 1.0F)
```

```
            {
                tmap.tetraIndex = i;
                tmap.barycentricCoords = b;
                break;
            }

            float dist = 0.0F;
            if (b.x + b.y + b.z > 1.0F) dist = b.x + b.y + b.z - 1.0F;
            if (b.x < 0.0F) dist = (-b.x < dist) ? dist : -b.x;
            if (b.y < 0.0F) dist = (-b.y < dist) ? dist : -b.y;
            if (b.z < 0.0F) dist = (-b.z < dist) ? dist : -b.z;
            if (i == 0 || dist < minDist)
            {
                minDist = dist;
                tmap.tetraIndex = i;
                tmap.barycentricCoords=b;
            }
        }

        mapping.push_back(tmap);
    }
}
```

In each update of the tetrahedral constraint, the current shear and stress values are obtained. These are then used to calculate the positional correction dp for each tetrahedral vertex. For space concerns, the UpdateTetrahedralConstraint() and UpdateBendingConstraint() function definitions have been omitted. The readers are referred to the TetrahedralMesh.cpp file in the accompanying demo source code for details.

12.7 Barycentric Interpolation

Once the updated tetrahedral vertex positions have been calculated, the obtained deformations are transferred to the surface enclosing the tetrahedral mesh. To accomplish this, barycentric coordinates are used. Each tetrahedral vertex is multiplied by its barycentric coordinates with respect to the current triangle vertex to obtain the interpolated position. The current surface mesh vertex position is then updated with the interpolated position. All of this is calculated in the UpdateMesh() function as shown in Listing 12.11.

Listing 12.11. Code snippet showing calculation of interpolated vertex position calculated from the deformed tetrahedra using barycentric interpolation.

```
void UpdateMesh(void)
{
    glm::vec3 *pVertices = mesh.GetPositionPointer();
    for (size_t i = 0; i < mapping.size(); ++i)
    {
        TetraMap tmap = mapping[i];
        int index = tmap.tetraIndex;
        int i0 = tetraIndices[index];
        int i1 = tetraIndices[index + 1];
        int i2 = tetraIndices[index + 2];
        int i3 = tetraIndices[index + 3];

        glm::vec3 p0 = X[i0];
        glm::vec3 p1 = X[i1];
        glm::vec3 p2 = X[i2];
        glm::vec3 p3 = X[i3];
        glm::vec3 b = tmap.barycentricCoords;
        glm::vec3 temp = p0 * b.x + p1 * b.y + p2 * b.z +
            p3 * (1.0F - b.x - b.y - b.z);

        pVertices[i].x = temp.x;
        pVertices[i].y = temp.y;
        pVertices[i].z = temp.z;
    }

    mesh.CalcNormals();
}
```

12.8 Experimental Evaluation

The strain based dynamics technique detailed in this chapter was evaluated on two machines:

1. A laptop ASUS K56CB with an Intel Core i7-3537U CPU @ 2 GHz with 4 GB RAM on a Windows 7 64-bit operating system. The laptop was equipped with an Nvidia GeForce GT 740M GPU.

12.8 Experimental Evaluation

2. A desktop PC with an Intel Core i7-4790K CPU @ 4 GHz with 16 GB RAM on a Windows 8.1 64-bit operating system. The desktop was equipped with an Nvidia GeForce Titan Black GPU.

For the cloth model, a set of cloth meshes with different mesh resolutions ranging from 21×21 vertices to 128×128 vertices were used.

Rendering results showing the cloth meshes during deformation with different anisotropic shear and stretch coefficients are shown in Figure 12.2. Varying the values of the stress and shear coefficients introduces anisotropic behavior. The cloth stretches and shears differently according to the values of the stretch and shear coefficients as can be seen in the middle and right columns in Figure 12.2.

Along with the anisotropic behavior, the overall performance of the method is also critical. Therefore, the experiments were extended to note the total time (including both deformation and rendering time) for cloth meshes. These are detailed in Table 12.1. As can be seen from the table, as the mesh resolution increases, the frame time also increases. The performance is comparable on both machines used in testing. The reason for this is that there is less geometry to process, and the entire simulation is implemented on the CPU using single-threaded code without taking advantage of additional CPU cores or the GPU.

Dataset	Total Vertices	Total Triangles	Total Time (ms per frame)	
			Machine 1	Machine 2
Cloth (21×21)	441	2646	6.44	6.38
Cloth (41×41)	1681	10086	9.54	9.21
Cloth (64×64)	4096	24576	16.20	14.88
Cloth (128×128)	16384	98304	53.14	43.84

Table 12.1. Performance of strain based dynamics for cloth mesh.

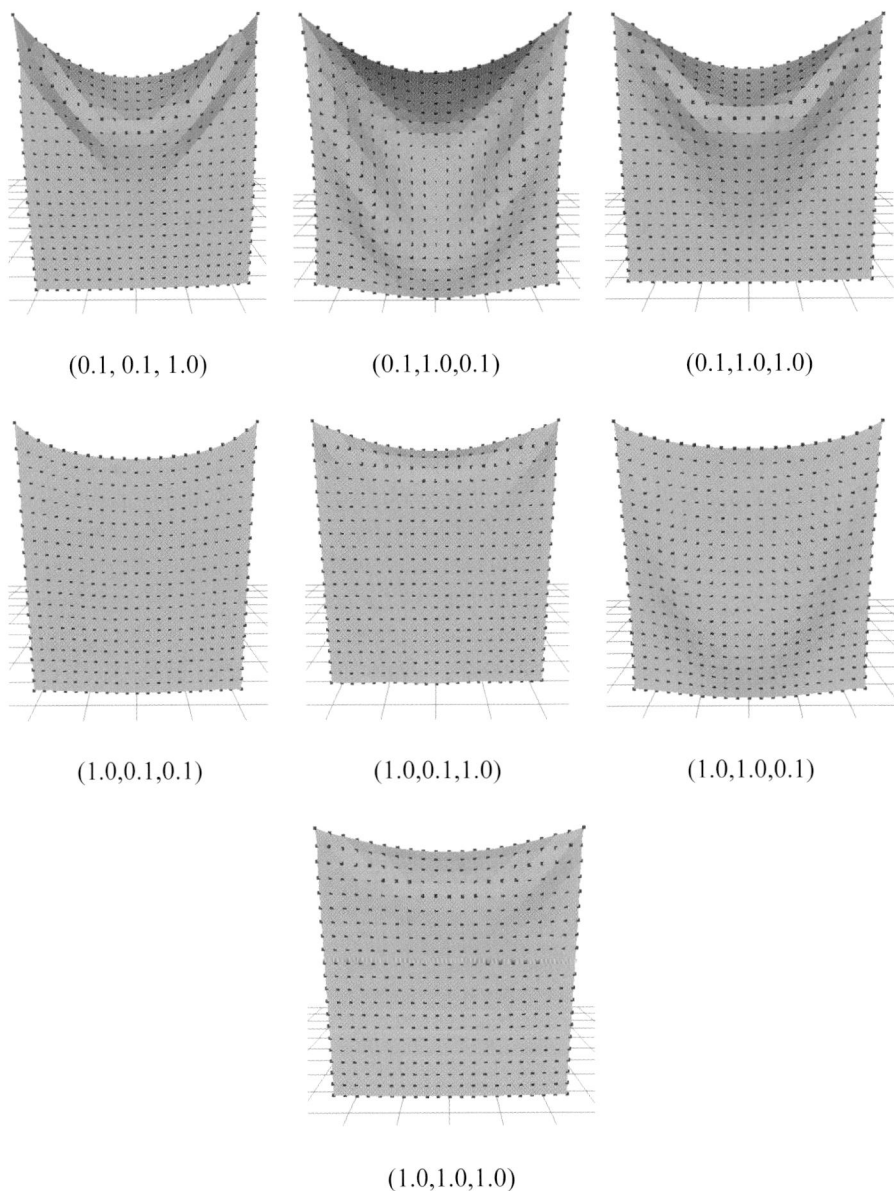

Figure 12.2. Rendering results of a cloth mesh using different values of stretch and shear coefficients to introduce anisotropic behavior. The values of the three coefficients, two stretch coefficients and one shear coefficient, are written as a tuple $(kS_{xx}, kS_{yy}, kS_{xy})$ below each image.

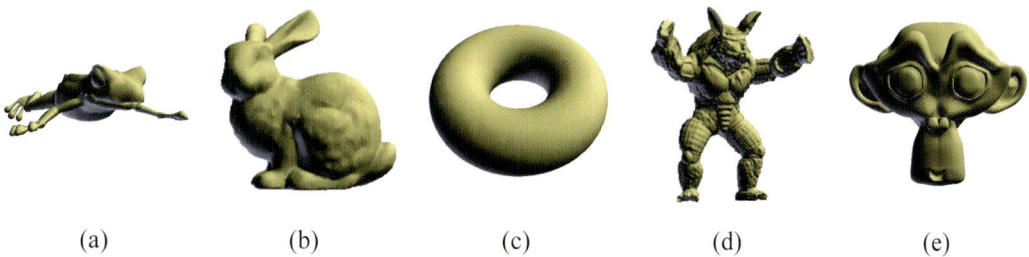

Figure 12.3. The different meshes used in the experimental evaluation: (a) frog, (b) bunny, (c) torus, (d) armadillo, and (e) Suzanne.

Additional experiments were carried out to incorporate tetrahedral meshes generated from the polygonal meshes shown in Figure 12.3. The meshes were downloaded from the Stanford 3D scanning repository. The tetrahedral approximations were obtained using the PhysXViewer application provided with the PhysX 2.8.4 SDK and stored in a separate file. Details about the mesh datasets are listed in Table 12.2. The total time required for deformation, barycentric interpolation, and rendering (in milliseconds per frame) is shown in Table 12.3.

The barycentric mapping step is carried out only once at initialization. In this process, for each tetrahedral vertex, the nearest polygonal mesh vertex is found and its barycentric coordinates are obtained. These coordinates are finally used to transfer the deformation from the tetrahedral mesh to the polygonal mesh through barycentric interpolation. As can be seen from the results shown in Table 12.3, the performance of strain based dynamics varies considerably as the number of tetrahedra increases. The main reason for this is that the entire deformation process is implemented on the CPU.

12.9 Future Work

A number of extensions are possible for the method discussed in this chapter. The first extension is utilizing the GPU for both deformation and barycentric interpolation. For deformation, the transform feedback mechanism could be used to implement strain based dynamics entirely on the GPU. The entire deformation may also be offloaded to the compute API (OpenCL, CUDA, or compute shaders in OpenGL or DirectX). The barycentric mapping and interpolation could also be carried out in the vertex or geometry shader stages of the GPU. Additional performance improvements may be achieved by calculating the deformation on a lower-resolution triangular or tetrahedral mesh, and then the obtained deformation could be transferred to the finer-resolution rendering mesh.

Dataset	Surface Mesh		Tetrahedral Mesh	
	Total Vertices	Total Triangles	Total Vertices	Total Tetrahedra
Frog	4010	7694	187	461
Bunny	4098	8192	1113	3614
Torus	1729	3458	1363	4387
Armadillo	106289	212574	1518	5094
Suzanne	7830	15492	1004	3229

Table 12.2. Datasets used in the performance assessment.

Dataset	Time (ms per frame)			
	Machine 1		Machine 2	
	Barycentric mapping	Deformation + Barycentric Interpolation + Rendering	Barycentric mapping	Deformation + Barycentric Interpolation + Rendering
Frog	41.58	7.15	30.14	6.94
Bunny	451.09	16.44	288.64	14.419
Torus	205.14	18.17	142.96	16.331
Armadillo	13781.60	28.56	9753.42	25.29
Suzanne	651.17	15.05	495.89	13.858

Table 12.3. Performance of strain based dynamics for tetrahedral mesh model.

References

[Jakobsen 2001] Thomas Jakobsen, "Advanced Character Physics". Game Developers Conference, 2001.

[Nealen 2006] Andrew Nealen, Mathias Müller, Richard Keiser, Eddie Boxerman, and Mark Carlson. "Physically Based Deformable Models in Computer Graphics". Computer Graphics Forum, Vol. 25, No. 4 (December 2006), pp: 809–836.

[Mathias 2007] Matthias Müller, Bruno Heidelberger, Marcus Hennix, and John Ratcliff. "Position based Dynamics". *Journal of Visual Communication and Image Representation*, Vol. 18, No. 2 (April 2007), pp. 109–118.

[Mathias 2014] Mathias Müller, Nuttapong Chentanez, Tae-Yong Kim, and Miles Macklin. "Strain Based Dynamics". *Eurographics / ACM SIGGRAPH Symposium on Computer Animation*, 2014.

Part III

General Programming

13

Generic, Lightweight, and Fast Delegates in C++

Stefan Reinalter
Molecular Matters

In game programming, we often have the need to couple two or more completely unrelated classes at a higher level, making one of them call into the other. While engine and game systems should be isolated at a lower level as much as possible, sooner or later these systems have to talk to each other by some means. As an example, consider a character walking through a 3D environment. While the skeletal animation is driven by the animation system, playing footstep sounds would be the responsibility of the sound system, but neither of the systems in question should know about the existence of the other.

In theory, this could be achieved by introducing interfaces as a bridge between unrelated classes. In practice, this is often frowned upon, because it creates coupling between the implementation and the corresponding interface and can have additional unwanted side effects. Furthermore, it leads to more boilerplate code being written and incurs extra function call overhead.

In languages that treat functions as first-class citizens, this problem can be solved easily by passing around functions among all parties that somehow need to communicate. Since C++11, `std::function` offers such a general-purpose mechanism for passing around, storing, and invoking functions, supporting lambdas, member functions, and other function objects.

While `std::function` is a welcome addition to the standard C++ library, this gem showcases a different solution to the underlying problem of tying unrelated types into a common interface. Most notably, this gem offers the following features, making it stand out from other implementations:

- **Lightweight.** The size of a delegate is typically between 8 and 16 bytes, depending on the compiler and the platform. The size of a delegate is always constant for a given compiler and platform no matter what function it is bound to.
- **Fast.** Calling a function bound to the delegate is as fast as calling a function through a pointer in all situations. In many cases, the invocation can even be optimized into a direct function call.
- **No dynamic memory allocation.** The delegate never needs to allocate any additional memory.
- **No virtual function call overhead.** The implementation does not rely on virtual function dispatch.
- **No C++11 or C++14 required.** The implementation does not make use of newer C++ features from the C++11 and C++14 standards. It works on older compilers not supporting C++11.
- **Standard C++.** The implementation uses standard-conformant, legal C++. No platform-specific hacks, assembly language programming, etc., are needed.
- **No third-party dependencies.** There is no requirement for STL, Boost, or any other third-party libraries.
- **Generic.** The delegate can be bound to both free functions and member functions that each accept an arbitrary number of arguments of any type.

13.1 Background

A delegate should lend itself to being bound to both free functions as well as member functions. This means that internally, the implementation needs to be able to accept both as a target, storing each through some kind of abstraction. C++ pointers-to-function and pointers-to-member-function would seem like promising candidates for getting the job done if it weren't for the C++ language throwing a monkey wrench in. Pointers-to-function and pointers-to-member-function are fundamentally different types! Neither of them can be converted into the other, nor can either of them be converted into a pointer to `void`. All such casts are illegal because pointers to functions are not necessarily represented in the same way as pointers to data. Furthermore, the size of a pointer-to-member-function might depend on the function to which it is pointing.[1]

The prevalent solution to this problem is to employ a technique known as *type erasure*. This erases the type of an object through a base class interface,

---

[1] This is the case for Microsoft's Visual C++ compiler (see also the `/vmm`, `/vms`, and `/vmv` compiler options).

13.1 Background

while making use of the concrete type in derived classes. To see how this works, consider the exemplary `Delegate` class implementation shown in Listing 13.1. This class is able to hold both a pointer-to-function as well as a pointer-to-member-function for any class as long as the function takes and returns an `int`.

Listing 13.1. Type erasure in action. Constructors, destructors, operators, and assertions have been removed for clarity.

```
class Delegate
{
    struct Wrapper
    {
        virtual int Invoke(int) = 0;
    };

    struct FunctionWrapper : public Wrapper
    {
        typedef int (*Function)(int);

        virtual int Invoke(int value)
        {
            return (*m_function)(value);
        }

        Function     m_function;
    };

    template <class T>
    struct MemFunctionWrapper : public Wrapper
    {
        typedef int (T::*MemFunction)(int);

        virtual int Invoke(int value)
        {
            return (m_instance->*m_function)(value);
        }

        MemFunction   m_function;
        T             *m_instance;
    };
```

```
    public:

        void Bind(int (*function)(int))
        {
            m_wrapper = new FunctionWrapper(function);
        }

        template <class T>
        void Bind(int (T::*memFunction)(int), T *instance)
        {
            m_wrapper = new MemFunctionWrapper<T>(memFunction, instance);
        }

        int Invoke(int value)
        {
            return m_wrapper->Invoke(value);
        }

    private:

        Wrapper    *m_wrapper;
};
```

Note how by using the `Wrapper` class we can hide the fact that pointers-to-function and pointers-to-member-function are incompatible types and have different invocation syntax. Derived classes know how to store and invoke the respective function objects, while the delegate implementation internally only uses the base interface. All differences between pointers to free functions and pointers to member functions have effectively been erased.

This works in the same spirit as the technique employed by `std::function`. However, there is a way to achieve the same effect without having to resort to type erasure.

13.2 The Delegate Technique

One of the lesser used (or known) features of C++ is the ability to pass a pointer-to-function and pointer-to-member-function as non-type template arguments,[2] as shown in Listing 13.2.

---

[2] See the C++ standard, §14.1 Template parameters.

13.2 The Delegate Technique

Listing 13.2. Passing a pointer-to-function as non-type template argument.

```
template <int (*function)(int)>
int CallMe(int value)
{
    return (*function)(value);
}

CallMe<&Add>(10);
```

While this feature seems inapplicable in the context of the example given in the previous section, it allows us to reconcile pointers-to-function and pointers-to-member-function and their differing syntax with one common signature, exemplified in Listing 13.3.

Listing 13.3. Two proxy functions for calling free functions and member functions using function pointers, but both sharing the same signature.

```
template <int (*function)(int)>
int FunctionProxy(void *instance, int value)
{
    return (*function)(value);
}

template <class C, int (C::*memFunction)(int)>
int MemFunctionProxy(void *instance, int value)
{
    return (static_cast<C *>(instance)->*memFunction)(value);
}
```

There are three things worth noting here. First, both `FunctionProxy()` and `MemFunctionProxy()` share the same signature, namely `int (void *, int)`. This means that we can store a pointer-to-function to either of them internally, no longer having to distinguish between the two of them.

Second, don't let the `void *` used for passing around the instance fool you. This does not compromise type safety in any way because the delegate implementation only deals with concrete (template) types. The given instance is cast to `void *` only for storage, and it is later cast back to its original type for performing the member function call. Casting to and from `void *` is legal and explicitly allowed by the C++ standard.[3]

Third, note that passing the pointer-to-function and pointer-to-member-function as template arguments offers excellent optimization opportunities to the compiler. As an example, when binding a small member function to a delegate, the compiler is able to inline the member function call into the proxy function, resulting in overhead similar to only that of an ordinary function call. Larger functions cannot be inlined, and thus have to make an extra jump through the delegate's proxy function.

Listing 13.4 shows a simplified `Delegate` class implementation incorporating the fundamental ideas of this chapter.

Listing 13.4. The fundamental technique in action.

```
class Delegate
{
    typedef int (*ProxyFunction)(void *, int);

    template <int (*Function)(int)>
    static int FunctionProxy(void *, int arg0)
    {
        return (Function)(arg0);
    }

    template <class C, int (C::*Function)(int)>
    static int MethodProxy(void *instance, int arg0)
    {
        return (static_cast<C *>(instance)->*Function)(arg0);
    }

    template <class C, int (C::*Function)(int) const>
    static int ConstMethodProxy(void *instance, int arg0)
    {
        return (static_cast<const C *>(instance)->*Function)(arg0);
    }

public:
```

---

[3] See the C++ standard, §4.10 Pointer Conversions and §5.2.9 Static cast.

13.3 Toward a Generic Solution

```
        template <int (*Function)(int)>
        void Bind(void)
        {
            m_instance = nullptr;
            m_proxy = &FunctionProxy<Function>;
        }

        template <class C, int (C::*Function)(int)>
        void Bind(C *instance)
        {
            m_instance = instance;
            m_proxy = &MethodProxy<C, Function>;
        }

        template <class C, int (C::*Function)(int) const>
        void Bind(const C *instance)
        {
            m_instance = const_cast<C *>(instance);
            m_proxy = &ConstMethodProxy<C, Function>;
        }

        int Invoke(int arg0) const
        {
            return m_proxy(m_instance, arg0);
        }

    private:

        void             *m_instance;
        ProxyFunction    m_proxy;
};
```

13.3 Toward a Generic Solution

So far, the delegate can only cope with functions that accept a single `int` parameter and return an `int`. In order to make the delegate accept an arbitrary number of parameters and return any type, we have to resort to partial template specialization. By using a base template that accepts only a single template argument, we can partially specialize the class template on different signatures, as shown in Listing 13.5. Note that the syntax of the class specialization expects us to pass a function signature as the template argument rather than individual types. This is illustrated in Listing 13.6.

The implementation shown in Listing 13.4 could serve as an implementation for the partial specialization `class Delegate<R (ARG0)>` shown in Listing 13.5 as long as all return values of type `int` are replaced by `R`, and all parameters of type `int` are replaced by `ARG0`.

Listing 13.5. Partial template specialization allows the delegate to accept an arbitrary number of parameters of any type.

```
// Base template.
template <typename T>
class Delegate {};

template <typename R>
class Delegate<R ()>
{
    // Implementation for zero arguments, omitted.
};

template <typename R, typename ARG0>
class Delegate<R (ARG0)>
{
    // Implementation for one argument, omitted.
};

template <typename R, typename ARG0, typename ARG1>
class Delegate<R (ARG0, ARG1)>
{
    // Implementation for two arguments, omitted.
};

// More partial specializations for 3, 4, or more arguments.
```

Listing 13.6. Using the `Delegate` class.

```
int AddOne(int value)
{
    return value + 1;
```

```
}

Delegate<int (int)>  del;

del.Bind<&AddOne>();
int value = del.Invoke(10);       // value == 11
```

13.4 Embracing C++11

When using a compiler that supports the variadic template feature introduced in C++11, we can omit all of the partial specializations and simply write one variadic template specialization instead. This is illustrated in Listing 13.7.

Listing 13.7. Delegate class implementation using variadic templates.

```
// Base template.
template <typename T>
class Delegate {};

// Variadic specialization.
template <typename R, typename... Args>
class Delegate<R (Args...)>
{
    typedef R (*ProxyFunction)(void *, Args...);

    template <R (*Function)(Args...)>
    static R FunctionProxy(void *, Args... args)
    {
        return Function(std::forward<Args>(args)...);
    }

    template <class C, R (C::*Function)(Args...)>
    static R MethodProxy(void *instance, Args... args)
    {
        return (static_cast<C *>(instance)->*Function)
                (std::forward<Args>(args)...);
    }
```

```cpp
        template <class C, R (C::*Function)(Args...) const>
        static R ConstMethodProxy(void *instance, Args... args)
        {
            return (static_cast<const C *>(instance)->*Function)
                    (std::forward<Args>(args)...);
        }

    public:

        template <R (*Function)(Args...)>
        void Bind(void)
        {
            m_instance = nullptr;
            m_proxy = &FunctionProxy<Function>;
        }

        template <class C, R (C::*Function)(Args...)>
        void Bind(C *instance)
        {
            m_instance = instance;
            m_proxy = &MethodProxy<C, Function>;
        }

        template <class C, R (C::*Function)(Args...) const>
        void Bind(const C *instance)
        {
            m_instance = const_cast<C *>(instance);
            m_proxy = &ConstMethodProxy<C, Function>;
        }

        R Invoke(Args... args) const
        {
            return m_proxy(m_instance, std::forward<Args>(args)...);
        }

    private:

        void           *m_instance;
        ProxyFunction  m_proxy;
};
```

13.5 Extensions

In its current implementation, the delegate does not take ownership of the instance used in the call to `Bind()`. If that poses a problem, the delegate could be extended to also accept the `std::` family of pointers, which includes types such as `std::shared_ptr`. Furthermore, depending on the use cases, it might be worthwhile to implement comparison operators as well as a function call operator.

13.6 Source Code

A complete implementation of the technique described in this chapter can be found in `Delegate.h` (pre-C++11 version) and `Delegate11.h` (C++11 version) on the book's website. These are both made available under the MIT license.

14

Compile-Time String Hashing in C++

Stefan Reinalter
Molecular Matters

Every now and then in game programming, there comes a need to look up some entity, component, or resource by name. Even though true string-based lookups are mostly avoided where possible, there are situations where they are the best solution to the problem at hand. Examples include looking up certain bones in an animated rig in order to attach special effects, or looking up hardcoded assets such as meshes or textures in case a resource is missing or could not be loaded correctly.

In professional game engines, expensive string operations such as `strcmp()`, `strlen()`, and others are avoided where possible in run-time code. Thus, the prevalent technique for performing string-based lookups is to use hash-based lookups instead. Note that this does not imply that a hash-based data structure is used for storing the data, but instead refers to the fact that all string-based identifiers such as resource names have been hashed by the engine's content pipeline in an offline process.

The benefits of this approach are two-fold. First, a hash is a single integer value of fixed size, which simplifies the data and memory layout. Second, lookups in the engine code can be performed by using integer comparisons rather than costly string comparisons, as exemplified in Listing 14.1.

While this approach is a vast improvement over using `std::string` or `const char *` for lookup purposes, there is still overhead present, namely in all code that calls functions that accept a hash as an argument, as shown in Listing 14.2. Every time the `FindBoneIndex()` function is called, a hash must be generated at run time from a given string first.

Listing 14.1. Hash-based lookup of bones in an animated skeleton with hashes stored in a flat array.

```
uint32_t Skeleton::FindBoneIndex(uint32_t hash)
{
    // Look up the bone index based on the hash of the bone's name.
    uint32_t *p = std::find(arrayOfHashes, arrayOfHashes + arraySize, hash);
    return (p - arrayOfHashes);
}
```

Listing 14.2. Hashing the string literal "neck" using a `HashString()` function.

```
uint32_t index = skeleton.FindBoneIndex(HashString("neck"));
```

One way to get rid of the run-time overhead is to let the compiler calculate hash values at compile time. This also opens up new possibilities like using the resulting values as case constants in switch statements or as template arguments. This chapter showcases a solution for generating hash values for string literals and character arrays at compile time.

14.1 Background

Before delving into the realm of C++ template programming, a suitable hash function needs to be defined first. This chapter works with the FNV-1a hash function,[1] but other functions would also be appropriate. A 32-bit implementation of the FNV-1a hash function in C++ is shown in Listing 14.3.

The implementation in Listing 14.3 can be used for strings of arbitrary lengths, and it allows chaining of hash values. It starts with an offset basis of 2166136261, and uses 16777619 as the prime value. The evaluation of the hash value only uses exclusive-or and multiplication operations, which makes it fast while maintaining a low collision rate.

Turning the hash function shown above into a compile-time construct using templates would not be hard if it weren't for the fact that C++ does not allow objects with internal linkage to be used as non-type template arguments.[2] C++11

---

[1] Named after Glenn Fowler, Landon C. Noll, and Phong Vo. See http://www.isthe.com/chongo/tech/comp/fnv/index.html.

[2] See C++ standard, §14.1 Template parameters.

Listing 14.3. The FNV-1a hash function.

```
uint32_t Fnv1aHash(uint32_t hash, const char *str, size_t length)
{
    for (size_t i = 0; i < length; ++i)
    {
        const uint32_t value = static_cast<uint32_t>(*str++);
        hash ^= value;
        hash *= 16777619u;
    }

    return hash;
}

uint32_t Fnv1aHash(const char *str, size_t length)
{
    return Fnv1aHash(2166136261u, str, length);
}

uint32_t Fnv1aHash(const char *str)
{
    return Fnv1aHash(str, strlen(str));
}
```

has lifted this restriction in certain cases but still does not allow string literals to be used as non-type template arguments.[3] This means that the code in Listing 14.4 will not compile. Keep in mind that the intrinsic type of a narrow string literal such as "abc" in this example is not `const char *`, but an array of N `const char` where N is the number of characters plus a terminating '\0' character.[4]

14.2 The Hash Technique

The solution to this problem is to make use of the C++11 `constexpr` keyword, instead of trying to somehow cram string literals into non-type template parameters. The particular implementation shown in this chapter also possesses additional features that prove to be beneficial even in pre-C++11 environments.

---

[3] See C++ standard, §14.3.2 Template non-type arguments.
[4] See C++ standard, §2.13.5 String literals.

Listing 14.4. Two non-working alternatives.

```
template <const char *>
struct Hash
{
    // Implementation omitted.
};

Hash<"abc">;    // Does not compile.

template <size_t N, const char [N]>
struct Hash
{
    // Implementation omitted.
};

Hash<4, "abc">;    // Does not compile.
```

One key realization is that by starting with the last rather than the first character in the string, the iterative process of evaluating the hash function can be turned into a recursion. This in turn can be expressed using a small template metaprogram, as shown in Listing 14.5.

Listing 14.5. Template metaprogram for calculating the FNV-1a hash of a string literal at compile time.

```
template <size_t I>
struct Hash
{
    template <size_t N>
    constexpr static uint32_t Generate(const char (&str)[N])
    {
        return (Hash<I - 1>::Generate(str) ^ str[I - 1]) * 16777619u;
    }
};

template <>
struct Hash<0u>
{
```

```
    template <size_t N>
    constexpr static uint32_t Generate(const char (&str)[N])
    {
        return 2166136261u;
    }
};
```

Starting with the last character in the string literal, the metaprogram works its way until it reaches the first character at index $I == 0$, which will end the recursion due to the corresponding specialization of the `Hash` struct. The following illustration breaks down the evaluation of the hash value for the string literal `"abc"` into single steps.

```
Hash<3>::Generate("abc") =

(Hash<2>::Generate("abc") ^ 'c') * 16777619 =

((Hash<1>::Generate("abc") ^ 'b') * 16777619) ^ 'c') * 16777619 =

(((((Hash<0>::Generate("abc") ^ 'a') * 16777619) ^ 'b') *
    16777619) ^ 'c') * 16777619 =

(((((2166136261u ^ 'a') * 16777619) ^ 'b') * 16777619) ^ 'c') *
    16777619
```

14.3 Toward a Generic Hash Function

In its current form, the implementation accepts string literals and arrays of constant and non-constant characters as arguments, but not `const char *` or `std::string`. While such runtime strings cannot be hashed at compile time, the implementation should be able to cope with these types as well in order to make the use of string hashes ubiquitous.

What is needed is a helper function that correctly forwards a given argument to either the run-time or compile-time variant of our implementation, based on the type of the argument. Alas, a simple function with two overloads does not suffice, as shown in Listing 14.6.

Listing 14.6. A nonworking attempt at a generic `GenerateHash()` function.

```
uint32_t GenerateHash(const char *str)
{
    return Fnv1aHash(str);
}

template <size_t N>
constexpr uint32_t GenerateHash(const char (&str)[N])
{
    return Hash<N - 1>::Generate(str);
}

// Calls (const char *) overload!
uint32_t hash = GenerateHash("abc");
```

This might come as a surprise, but it is the outcome dictated by the C++ standard. Even though the template overload provides a perfect match for the type of argument given, the compiler considers the non-template overload to be a better match, due to the associated rank[5] of the array-to-pointer conversion[6] that is necessary in order to call the non-template overload. This effect can be bypassed by introducing a helper class template, along with necessary specializations, as exemplified in Listing 14.7.

Listing 14.7. A generic `GenerateHash()` function using a helper template.

```
template <typename T>
struct HashHelper {};

template <>
struct HashHelper<const char *>
{
    static uint32_t Generate(const char *str)
    {
        return Fnv1aHash(str);
    }
```

---

[5] See C++ standard, §13.3.3.1.1 Standard conversion sequences, Table 11.
[6] See C++ standard, §4.2 Array-to-pointer conversion.

14.3 Toward a Generic Hash Function

```
};

template <size_t N>
struct HashHelper<char [N]>
{
    constexpr static uint32_t Generate(const char (&str)[N])
    {
        return Hash<N - 1>::Generate(str);
    }
};

template <typename T>
constexpr static uint32_t GenerateHash(const T& str)
{
    return HashHelper<T>::Generate(str);
}
```

There are four things worth noting here. First, the `GenerateHash()` function accepts a constant reference to ensure that no array-to-pointer decay takes place when passing arguments.

Second, note that `HashHelper` offers a specialization for `char [N]`, and not `const char (&)[N]`. This is owed to the fact that the type `T` is being deduced as `char [N]` when a string literal (of type `const char [N]`) is passed as an argument to `GenerateHash()`.

Third, using the generic function allows users to pass both string literals as well as runtime strings into the function, and the compiler "does the right thing". String literals and character arrays are hashed at compile time, while other strings are hashed at run time.

Fourth, note that for strings hashed at compile time, the resulting value is marked as being `constexpr`, which makes it possible to use the result of `GenerateHash("abc")`, for example, as case constant in a switch statement or as nontype template argument. In a sense, this provides the functionality to make templates accept strings (or at least their hashes) as well as provide specializations for specific string literals, something that is otherwise impossible to do in C++ without jumping through additional hoops.

14.4 Implementation Notes

Even on platforms that do not support the C++11 `constexpr` keyword, the compiler is often smart and aggressive enough to fold the computation of the hash value into a single constant in the executable, given proper optimization settings. The implementation in this chapter was written specifically to give the compiler a great amount of optimization opportunities.

In a production environment, appropriate measures should be taken to ensure that no hash collisions occur among strings which are hashed by a call to `GenerateHash()`. This can most easily be accomplished by introducing an auxiliary class that is used for passing around hash values, as shown in Listing 14.8.

By using a non-explicit constructor, code that expects a hash value (such as the `FindBoneIndex()` function) can be called with string literals as well as runtime strings as arguments, without the user having to care or know about any of the underlying details. The technique still works the exact same way as described above.

Listing 14.8. An auxiliary class used as aid in checking string hashes for collisions.

```
class StringHash
{
    public:

        template <typename T>
        StringHash(const T& str) : m_hash(GenerateHash(str))
        {
            // Check against database of string hashes.
        }

        uint32_t Get(void) const
        {
            return m_hash;
        }

    private:

        const uint32_t    m_hash;
};
```

```
uint32_t Skeleton::FindBoneIndex(StringHash hash)
{
    uint32_t *p = std::find(arrayOfHashes, arrayOfHashes + arraySize,
            hash.Get());
    return (p - arrayOfHashes);
}
```

14.5 Source Code

A complete implementation of the technique described in this chapter can be found in `StringHash.h` on the book's website. This is made available under the MIT license.

15

Static Reflection in C++ Using Tuples

Nicolas Guillemot
Intel

It is common for game engines to be built with C++, and these C++ engines often need to convert objects from their C++ representation to alternate representations. For example, one may want to convert a C++ object member-by-member into a JavaScript object using a JSON encoding. One may also want to send an object through a network protocol which requires a byte order swap of each member of the object. It might also be interesting to check if a given object has a member with a specific name.

All of the above operations could be implemented in general ways if the C++ programming language allowed us to perform the generic operation of iterating over the members of an object. In order to minimize run-time overhead, it is desirable to perform these operations compile time, and this would require that we have the ability to statically inspect the structure of objects. In other words, we would require *static reflection* (as opposed to reflection in languages like Java or C#, which is generally done at run time.)

Although the C++ programming language does not currently have a built-in feature to inspect the members of objects in a generic way, such a feature is currently being designed for a future version of C++. Don't hold your breath—we would be lucky to have this feature in C++ in the distant year 2020. Instead, let's see how far we can get using today's compilers. This gem explores a solution using the C++11 `std::tuple` class as an alternative implementation of static reflection in the absence of proper language support.

15.1 Rethinking Composition Using Tuples

Instead of just spoiling the solution, let's work our way through the thought process that leads to it. Our quest is to answer the following question. Given a class type, how can we iterate over its members? It might sound like it should be easy, but C++ has no built-in facilities for such an operation. We could generate the code using a library like `libclang`,[1] but it would be nice to accomplish this goal within the language instead of through extra build tools.

With C++11 and C++14, many new interesting features were added to the language. Among these features is variadic templates, which make it possible to declare a template that accepts a variable number of template arguments. Using this feature, a new standard library type was added: `std::tuple`. This type is similar to `std::pair`, but uses variadic templates to have a variable number of members instead of being restricted to two members as `std::pair` is. For example, `std::tuple` can be used like `std::tuple<int, float, std::string>`, which declares a tuple containing three members of the listed types.

In C++11, accessing members of a tuple was done using integer indices. For example, to access the first member of a tuple, one would use `std::get<0>(tup)`. Similarly, to access the second member of a tuple, one would use `std::get<1>(tup)`, and so on. This opens a solution to our earlier problem. Instead of declaring composite types as structs, we can use tuples, as in Listing 15.1.

After defining the object's type as a `std::tuple`, we can access its members using indices as shown earlier. Unfortunately, this solution has many problems:

Listing 15.1. Comparison of a `struct` and tuple that store two members.

```
// As a struct
struct Person
{
    std::string   Name;
    int           Age;
};

// As a tuple (using a typedef)
using Person = std::tuple<std::string, int>;
```

---

[1] See "libclang: C Interface to Clang". http://clang.llvm.org/doxygen/group__CINDEX.html

15.1 Rethinking Composition Using Tuples

- Accessing members by index makes for unreadable code. "What was index 3 again?" A matching list of named constants can fix this at the cost of more boilerplate.
- The declaration of the tuple is hard to understand. "What is the meaning of that `int`?"
- The tuple declaration is verbose, which motivates a `typedef`.

Furthermore using a simple `typedef` is not enough: We can't safely overload functions with the `typedef` due to the possibility of two different objects having the same actual type. For example, `std::tuple<std::string, int>` could represent something other than a `Person`.

Fortunately, C++14 introduced a feature that enables a solution to many of these problems, `std::get<T>`. This function is used to access members of a tuple based on their type instead of their index. For example, we can call `std::get<std::string>(person)` to access the name of a person. This removes the need of accessing tuple members using magic numbers, but doesn't yet solve all our problems: Now we're using magic types instead of magic numbers with the added restriction that no two members of a tuple have the same type. As a solution to this problem, we create a new type for each member, as in Listing 15.2.

With this new design, it is now possible to access the properties of `person` in a readable way. For example, we can access its name using `std::get<Name>(person)`. This tuple now closely resembles a C `struct`, but has the added feature of iteration over its members thanks to its `std::tuple` nature. (Iteration will be discussed later in this chapter.) Finally, the `std::tuple<Name, Age>` type can itself be wrapped in a `struct` (as shown in Listing 15.3), allowing functions to be overloaded unambiguously on the `Person` type. This also enables generic recursive traversals of objects thanks to the naming convention of the `value` member (as explained in the next section). This is the basis of this chapter's static reflection system.

Listing 15.2. Tuple elements are given unique types to facilitate accessing them through `std::get<T>`.

```
struct Name {std::string value;};
struct Age {int value;};

std::tuple<Name, Age> person{Name{"Alfred"}, Age{31}};
```

Listing 15.3. Creating a unique type for `Person` makes it possible to overload functions on the `Person` type and makes it possible to apply recursive functions on the `value` member of objects represented this way.

```
struct Name {std::string value;};
struct Age {int value;};

struct Person
{
    std::tuple<Name, Age>   value;
};

Person person{std::make_tuple(Name{"Alfred"}, Age{31})};
```

The use of `std::make_tuple` in Listing 15.3 may be considered ugly, as it would be more concise to initialize it with braces as in Listing 15.2. There exists a proposal to fix this with a library solution.[2]

15.2 Recursive Member Iteration

One basic application of this design is to load and save an object through a JSON representation, which can be done by traversing an object recursively and reading or writing its members. This recursive traversal can be implemented with function overloading. In our case, a function named `SaveJSON()` will be overloaded to serialize any given type into an equivalent JSON representation. To start with something simple, Listing 15.4 shows the implementations of `SaveJSON()` for the built-in `int` and `std::string` types, which are straightforward.

The `int` and `std::string` overloads required no recursion, since they are leaf types. On the other hand, implementing `SaveJSON()` for arrays or objects requires recursive calls in order to print their members. We'll tackle the array implementation first because it is easier. The implementation for arrays is shown in Listing 15.5. Note that this function can be generalized for a `std` algorithm-style pair of iterators, which can be reused to implement other array-like containers such as `std::array` and `std::vector`.

---

[2] See document number N4387, The C++ Standards Committee. http://www.open-std.org/jtc1/sc22/wg21/docs/papers/2015/n4387.html

15.2 Recursive Member Iteration

Listing 15.4. Translating basic types into JSON.

```
void SaveJSON(std::ostream& os, int x)
{
    os << x;
}

void SaveJSON(std::ostream& os, const std::string& s)
{
    os << "\"" << s << "\"";
}
```

Listing 15.5. Converting a C array into a JSON array.

```
template <class T, size_t N>
void SaveJSON(std::ostream& os, const T(&a)[N])
{
    os << "[";
    for (size_t i = 0; i < N; i++)
    {
        if (i != 0)
        {
            os << ",";
        }

        SaveJSON(os, a[i]);
    }

    os << "]";
}
```

Next, we'll implement `SaveJSON()` for objects. According to the object system described in this chapter, an object is a type that has one member variable called `value`. If the type of `value` is `std::tuple`, then this object represents a composition of named subobjects that will be represented as key/value pairs in a JSON object. The implementation of `SaveJSON()` for these objects is shown in Listing 15.6.

Listing 15.6. Converting a tuple (made out of types that represent object members) into a JSON object.

```
template <class... Ts>
void SaveJSON(std::ostream& os, const std::tuple<Ts...>& tup)
{
    os << "{";
    bool first = true;
    auto saveOne = [&first, &os](const auto& x)
    {
        if (!first)
        {
            os << ",";
        }
        else
        {
            first = false;
        }

        SaveJSON(os, x);
    };

    int saveAll[] = {0, (saveOne(std::get<Ts>(tup)), 0)...};
    os << "}";
}
```

From a high-level view, this function is simple. It simply applies the function `saveOne()` to each member of the tuple, which outputs the members with proper comma separation. However, the `saveAll` statement deserves some explanation. The goal here is to iterate over members of a tuple and apply a function on each one, so let's step through the thought process.

One might think that it's possible to iterate over the members of a tuple by simply using the ellipsis (...) operator to expand the variadic argument, resulting in a statement as in Listing 15.7.

Listing 15.7. An incorrect first guess of how to apply a function over a tuple.

```
saveOne(std::get<Ts>(tup))...;
```

15.2 Recursive Member Iteration

Unfortunately, this notation is not a valid use of parameter pack expansion as far as the current C++ grammar is concerned. Besides, if `saveOne()` happened to have a return value, this use would be throwing them away, which is not ideal. One place where parameter pack expansion is valid is in array initialization, which conveniently also allows us to store the return values and guarantee left-to-right order of execution (as opposed to expanding it within a function call, similarly to `std::make_tuple(f(args)...)`). This leads us to the second attempt in Listing 15.8.

Listing 15.8. An almost valid application of a function on a tuple, if the type wasn't `void`.

```
void saveAll[] = {saveOne(std::get<Ts>(tup))...};
```

Unfortunately, arrays of type `void` are not allowed. This wouldn't be a problem if `saveOne()` didn't have a `void` return type, but in this case we have to switch the type of the expression. One way to do this is to use the comma operator, as in Listing 15.9.

Listing 15.9. Applying a function that returns `void` to a tuple.

```
int saveAll[] = {(saveOne(std::get<Ts>(tup)), 0)...};
```

There's one last problem. If the tuple is empty, then this statement fails to compile due to zero size arrays being disallowed. This can be fixed by adding a placeholder value as in Listing 15.10, which completes the implementation.

Listing 15.10. Adding a placeholder makes the array size never be zero, so this works with empty tuples.

```
int saveAll[] = {0, (saveOne(std::get<Ts>(tup)), 0)...};
```

This idiom is a relatively convenient and reusable way to map a function over a tuple. It doesn't require any fancy metaprogramming libraries and doesn't require potentially tricky/inefficient recursion. If `saveOne()` did return a result, this would also be a convenient way to access it. Also, note that if `saveOne()`

returns a different type based on its operand, the result could be stored in a `std::tuple` instead of an array.

To complete the implementation of `SaveJSON()`, two more functions will be defined. First, the default overload of `SaveJSON()` will be considered to be operating on a type that represents an object's member. JSON's object property notation will be used to serialize object members, which consists of the member's name followed by a colon and its value. This is complemented by a `SaveJSON-TopLevel()` function, which creates the entry representing the whole object being serialized. Their implementations are available in Listing 15.11.

You might have noticed that the code calls `GetJSONName()` on each object. This is a function that must be defined for each type passed to the system. For example, one could define it for the earlier `Name` class as in Listing 15.12. Since C++ has no portable way to get a class's name, this binding may require manual work. A macro system could be used to automatically convert the class's name to a string, but it's worth considering if this one-to-one mapping is really what you

Listing 15.11. Converting object members and top-level objects into JSON.

```
template <class T>
void SaveJSON(std::ostream& os, const T& obj)
{
    os << "\"" << GetJSONName(obj) << "\": ";
    SaveJSON(os, obj.value);
}

template <class T>
void SaveJSONTopLevel(std::ostream& os, const T& obj)
{
    os << "{";
    SaveJSON(os, obj);
    os << "}";
}
```

Listing 15.12. A simple way to associate a string to a C++ type.

```
const char *GetJSONName(const Name&)
{
    return "name";
}
```

want in any practical cases. In the simple `Name` example, the level of indirection allows us to switch to a JavaScript naming convention ("camelCase"), and also makes it possible to modify the C++ class's name without breaking backwards compatibility with the schema of previously written JSON files. If you're looking for a quick non-portable way to get a class's name, consider using C++'s RTTI, `typeid(x).name()`. Better static reflection in C++'s future could make it easier to automate this.[3]

15.3 Practical Concerns

This way of designing objects may be an unfamiliar way of thinking, and it does require a good level of language mastery due to its metaprogramming nature. One immediate source of confusion in this design is the fact that C++ types are now used for two purposes. Some represent classic C++ data-types such as `std::string`, and others represent member names (e.g., `Name` and `Age`). Depending on your use, keeping this distinction in mind is necessary to correctly build types. For example, consider the correct and incorrect uses in Listing 15.13. The incorrect solution uses `Point` as if it was a data type, which is wrong because `Point` is supposed to be the name of an object's member. If you look at the output of `SaveJSON()`, it's immediately noticeable that something is wrong.

Naturally, the approach presented in this chapter is not the only way to implement a recursively traversable type system using tuples. Programmers seeking to use a similar solution are encouraged to explore the design space and, in the future, consider how newer versions of C++ can improve this kind of design.

As an additional practical concern, it seems unreasonable to suggest that every class in a project be written this way, but this technique can still be applied in a single subsystem where its features are worth the extra complexity. One of the most important things to take from this chapter is that it is possible to iterate over tuples to perform generic operations on objects, opening up new interesting designs.

There are many other possible extensions of this technique. A scripting language could be automatically hooked up to C++ objects, or the layout of objects could be switched between struct-of-arrays and array-of-structs. A more ambitious use is an embedded DSL for statically typed SQL-like relational algebra operations on containers. For example, an SQL query like `SELECT Name FROM people WHERE Age = 30` could be implemented by extracting the `Name` member

---

[3] For example, see document number N4451, The C++ Standards Committee. http://www.open-std.org/jtc1/sc22/wg21/docs/papers/2015/n4451.pdf

of a list of `Person` objects and applying a filter based on the value of the `Age` member.

Techniques using the tuple-based designs shown in this chapter will be facilitated more as the C++ programming language is improved, and we may find ourselves one day totally abandoning tuple-based designs for a true static reflection system.[4] Until then, this solution ought to be a decent option.

Listing 15.13. Example of the error caused by using a type representing a member as if it were a normal data type.

```
// Deceivingly incorrect design.
// -------------------------------

struct Point {float value[2];};
struct Quad {Point value[4];};

// SaveJSONTopLevel output (pretty printed):
// {
//    "quad":
//    [
//       "point": [0,0],
//       "point": [0,1],
//       "point": [1,1],
//       "point": [1,0]
//    ]
// }


// One possible correct design.
// -------------------------------

struct TopLeft {float value[2];};
struct BottomLeft {float value[2];};
struct BottomRight {float value[2];};
struct TopRight {float value[2];};

struct Quad {std::tuple<TopLeft, BottomLeft, BottomRight, TopRight> value;}
```

---

[4] In addition to N4451, see document number N4447, The C++ Standards Committee. http://www.open-std.org/jtc1/sc22/wg21/docs/papers/2015/n4447.pdf

```
// SaveJSONTopLevel output (pretty printed):
// {
//    "quad":
//    {
//       "topLeft":     [0,0],
//       "bottomLeft":  [0,1],
//       "bottomRight": [1,1],
//       "topRight":    [1,0]
//    }
// }
```

16

Portable SIMD Programs Using ISPC

Nicolas Guillemot
Marc Fauconneau Dufresne
Intel

Before it became accelerated in hardware in the late 1990s, games did vertex transformation and lighting in software on the CPU. As 3D gaming became mainstream, SIMD (Single Instruction Multiple Data) instruction sets like SSE (Streaming SIMD Extensions) were added to CPUs to accelerate geometry processing and other computationally expensive tasks. Unlike regular floating-point instructions that perform *scalar* operations, SSE instructions perform *vector* operations that can operate on groups of four floating-point numbers in parallel, as in Figure 16.1. SSE's wide applicability in game programming made such SIMD instruction sets an essential part of any high-performance game engine. SIMD instruction sets have since seen great evolution, but an open question remains: How can we best take advantage of SIMD instruction sets?

This gem's topic is ISPC. ISPC stands for "Intel SPMD Program Compiler", and SPMD stands for "Single Program Multiple Data". ISPC allows you to write portable, maintainable, and efficient SIMD code. Note that despite the Intel branding, ISPC is not exclusive to Intel's architectures. ISPC is an LLVM-based open-source compiler currently hosted on GitHub, and it is supported on

$$[1 \ 2 \ 3 \ 4] + [5 \ 6 \ 7 \ 8] = [(1+5) \ (2+6) \ (3+7) \ (4+8)]$$
$$= [6 \ 8 \ 10 \ 12]$$

Figure 16.1. An example of parallel addition.

Windows, Mac OS X, and Linux. ISPC can target various instruction sets including SSE2, AVX2, and NEON. It also features an experimental PlayStation 4 cross-compiler for Windows. A detailed technical introduction can be found in an InPar 2012 paper [Pharr and Mark 2012]. The project is hosted at https://ispc.github.io/.

16.1 The Problem

Since SIMD was introduced to home PCs, more and more SIMD instruction sets have been added to processors over the years. Depending on how recent a CPU is, it may or may not support some of these instruction sets, which can make it hard to write portable SIMD code. One solution used by game developers [Fredriksson 2015] is to target the SSE2 (Streaming SIMD Extensions 2) instruction set, which has existed since the early 2000s and is currently supported ubiquitously by hardware used by PC gamers [Valve 2015]. While this allows game developers to use SIMD with few portability problems, it means that performance is left on the table for users with more advanced CPUs.

In addition to the portability issues, it is also difficult to write SIMD code using currently available tools. Some commonly used approaches are:

- Assuming your C/C++ compiler automagically transforms scalar code into vector code.
- Using 3D linear algebra classes that use SIMD for their operations (e.g., `float4`, `matrix4x4`).
- Using intrinsics, special functions recognized by the compiler and converted directly into SIMD instructions.

Unfortunately, all of these methods have major issues:

- Compilers cannot reliably apply auto-vectorization, as small changes to your code can break it. Ideally, we would like a guarantee that vectorization is happening.
- 3D linear algebra classes like `float4` expose limited parallelism due to their array-of-structs nature, as opposed to struct-of-arrays (see Listing 16.1). Storing the *x*, *y*, *z*, and *w* components of a `float4` sequentially in memory makes ineffective use of SIMD in common operations like the dot product [Fredriksson, 2015]. The approach also doesn't scale to instruction sets with wider vectors.

16.1 The Problem

- Intrinsics are not portable. Also, while explicit control of generated assembly might help improve your tightest loops at a micro scale, it becomes more difficult to implement algorithmic improvements at macro scale due to the decrease in productivity.

Ideally, we would like to write programs that make good use of current (and future) instruction sets. This code should be maintainable, easy to write, and uncompromising in performance whenever practical. To this end, we introduce ISPC, a compiler for a C-like language that makes it easy to write portable and efficient code using SIMD through a thin abstraction layer.

Listing 16.1. Comparison of array-of-structs design and struct-of-arrays design. The struct-of-arrays design tends to lend itself better to SIMD operations.

```
// Array-of-structs design.
struct float4
{
    float x;
    float y;
    float z;
    float w;
};

float4    mystructs[N];

// Struct-of-arrays design.
struct Float4Arrays
{
    float xs[N];
    float ys[N];
    float zs[N];
    float ws[N];
};

Float4Arrays myarrays;
```

16.2 ISPC Basics

The SPMD programming model is similar to GPU shaders. Programs are written as if they operate on a single value, but the program is actually being executed many times in parallel. ISPC implements this efficiently using SIMD instructions.

In ISPC terms, each execution of the program is called a *program instance*, and the group of all simultaneously executing programs is called a *gang*. In ISPC, the size of the gang is known at compile time and is based on the target SIMD instruction set. When writing ISPC code, algorithms are described from the view of a single program instance.

ISPC is syntactically similar to C with some added semantics. For example, ISPC adds the `uniform` and `varying` qualifiers, which are used in variable declarations. These qualifiers describe how the variable behaves across program instances. A uniform variable has the same value in each program instance of the gang, and a varying variable has an independent value in each program instance. This difference has an interesting effect because varying variables can cause control flow to diverge between program instances.

To implement divergent control flow with SIMD instructions, ISPC uses predication. All possible paths of control flow are taken, but ISPC keeps track of which set of program instances satisfy the conditions at any point in the code. Side effects are only executed for this set of program instances, and the results are merged when control flow converges. Predication is also used to handle the case of a loop's iteration count not being a multiple of the program instance count.

16.3 ISPC Example Programs

As an introduction, we give a walkthrough of the `simple.ispc` program in Listing 16.2. This program should be mostly intuitive to C programmers, since the equivalent C program is almost identical. The only differences between this program and the C equivalent are:

- The `export` keyword, which tells ISPC to generate a C entry point for the function to which it's applied.
- The `uniform` keyword on inputs, since inputs come from C where everything is uniform.
- The `foreach` loop, which runs multiple instances of the loop in parallel.

16.3 ISPC Example Programs

Listing 16.2. A simple ISPC program: `simple.ispc`.

```
export void simple(uniform float vin[], uniform float vout[],
                   uniform int count)
{
    foreach (index = 0 ... count)
    {
        float v = vin[index];
        if (v < 3)
        {
            v = v * v;
        }
        else
        {
            v = sqrt(v);
        }

        vout[index] = v;
    }
}
```

The `foreach` loop deserves more explanation. It generates a varying variable named `index`. Because the index is varying, it has a different value in each program instance. For example, if the program instance count is 4, then `index` would be [0 1 2 3] in the first iteration. Thus, reading `vin[index]` actually reads up to four floats into `v` (which is a `varying float`.) The computation is carried out on these four floats in parallel, and they are then written into `vout`. Due to the `if...else` inside the loop, some program instances will square `v`, and others will compute its square root. These results are merged using predication.

When compiling this program, a header is created that contains the declaration in Listing 16.3. This function can be called by using the example C code in Listing 16.4.

Listing 16.3. Declaration of `simple` in the header generated by compiling `simple.ispc`.

```
extern void simple(float vin[], float vout[], int32_t count);
```

Listing 16.4. Example invocation of the `simple.ispc` program.

```
#include <stdio.h>
#include "simple.h"

int main()
{
    float vin[16], vout[16];

    for (int i = 0; i < 16; ++i)
    {
        vin[i] = i;
    }

    simple(vin, vout, 16);

    for (int i = 0; i < 16; ++i)
    {
        printf("%d: simple(%f) = %f\n", i, vin[i], vout[i]);
    }
}
```

As a more practical example of the language, consider the ISPC code in Listing 16.5. This code takes a list of spheres and six frustum planes as input and computes for each sphere whether it is outside the frustum. This code can be used to detect objects outside the camera's field of view, which is a very effective basic culling technique. The most interesting thing about this program is its demonstration of the power of struct-of-arrays. If the sphere coordinates were supplied as a single array (as array-of-structs), then it wouldn't be possible to perform the dot product in the inner loop as efficiently because it would be processing one sphere at a time rather than many. The advantages of the struct-of-arrays approach for dot products are further explained in [Fredriksson 2015].

16.4 Integration in a Game Engine

ISPC can be used for various tasks in a game, game engine, or game asset pipeline. The most common use is computationally heavy algorithms because ISPC makes it easier to generate SIMD code by automating tedious constructs like conditional execution and the ends of loops.

16.4 Integration in a Game Engine

Listing 16.5. ISPC code to frustum cull a list of spheres.

```
export void FrustumCull(uniform int numSpheres,
        uniform const float sphereCenterXs[],
        uniform const float sphereCenterYs[],
        uniform const float sphereCenterZs[],
        uniform const float sphereRadii[],
        uniform const float frustumPlaneEqns[6][4],
        uniform int cullingOutput[])
{
    foreach (sphereIdx = 0 ... numSpheres)
    {
        int culled = 0;

        for (uniform int planeIdx = 0; planeIdx < 6; planeIdx++)
        {
            float outsideDistanceFromPlane
                = sphereCenterXs[sphereIdx] * frustumPlaneEqns[planeIdx][0]
                + sphereCenterYs[sphereIdx] * frustumPlaneEqns[planeIdx][1]
                + sphereCenterZs[sphereIdx] * frustumPlaneEqns[planeIdx][2]
                + frustumPlaneEqns[planeIdx][3];

            if (outsideDistanceFromPlane > sphereRadii[sphereIdx])
            {
                culled = 1;
            }
        }

        cullingOutput[sphereIdx] = culled;
    }
}
```

It's tempting to offload heavy computations to the GPU, but using ISPC instead for shader-like workloads has some distinct advantages. Because it runs on the CPU, ISPC directly shares data structures with your C/C++ program. In addition, ISPC allows you to use the CPU's low latency, in contrast to using the GPU's latency hiding mechanisms. You can efficiently call a short ISPC function from C++ or make a callback from ISPC into C++ code, and these are the kinds of workloads that put GPUs to shame.

Since the same ISPC code can be compiled for different architectures, it makes effective use of a heterogeneous server farm used for compiling assets, where code can be compiled to exploit any given processor's SIMD capabilities. You can even share the same ISPC code between your game and your asset pipeline.

Adding ISPC to an existing C/C++ project is easy. ISPC builds `.obj` files that can be simply linked into your binary, and it also generates a header that you can simply `#include` in order to call exported functions.

As a quick setup guide, ISPC can be integrated in a Visual Studio project as follows:

1. Download `ispc.exe` from http://ispc.github.io/.
2. Put `ispc.exe` into your project's directory.
3. Add your `.ispc` source file to your project.
4. Right click on your `.ispc` file in Visual Studio, and choose Properties.
5. Under "Configuration Properties > General", set "Item Type" to "Custom Build Tool".
6. Under "Configuration Properties > Custom Build Tool > General", configure similarly to that shown in Figure 16.2.

The target architecture, the instruction set, and the description of the task may be freely changed. In a project that uses ISPC heavily, or on various platforms, it might be interesting to automate this process. This automation can be done through a higher level build system, or by associating the `.ispc` extension to a custom build step in Visual Studio.

Command Line	ispc.exe %(FullPath) -h %(Filename)_ispc.h -o $(IntermediateOutputPath)%(Filename)_ispc.obj --arch=x86-64 --target=avx2
Description	Compiling ISPC frustum culling code
Outputs	%(Filename)_ispc.h;$(IntermediateOutputPath)%(Filename)_ispc.obj
Additional Dependencies	
Link Objects	Yes
Treat Output As Content	No
Execute After	
Execute Before	

Figure 16.2. Options for adding an ISPC file to a Visual Studio project. This can be made automatic with a custom build step.

16.5 Tips & Tricks

What follows are some tips for getting the most out of ISPC, based on our experience using it.

Prefer uniform, and don't use varying unless you need to

Since `varying` is the default qualifier for variables, it's possible to accidentally use a varying variable in a case where all program instances have the same value. Using `varying` in that case will yield worse performance than explicitly marking it as `uniform`.

Build for all instruction sets, and choose the best available at runtime

The same ISPC program can be compiled for many target instruction sets simultaneously, and all of these different compiled programs can be linked together into the same executable. This makes it possible to dynamically decide which instruction set to use at runtime, which is interesting for things like PC games where your users have a wide variety of hardware capabilities. This is implemented automatically by passing multiple comma-separated targets to the ISPC command line. The generated entry points for the exported functions will check your CPU's capabilities and invoke the most appropriate implementation.

Consider the effects of divergence

SPMD can interact poorly with algorithms that use branching. Consider the case of an algorithm that iteratively refines its results. The core of the algorithm is a loop that ends either when the value converges or after a maximum number of iterations. When running the loop, some program instances of an SPMD gang of size N will converge earlier than others. It is possible for the loop to keep iterating even if only a single program instance is active, which means that the other $N-1$ program instances are waiting for reconvergence. For this reason, algorithms should be designed to minimize divergence in order to achieve higher throughput. Advanced solutions exist to handle divergence by refilling lanes that have converged early.

Avoid gathers

Load/store using varying indices may result in gather/scatter operations. When this happens, ISPC will generate a performance warning because those are inherently slow operations. This affects the balance in performance between table lookups and computation. It can often be slower to lookup the result of a function in a table, due to the required gather operation, than to compute the function. Finding creative ways to convert tables into equivalent functions can yield performance benefits, despite the seemingly redundant computation.

References

[Fredriksson 2015] Andreas Fredriksson. "SIMD at Insomniac Games: How We Do the Shuffle". Game Developers Conference 2015. Available at http://www.gdcvault.com/play/1022249/SIMD-at-Insomniac-Games-How.

[Pharr and Mark 2012] Matt Pharr and William R. Mark. "ispc: A SPMD Compiler for High-Performance CPU Programming. Innovative Parallel Computing". *Innovative Parallel Computing*, 2012.

[Valve 2015] Valve Steam Hardware & Software Survey, July 2015. Available at http://store.steampowered.com/hwsurvey/.

17

Shared Network Arrays as an Abstraction of Network Code from Game Code Logic

João Lucas Guberman Raza
Microsoft

17.1 Introduction

This chapter discusses the concept of a shared network array (SNA), a data structure aimed at abstracting underlying network code while one writes game logic code. This comes from the fact that SNAs synchronize their nodes' data across all clients while still allowing a developer to use them as if they were a local array. As an example of their applicability, in multiplayer games it is common for game logic code to iterate over objects that are shared across all clients. This occurs when each client iterates over the list of enemies and players present in a map to determine their visibility and rendering effects. This also occurs when a server iterates over a list of projectiles to determine collisions.

As each client and server retrieves and/or updates the state for these objects, a host of underlying network operations need to ensue, such as broadcasting, updating, and refreshing state changes across all clients. Historically, games have kept all clients and server data structures coordinated via numerous mechanisms, such as through reliable messages [Brownlow 2005]. Although such mechanisms are functional in themselves, they rely on tight integration between the network stack and the game logic. Consequently, this forces tight coordination among the involved teams that own those corresponding components.

SNAs serve as a method for abstracting these interdependencies. Suppose a developer is writing game logic code to check whether enemies are near any player, and if so, alert the corresponding player. With SNAs, a developer could write the following code.

```
while (true) // core game loop
{
    /* players is an object of type SharedNetworkArray<CPlayer> */
    for (int i = 0; i < players.ARRAY_SIZE; i++)
    {
        if (players[i]->isNearEnemies())
        {
            players[i]->alert();
            /* ... do extra game logic when near an enemy ... */
            players[i]->propagateChange();
        }
    }

    /* ... perform rest of game logic ... */
}
```

This example highlights the key advantages to using SNAs. The first one is that the developer does not need to understand how clients synchronize data. The SNA framework automatically propagates any changes to the objects across all clients. The second advantage is that SNAs use templates, allowing the gameplay programmer to construct an SNA out of any game object. The third advantage is that SNAs allow a developer to write algorithms as if the objects are all local, thus simplifying their implementation.

The remainder of this chapter focuses on how the internals of SNAs work. Source code for a C++ implementation using Winsock is available on the book's website.

17.2 How SNAs Work

Each SNA contains an array composed of nodes that the application can access linearly. Each node contains metadata that details the node's age (used for synchronization disputes), its index in the array, and its propagation state (set to false by default). Each node also contains an object, which is an instance of the provided template object from the application. Each SNA also has an identifier that is equal across all SNA instances on each machine. This is so that when synchronizing data, the framework knows to which SNA the new data pertains.

SNAs rely on connection manager classes to propagate and synchronize changes. There are two types of connection managers, the client connection manager and the server connection manager. The client connection manager runs on each client instance (the game running on users' machines), while the server connection manager runs on the game host (the server). Each client and server needs only one connection manager for all its SNAs. Each client must also register its SNA (i.e., keep an internal pointer to the SNA) with its local connection manager so that automatic synchronizations may occur.

The client connection manager is responsible for uploading local changes that the client has made to the server connection manager. It is also responsible for establishing and maintaining a connection with the machine that is running the server connection manager. Whenever the client connection manager detects that an SNA's node propagation state is set to true, it sends an "update request" message to the server connection manager with the new state of the node's object. That message also contains the node's age from the client as well as its index so that the server connection manager may assess to which node the message pertains. Lastly, the client connection manager also locally merges data that the server connection manager has sent whenever it receives a "node update" message. Clients treat "node update" messages from the server as law—whatever the server says the state of a node is, the client accepts as is by overriding its local value. When a client successfully sends an "update request" message to the server, it resets the propagation state for the corresponding node.

The server connection manager is responsible for receiving update requests from the client connection manager. It is also responsible for accepting and registering incoming connections from all machines that are running a client connection manager. Whenever the server connection manager receives an "update request" message from a client, it checks the node to which the message pertains. (The servers contains a local copy of the SNA as a main reference.) If its age is equal to or younger than the received message, then the server adds the "update request" to its internal update backlog. If the server receives a new "update request" for a node that already has an "update request" in its update backlog, the server connection manager compares the ages of the messages. Whichever has the youngest age wins and remains in the update backlog. The server connection manager discards the older message. If both messages have the same age, then the server discards the newly received message in favor of the one currently in the backlog.

The server connection manager also periodically broadcasts the contents from its update backlog to all registered clients. It sends, for each connected client, an "update node" message, which contains the node's new age, its new state as reflected in the server, and its index. Messages that are successfully sent are removed from the update backlog. The ages of their nodes are also increased by one, both locally (on the resident SNA on the server) and on all clients.

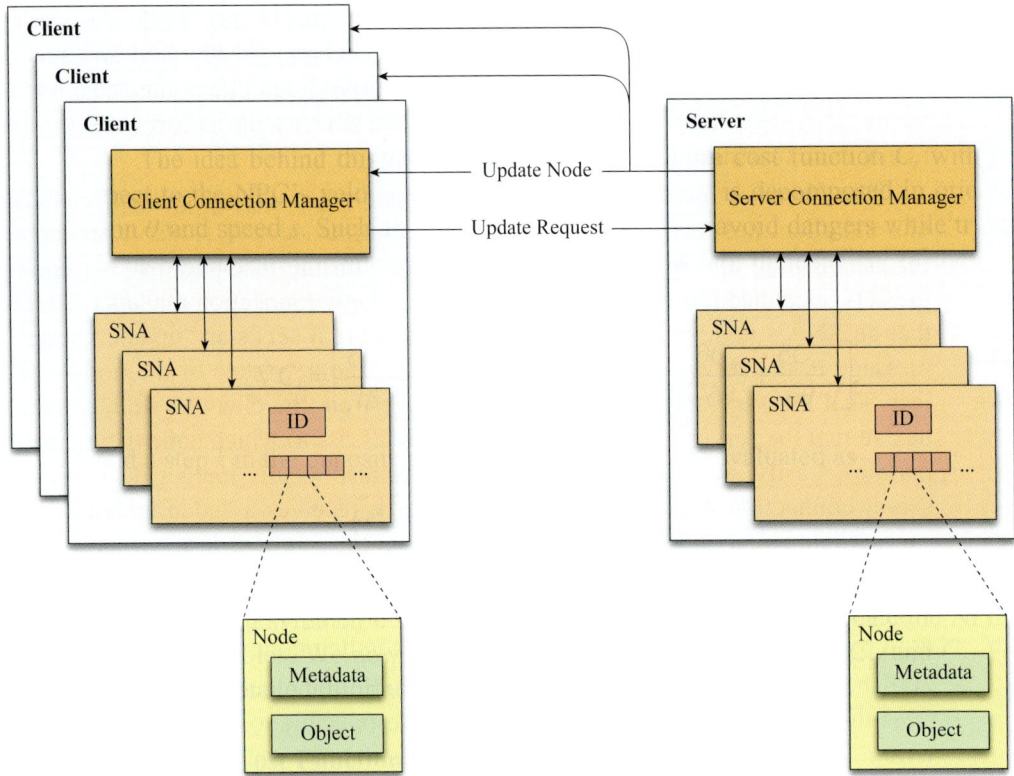

Figure 17.1. Connection manager interactions.

The diagram shown in Figure 17.1 serves to illustrate the connection manager interactions and topology.

17.3 How a Gameplay Programmer Uses SNAs

To help exemplify how SNAs work in real world scenarios, this section and the next highlight how to use the SNA framework provided in the accompanying source code.

When creating a new SNA, a developer supplies an identifier that must be equal across the instances of that SNA on all clients. The SNA framework enforces this by having the developer provide the SNA identifier at its instantiation as follows.

17.3 How a Gameplay Programmer Uses SNAs

```
const unsigned int PLAYER_ARRAY_NETWORK_ID = 20;
SharedNetworkArray<CPlayer> players(PLAYER_ARRAY_NETWORK_ID);
```

The client application must also contain a local client manager instance and initialize it as follows.

```
ClientConnectionManager clientCM;
clientCM.start();
```

Once created, the SNA's corresponding connection manager must register it. The following line registers the players SNA with its client connection manager.

```
clientCM.registerArray(&players);
```

Once registered, the developer has the equivalent of a fixed array of the provided template objects. The developer may interact with each object in that array using the brackets operator as follows. The SNA framework returns a pointer to the object at the specified index.

```
if (players[i]->isNearEnemies())
{
    players[i]->alert();
    /* ... do extra game logic when near an enemy ... */
}
```

In communication with its counterpart on the server, the client connection manager must also receive messages as well as send messages to be broadcast to the other clients. Such activities occur when the application invokes the client manager's `sync()` method. The application may call this method in a multithread safe manner using the following line.

```
clientCM.sync();
```

Finally, the gameplay developer must call the `propagateChange()` method for each object they wish the framework to propagate changes across all clients.

Other than that, the developer may rely on SNAs as if they were any other array in the system.

On the server, the developer must also create an instance of the same SNA having the same identifier as used on clients, initialize its server connection manager, and regularly synchronize for data as shown in the following code.

```
const unsigned int PLAYER_ARRAY_NETWORK_ID = 20;
SharedNetworkArray<CPlayer> players(PLAYER_ARRAY_NETWORK_ID);

ServerConnectionManager    serverCM;

serverCM.start();
serverCM.registerArray(&players);

while (true) // core game loop
{
    serverCM.sync();
    /* perform other game logic */
}
```

17.4 How a Network Programmer Uses SNAs

The network programmer building and using SNAs has to abide by a set of implementation interfaces required for SNAs to work. The first one is that any object used as a template parameter for an SNA (such as the `CPlayer` object in the code examples above) must inherit from the abstract `SharedObject` class. This ensures that the implementation is required to override its `copySharedObjectData()` and `setSharedObjectData()` methods.

The framework calls these methods whenever an internal synchronization event occurs, such as sending and receiving messages across connection managers. The application must copy whatever data it needs to propagate across all clients in the `copySharedObjectData()` method. Meanwhile, it must set whatever data it wishes to override locally with the `setSharedObjectData()`. An application cannot make any assumptions of how or when the connection managers call those methods.

These methods exist so that one can fine tune the information shared across clients. One may choose to select what content the framework broadcasts vs. what is local only. For example, a player's total life is shared across all clients,

17.4 How a Network Programmer Uses SNAs

while the player's control settings are not. The code below exemplifies a mock implementation for the `CPlayer` class, which contains a shared value across connected SNAs.

```cpp
class CPlayer : public SNA::SharedObject
{
    public:

        CPlayer() : value(0)
        {
        }

        virtual ~CPlayer()
        {
        }

        bool copySharedObjectData(char *buffer,
            const unsigned int sizeofBuffer, unsigned int& packageSize)
        {
            if (sizeofBuffer > packageSize || !buffer)
            {
                memcpy(buffer, &value, sizeof(value));
                packageSize = sizeof(value);
                return true;
            }

            return false;
        }

        bool setSharedObjectData(char *buffer,
                const unsigned int sizeofBuffer)
        {
            if (sizeofBuffer == sizeof(value))
            {
                memcpy(&value, buffer, sizeofBuffer);
                return true;
            }

            return false;
        }
```

```
    private:

        int   value; /* a dummy value that this object holds */
};
```

17.5 Further Discussion

The SNA proposal in this chapter makes three assumptions that one may wish to extend in terms of implementation. The first assumption is that all SNAs are of fixed size. One may enhance the SNA framework implementation so that it contains a dynamic size. To do so would require adding new messages to the connection managers that cause new nodes to be created and destroyed. It would also require adding a size method to the SNA class.

The second assumption is that synchronization disputes about the age (with messages discards) suffice as an introductory scenario. More complicated scenarios would likely need to enhance this dispute by using either an external clock system (such as the actual time in which the events were triggered), or an internal clock system, such as the game's local reference time. For further insight into clock synchronizations and disputes, see [Lamport 1978].

The third assumption is that the clients and the server are able to know which SNAs they wish to share beforehand. In scenarios where that may not hold true, one would likely need to implement a query system where a client is able to retrieve array IDs and types at runtime from the server connection manager.

References

[Brownlow 2005] Martın Brownlow. "A Reliable Messaging Protocol". *Game Programming Gems 5*, edited by Kim Pallister. Charles River Media, 2005.

[Lamport 1978] Leslie Lamport. "Time, clocks, and the ordering of events in a distributed system". *Communications of the ACM*, Vol. 21, No. 7 (July 1978), pp. 558–565.

Part IV

Character Control and Artificial Intelligence

18

Vision Based Local Collision Avoidance

Teófilo Bezerra Dutra
Universidade Federal do Ceará

Ricardo Marques
Universitat Pompeu Fabra

Julien Pettré
INRIA

Jan Ondřej
Disney Research

18.1 Introduction

Video games have traced a remarkable history since their emergence and popularization. Many major revolutions occurred in this ever-changing market. Nowadays, games take place in always-larger scenes, and the environments are becoming more and more dynamic. Game worlds need to be populated by non-player characters (NPCs) so as to not look devoid of life. Once those NPCs can freely wander through the environment, their ability to autonomously move and react to both static and dynamic obstacles has become a crucial feature in game development. Notwithstanding, local collision avoidance between moving NPCs is one of the most difficult tasks to perform.

For an efficient navigation, NPCs must plan their paths within complex scenarios in order to reach their goals, avoiding both moving and static obstacles. This is achieved by resorting to information provided by the game engine that is

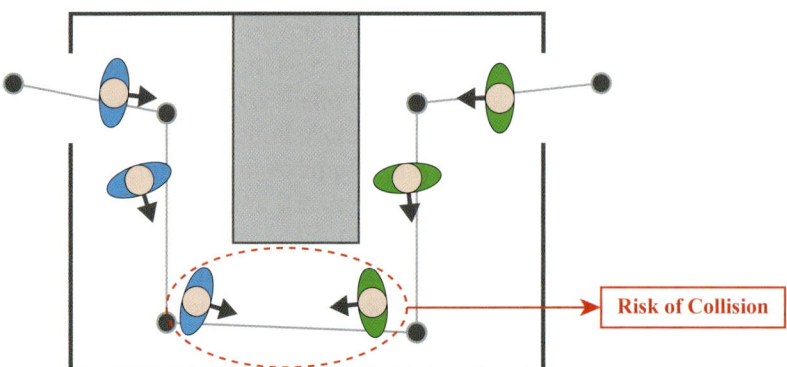

Figure 18.1. An example of a GPP is represented through the gray dots and their connections on the image. The situation highlighted illustrates a risk of collision, in which case an LPP is used to modify the path of the NPCs for collision avoidance.

usually fed to a pair of game components, a global path planner (GPP) and a local path planner (LPP). GPPs possess information about the whole scene in order to identify the traversable areas to the goals and to produce a set of intermediate waypoints, as shown in Figure 18.1. For their part, LPPs steer NPCs through these waypoints while making fine-grain adaptations to avoid collisions and other kinds of danger.

Regarding local path planning, game developers commonly resort to rule based approaches or to the recently introduced velocity based algorithms. Both of these classes of algorithms provide interesting results, but the literature has shown that further improvements are possible by using valuable hints provided by the NPC's visual flow [Ondřej et al. 2010, Dutra et al. 2014, Dutra 2015]. In the following section, we briefly present the concepts of rule based and velocity based approaches. Then, the remainder of this chapter is devoted to discussing vision based techniques and how they can be implemented.

18.2 Local Path Planning in Games

One of the most straightforward ways of simulating interactions between NPCs during navigation is to consider them as particles that are subject to attraction and repulsion forces in a particle system [Helbing and Molnár 1995]. In this case, NPCs should repulse each other to avoid collisions and be attracted to their goals (e.g., the waypoints provided by the GPP) so as to reach their objectives. In those approaches, the closer the characters, the stronger the adaptations. However, real life is different, because real humans allow themselves to either anticipate their avoidance or pass at closer distances to the obstacles. In this kind of approach, strong adaptations combined with lack of motion anticipation lead to visually unpleasant behaviors.

A simple way of avoiding those kinds of artifacts is to define behavioral rules for the particles in the system such as the several steering behaviors introduced by [Reynolds 1999] for simulating autonomous characters. These behaviors are described through atomic rules and their combinations. In the particular case of obstacle avoidance behavior, the danger (meaning the risk of collision in the near future) is anticipated, and consequently, the NPC's motion is adapted by extrapolating its trajectory to detect potential collisions in the near future. Rule based techniques are quite popular given the fair results achieved through the combination of simple and noncontradictory rules. An example of a good-quality C++ library for simulating steering behaviors can be found on the OpenSteer website.[1]

Other LPP techniques based on the principle of extrapolating the NPC's trajectory (according to its current velocity) for motion anticipation have been proposed [Paris et al. 2007, van den Berg et al. 2008, Karamouzas et al. 2009, Pettré et al. 2009]. Those so-called *velocity based* techniques have demonstrated visually appealing results as well as better level of realism, especially in semi-dense areas where anticipation plays an important role. A particular representative of such techniques, proposed in the field of robotics [Fiorini and Shiller 1998], resorts to the concept of *velocity obstacles*. This method works in velocity space and consists in selecting, for each robot, a velocity that guarantees that the future distance of closest approach to other obstacles over a short time window is above a collision threshold. That concept has evolved since then. A recent evolution is represented by the *optimal reciprocal collision avoidance* (ORCA) approach [van den Berg et al. 2011], which efficiently computes the optimal solution, i.e., the maximum collision-free velocity closest to a comfort velocity[2] in velocity space, hence reciprocally avoiding collisions between NPCs in the near future. This kind of velocity based technique suffers from problems such as the binary notion of collision that results in strictly minimal avoidance maneuvers and weird interaction distances where personal space is not taken into account. A C++ library implementing the ORCA velocity based technique can be found in the RVO2 website.[3]

---

[1] http://github.com/meshula/OpenSteer
[2] Comfort velocity is the velocity the NPC would use in an environment without obstacles, i.e., a vector pointing towards the goal with length equal to a predefined scalar comfort speed.
[3] http://gamma.cs.unc.edu/RVO2/

18.3 Vision Based Obstacle Avoidance

Overview

Recently, a new category of techniques that resort to using the NPC's visual flow to detect collisions with anticipation has demonstrated that the results achieved with velocity based techniques could be further improved [Ondřej et al. 2010, Dutra et al. 2014, Dutra 2015]. Vision-aided navigation is inspired by cognitive science literature, which acknowledges the role of the human vision system in the locomotion perception-action loop [Cutting et al. 1995, Warren and Fajen 2004, Rio et al. 2014]. Despite its clear importance for locomotion, the visual information has been a neglected feature by the existing techniques until recently, mostly for performance reasons.

In these vision based local path planning (VBLPP) techniques, the environment is rendered from the point of view of each NPC, and the resulting image is processed to determine how that NPC should react to the potentially dangerous obstacles within its field of view. The need for rendering and processing the vision of each NPC for each frame is a challenging task in terms of performance, given the amount of data to deal with. However, the capabilities of the modern graphics cards have made the simulation of several NPCs endowed with synthetic vision no longer impracticable. Despite the limited performance of VBLPP techniques when compared to other velocity based approaches, the former allow a more realistic perception of the virtual environment and open several new possibilities for dealing with the information acquired.

In this section, we present the technical aspects involved in VBLPP techniques. Afterward, we scrutinize the details of two representatives of such techniques and their implementations.

Implementation Guidelines

As stated before, the use of the NPC's vision to adapt its trajectory involves a rendering step and a processing step, as shown in Figure 18.2. In the rendering step, the camera is placed at the eye location of the NPC, and then the surrounding environment is rendered to a texture from this point of view. However, instead of rendering the visual aspect of the obstacles such as color, texture, and surface normal, some kinematic properties are associated with each pixel, such as relative position and relative velocity. The vision based technique employs programmable shaders in order to efficiently compute some motion variables with respect to each obstacle from the NPC's perspective. Therefore, this process aims

18.3 Vision Based Obstacle Avoidance

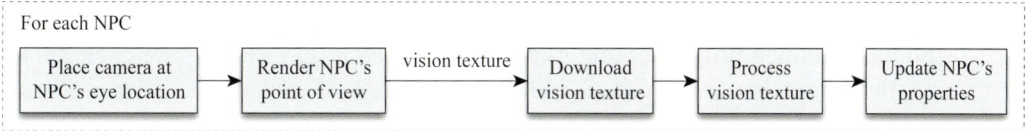

Figure 18.2. Algorithm overview for VBLPP techniques.

at producing a texture endowed with data meaningful enough to allow the NPC's reasoning with respect to the dangerous obstacles perceivable in its field of view. Since the resulting data does not represent colors, it is usually necessary render to a the texture storing unnormalized floating-point numbers.

Once the rendering is finished, the resulting texture is downloaded from the GPU to the CPU and processed. The processing step depends on the particular technique, but basically, background pixels are discarded, and a motion adaptation algorithm processes the remaining pixels. In Figure 18.3, we describe a base class for vision based techniques. The implementation of the techniques described in the following sections inherit from this base class.

In this class, the texture for synthetic vision is defined along with its dimensions. Other important properties are the camera to be used by the NPC and the shader used during the rendering from the NPC's point of view. The class has a method `ProcessAgents()` that is responsible for setting up the shader and processing the NPC's texture output. The `SetupVisionShader()` and `ProcessAgent()` methods are abstract in order to force them to be implemented by concrete derived classes.

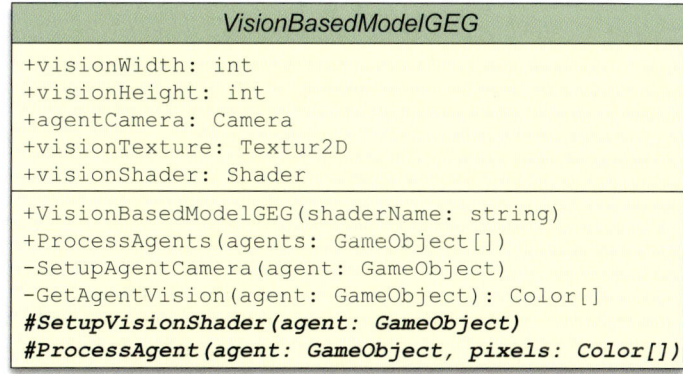

Figure 18.3. Base class for vision based techniques.

The code accompanying this chapter is written in C#, and it runs in Unity. Some undefined properties and methods presented in this chapter are encapsulated by Unity. In the `VisionBasedModelGEG` class, for example, `Camera`, `Texture2D`, and `Shader` are classes defined by Unity. Moreover, the shader snippets presented in the following sections are written in ShaderLab, a shading language used in Unity that has similarities with Cg and HLSL.

Common example evaluation scenarios usually define two NPC groups with the objective of swapping positions, e.g., where the initial positions of a group on the left are the goal positions for another group on the right and vice-versa. The main idea behind this is to bring forth situations where there are potential collisions, which are inevitable if the NPCs are unable to steer properly. Useful scenario scripts such as `OppositeScenario` are provided for this purpose.

After setting up the scenario, it is necessary to implement a means for creating the VBLPP technique object and for processing the NPCs with the collision avoidance technique at each application step. The `GEG` script inherits from `MonoBehavior` in order to do so. Moreover, a good demo is never complete without some user interaction. The `Player` script can be attached to the player's model in order to allow its representation and control. That model's shader has the "Obstacle" tag set in order to be perceived by the NPCs. The `Update()` method synchronizes information between the model and its shader.

The next two sections are devoted to detailing two VBLPP techniques and their implementations. First, we examine the purely reactive technique proposed by [Ondřej et al. 2010], which was the first vision based technique specifically designed for simulating crowds. In that case, NPCs react to the risk of collision identified through synthetic vision. A collision threshold is used to determine when to adapt the NPC's motion in order to escape the danger of collision. Second, we examine the gradient based technique introduced by [Dutra 2015], which represents an advance over the previous one where NPCs move so as to always minimize the risk of collision by taking into account all the information produced by the visual flux instead of merely reacting to the most imminent danger.

18.4 Purely Reactive Technique

Overview

The first technique scrutinized in this chapter was introduced by [Ondřej et al. 2010]. This purely reactive VBLPP algorithm extracts two indicators, $\dot{\alpha}$ and *tti*, from each pixel representing an obstacle in the synthetic optic flow. The first indicator, $\dot{\alpha}$, represents the time-derivative of the bearing angle α under which the obstacle is perceived. The second indicator, *tti*, or time-to-interaction, is the remaining time until a collision occurs with an obstacle. The NPC's reaction to visual stimuli is taken by means of the following two actions while ignoring the background pixels that are not processed during the rasterization stage:

- For each pixel indicating a future collision (i.e., with α close to zero), a turning angle is computed based on a symmetric threshold function that is inversely proportional to *tti*. That threshold function can be parameterized in order to control the NPC's safety distance from obstacles and how far ahead in time it can anticipate collisions (see [Ondřej et al. 2010] for more details). This action aims at choosing the turning angle that avoids all the obstacles and deviates less from the goal.
- The speed is adjusted according to the minimum *tti* when a collision is imminent, such as when there is at least one obstacle pixel with *tti* smaller than three seconds. This action slows down the NPC in order to prevent collisions from happening.

Implementation

In Figure 18.4, we derive the purely reactive technique from the base class introduced in the previous section. The derived class implements the two virtual methods defined in the base class and defines a private method for updating the NPC's properties. The properties of the shader used by the technique are also shown in Figure 18.4. The output of the vertex shader, which is the input of the fragment shader, are stored in the v2f structure. Finally, the value of the properties in PRMVisionShaderGEG and VisionShaderDefs are configured in SetupVisionShader() method of the model. For more details regarding this particular technique, please refer to [Ondřej et al. 2010].

Before describing an example using the purely reactive technique, it is important to characterize the NPCs and to define the obstacles in the environment that are considered during processing. First, to characterize an NPC, we create a C# script (AgentScript in Figure 18.5) that is attached to the 3D model representing the NPC and used to set the NPC's properties needed by the shader and the technique. AgentScript inherits from the base scripted behavior MonoBehavior within Unity's framework to define the Start() and Update() methods. Update() is invoked every frame in order to compute the NPC's properties using the underlying shaders. Finally, a material possessing the "Obstacle" tag in its shaders is used in order to specify the game objects that are considered as obstacles. Some results are shown in Figure 18.6.

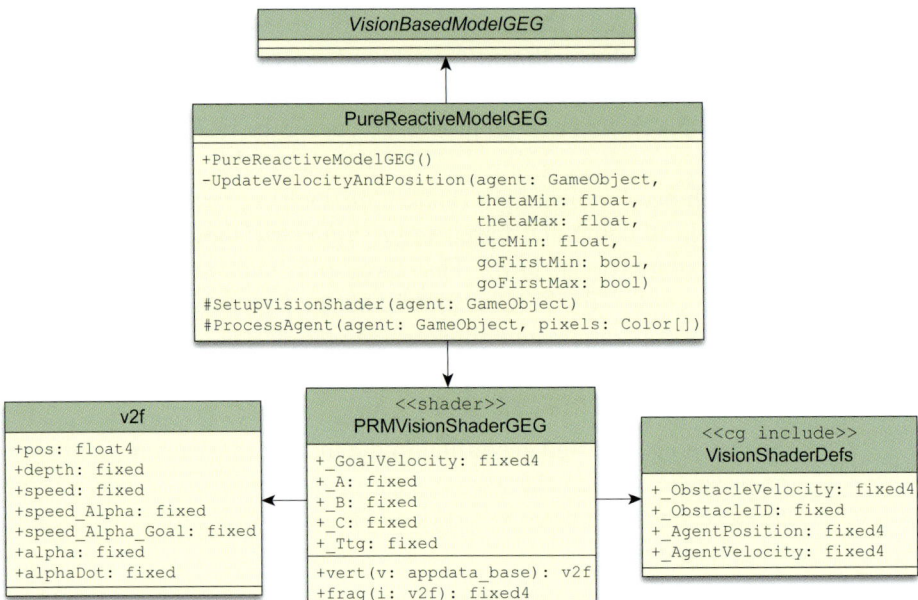

Figure 18.4. Description of the purely reactive technique.

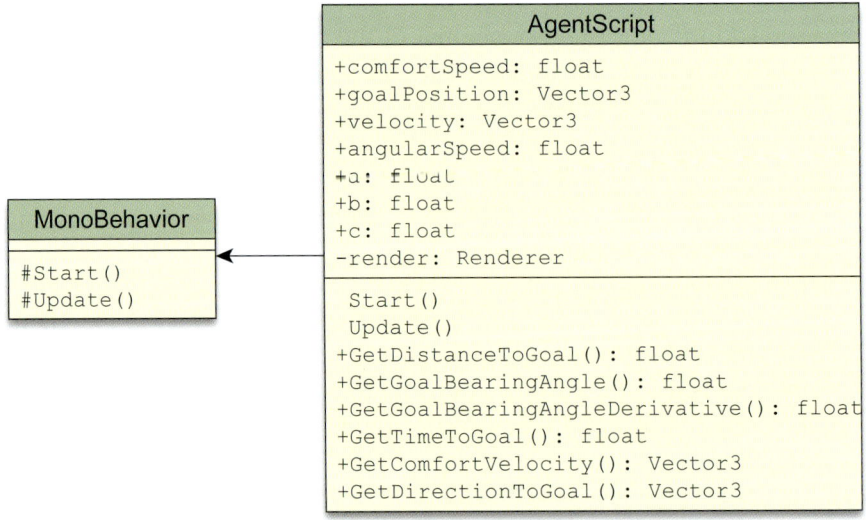

Figure 18.5. Script used to characterize an NPC.

18.5 Gradient Based Technique

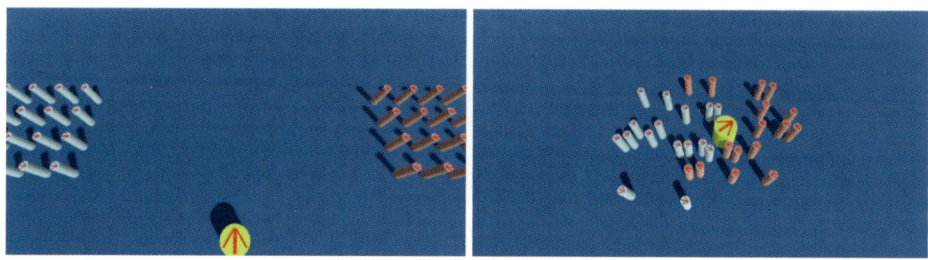

Figure 18.6. The initial state of the NPCs is shown on the left, where the player controls the yellow cylinder. On the right, the interaction of the player with the NPCs is shown when using the purely reactive technique.

18.5 Gradient Based Technique

Overview

In the purely reactive technique, the NPCs focus on avoiding only the most imminent danger and neglect the consequences of their actions on other potential threats. Moreover, behaviors such as accelerating for avoiding collisions are absent. In this section, we introduce an alternative technique that explores a wider range of possible motion adaptations for each NPC and retains the locally optimal one. Convincing behaviors are achieved as a result of this exploration.

The gradient based technique introduced by [Dutra 2015] extracts two indicators from each pixel representing an obstacle in the synthetic optic flow:

- *dca*, or distance at closest approach, represents the minimum reachable distance between an obstacle and an NPC, assuming that they keep their current velocities over time.
- *ttca*, or time to closest approach, is the remaining time until an obstacle reaches the *dca*. This indicator complements the previous one because it helps to determine the urgency for taking collision avoidance actions.

These indicators correspond to instant metrics for determining danger such that low values on both indicators mean that a collision is likely to occur in the near future.

The technique employs a cost function C_t to evaluate the current situation of the NPC. It is composed of two terms, so that $C_t = C_m + C_o$. The movement cost C_m considers the current state of the NPC, given by its orientation with respect to the goal and its current speed relative to its comfort speed. C_m accounts for whether the NPC is heading toward the goal at its comfort speed. The obstacles cost C_o considers the vision of the NPC, accounting for the (*dca*, *ttca*) pair for each pixel detected, and evaluates the importance of collision risk with obstacles.

The idea behind this technique is to minimize the cost function C_t with respect to the NPC's velocity. To this end, the velocity is decomposed in orientation θ and speed s. Such an approach makes the NPC avoid dangers while trying to move toward its goal at its comfort speed. To do so, the gradient of the cost function is computed as

$$\nabla C_t = \left[\frac{\partial C_t}{\partial s}, \frac{\partial C_t}{\partial \theta} \right] = \left[\left(\frac{\partial C_m}{\partial s} + \frac{\partial C_o}{\partial s} \right), \left(\frac{\partial C_m}{\partial \theta} + \frac{\partial C_o}{\partial \theta} \right) \right],$$

and a step k in the opposite direction of the gradient is evaluated as

$$(s', \theta') = (s, \theta) - \lambda_k \nabla C_t(s, \theta) + (0, \varepsilon),$$

where λ_k is the step size and ε is a noise that is added to the angle in order to disrupt undesired symmetric situations. The (s', θ') pair is used to update the NPC's motion variables. We now discuss the underlying cost functions C_m and C_o. For even more detailed information, please refer to [Dutra 2015].

Movement Cost Function

The movement cost function C_m is designed to be minimal when the agent is heading toward its goal at its comfort speed. It is defined as

$$C_m = 1 - \frac{e^{-\frac{1}{2}\left(\frac{\alpha_g}{\sigma_{\alpha_g}}\right)^2} + e^{-\frac{1}{2}\left(\frac{s - s_{\text{comf}}}{\sigma_s}\right)^2}}{2},$$

where σ_{α_g} and σ_s control the width of the Gaussian functions with respect to the bearing angle and the deviation of the NPC's speed s from the comfort speed s_{comf}, respectively. The parameterization of these Gaussians allows making an adjustment to the tradeoff between adapting the orientation or the navigation speed. This is useful for modeling different maneuvering capabilities of distinct entities such as people, cats, cars, horses, etc.

Obstacles Cost Function

The obstacles cost function C_o makes use of the NPC's vision, and it is designed to be maximal when both *dca* and *ttca* are zero. This function considers all obstacle pixels i within the view range in order to compute an average based on each individual pixel's contribution C_{o_i} to the overall cost, yielding

$$C_o = \frac{1}{n} \sum_{i=1}^{n} C_{o_i},$$

$$\text{with } C_{o_i} = e^{-\frac{1}{2}\left[\left(\frac{ttca_{o_i}}{\sigma_{ttca}}\right)^2 + \left(\frac{dca_{o_i}}{\sigma_{dca}}\right)^2\right]},$$

where σ_{ttca} and σ_{dca} are used to adjust the shape of the two-dimensional Gaussian. More specifically,

- σ_{ttca} adjusts the motion anticipation time such that low values cause the NPC to delay its reaction to eventually detected future collisions. On the other hand, high values cause the NPC to avoid collisions earlier and more smoothly. Hence, this parameter can model the NPC's attention to dangers or carefulness level.
- σ_{dca} adjusts the comfort distance to keep from obstacles, influencing how far the NPC tries to stay from obstacles while navigating. Therefore, it can be used to model a personal safe area that the NPC tries to preserve, often for animation purposes.

Implementation

We derive the gradient based technique by implementing the interface introduced in Section 18.3. The properties of the shader used by the technique are shown in Figure 18.7. A `v2f` structure possessing the specific properties for this technique is shown in a way similar to the purely reactive technique in the previous section. The values of the properties in the `GBMVisionShaderGEG` shader and the `VisionShaderDefs` structure need to be configured in the model's `SetupVisionShader()` method.

The example scenarios described in Section 18.3 are compatible with our implementation of this technique, given that a proper object implementing the technique is instantiated. Finally, `AgentScript` now has the properties demanded by the gradient based technique, shown in Figure 18.8. Some results can be seen in Figure 18.9.

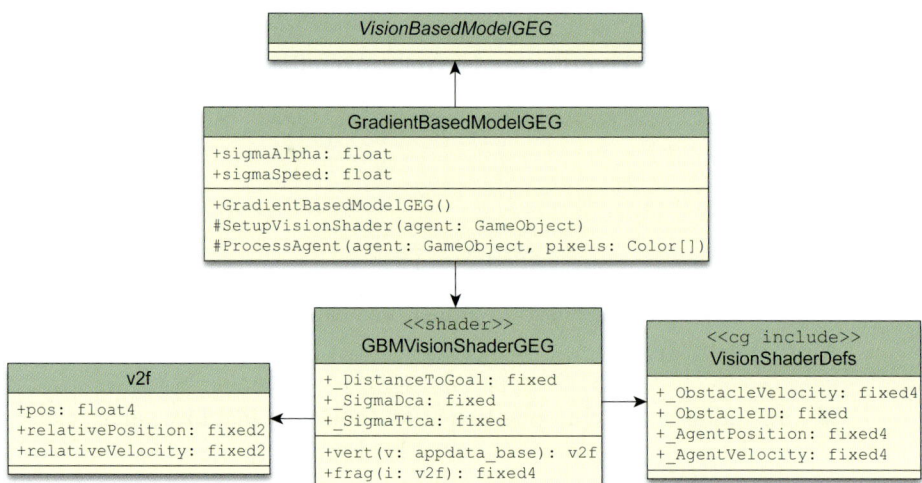

Figure 18.7. Description of the gradient based technique.

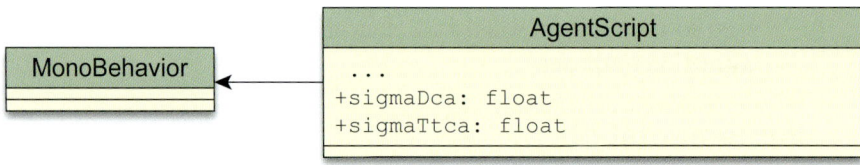

Figure 18.8. New properties in the NPC's script.

18.6 Final Considerations

Vision based techniques are an emerging technology for local path planning. VBLPP techniques prove how utilizing synthetic vision for locomotion can lead to convincing results. These kind of techniques can go further by expanding the reasoning of the NPCs so that they are able to deal with more complex entities and situations. Since the real point of view of the NPC is retrieved, a lot of information could be considered to determine its next move or reaction. For example, taking into account the environment and other NPCs in the vision, an NPC could determine if it needs to crouch, jump, or dash in addition to just turning or accelerating.

18.6 Final Considerations

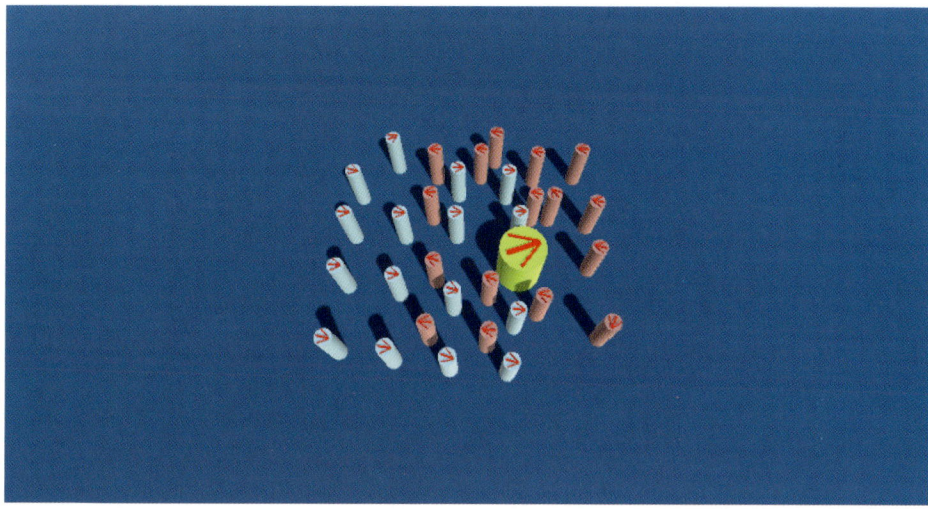

Figure 18.9. Example of interactions among the player and the NPCs using the gradient based technique.

Another interesting extension of these techniques would be the addition of 3D motion, which would be useful for simulating flying and swimming entities, for example. The use of synthetic vision in games opens several possibilities beyond those related to locomotion since any information perceived from the point of view of an NPC could be used as stimuli for its reasoning system.

In this chapter, we introduced the general concept behind VBLPP, and we described two methods that are representative of this approach. These kinds of techniques have a higher computational cost than their conventional counterparts. However, the power of the current graphics cards allows VBLPP techniques to be used for real-time applications with a moderate number of NPCs. As graphics hardware evolves along with the associated programming interfaces, these kinds of LPP methods will become more feasible for enhancing the quality of NPCs in upcoming games. Moreover, better performance can be obtained by resorting to hybrid techniques or adaptive methods where the vision based information would be used just in key frames for faster reasoning.

The two methods shown in this chapter employ functions that model how the NPCs reason about their movements. The first one uses a threshold function, and the second one uses a cost function. Those functions' parameters can be set to produce multiple behaviors. Moreover, dynamic weights can be applied per NPC to the C_m and C_o components of the cost function C_t for the sake of modeling a wider diversity of personality traits. For example, a bold NPC may prioritize reaching its goal over avoiding collisions and, therefore, may force its way through a crowd.

The implementation provided with this chapter on the book's website is a reference for study and experimentation. For commercial usage, we kindly suggest to contact the respective authors.

Acknowledgements

We would like to thank Dr. Creto Auguto Vidal (Federal University of Ceará, Brazil), Dr. Joaquim B. Cavalcante Neto (Federal University of Ceará, Brazil), Dr. José Gilvan Rodrigues Maia (Federal University of Ceará, Brazil), and CAPES (Coordenação de Aperfeiçoamento de Pessoal de Nível Superior) for their financial support (Teófilo) and the project funded by the French research agency ANR JCJC PERCOLATION also for their financial support (Ricardo).

References

[Berg et al. 2011] Jur van den Berg, Stephen J. Guy, Ming Lin, and Dinesh Manocha. "Reciprocal n-body collision avoidance". *Robotics Research*, Volume 70, Springer, 2011, pp. 3–19.

[Dutra et al. 2014] Teófilo Bezerra Dutra, Gurvan Priem, J. B. Cavalcante-Neto, Creto Vidal, and Julien Pettré. "Synthetic vision-based crowd simulation: reactive vs. reactive planning approaches". *Proceedings of the 27th Conference on Computer Animation and Social Agents*, 2014.

[Dutra 2015] Teófilo Bezerra Dutra. "Gradient-Based Steering for Vision-Based Crowd Simulation Algorithms". PhD thesis, Fortaleza, 2015. Available at http://www.mdcc.ufc.br/teses-e-dissertacoes/teses-de-doutorado/doc_download/283.

[Cutting et al. 1995] James E. Cutting, Peter M. Vishton, and Paul A. Braren. "How we avoid collisions with stationary and moving objects". *Psychological Review*, Vol. 102, No. 4 (1995), pp. 627–651.

[Fiorini and Shiller 1998] Paolo Fiorini and Zvi Shiller. "Motion planning in dynamic environments using velocity obstacles". *The International Journal of Robotics Research*, Vol. 17, No. 7 (1998), pp. 760–772.

[Helbing and Molnár 1995] Dirk Helbing and Péter Molnár. "Social force model for pedestrian dynamics". *Physical Review E*, Vol. 51, No. 5 (May 1995), pp. 4282–4286.

References

[Karamouzas et al. 2009] Ioannis Karamouzas, Peter Heil, Pascal van Beek, and Mark H. Overmars. "A predictive collision avoidance model for pedestrian simulation". *Motion in Games*, Vol. 5884, pp. 41–52.

[Ondřej et al. 2010] Jan Ondřej, Julien Pettré, Anne-Hélène Olivier, and Stéphane Donikian. "A synthetic-vision based steering approach for crowd simulation". *ACM Transactions on Graphics*, Vol. 29, No. 4 (July 2010), Article 123.

[Paris etal. 2007] Sébastien Paris, Julien Pettré, and Stéphane Donikian. "Pedestrian reactive navigation for crowd simulation: a predictive approach". *Eurographics*, Vol. 26, No. 3 (2007), pp. 665–674.

[Pettré et al. 2009] Julien Pettré, Jan Ondřej, Anne-Hélène Olivier, Armel Cretual, and Stéphane Donikian. "Experiment-based modeling, simulation and validation of interactions between virtual walkers". *Proceedings of the 2009 ACM SIGGRAPH/ Eurographics Symposium on Computer Animation*, pp. 189–198.

[Reynolds 1999] Craig Reynolds. "Steering behaviors for autonomous characters". *Proceedings of the Game Developers Conference 1999*, pp. 763–782.

[Rio et al. 2014] Kevin W. Rio, Christopher K. Rhea, William H. Warren. "Follow the leader: Visual control of speed in pedestrian following". *Journal of Vision*, Vol. 14, No. 2 (February 2014).

[Van den Berg et al. 2008] Jur van den Berg, Ming C. Lin, and Dinesh Manocha. "Reciprocal velocity obstacles for real-time multi-agent navigation". *Proceedings of the IEEE International Conference on Robotics and Automation*, 2008, pp. 1928–1935.

[Warren and Fajen 2004] William H. Warren and Brett R. Fajen. "From Optic Flow to Laws of Control". *Optic Flow and Beyond*, edited by Lucia M. Vaina, Scott A. Beardsley, and Simon K. Rushton. Kluwer Academic Publishers, 2004.

19

A Programming Framework for Autonomous NPCs

Artur de Oliveira da Rocha Franco
José Gilvan Rodrigues Maia
Fernando Antonio de Carvalho Gomes
Federal University of Ceará

19.1 Introduction

Game engines have usually focused on plausible physics and cutting-edge graphics. Modern engines also deliver mechanisms for controlling non-player characters (NPCs), but these are typically not deep enough to yield a compelling experience, especially considering that some games may require complex NPCs that behave in a rich, coherent fashion. Following that trend, many recent titles such as Monolith Productions' *Middle-earth: Shadow of Mordor*[1] adopted sophisticated systems for NPC interaction allowing for rich, awful enemies that players can face. Players who enjoy stories are like book readers—they need good quality NPCs to love and hate as the game progresses.

It is arguable that a considerable part of the interactive storytelling features found on video games was inspired by role playing games (RPGs) that emerged in the 1970s and whose creation is attributed to Gary Gigax and Dave Arneson. RPGs are derived from board games, and they introduced an interpretative aspect—an RPG player essentially personifies a character of a story narrated and managed by a new kind of player called the "master". Adventures are faced by a player group controlling the protagonists as the story develops through game sessions. The control of a character's actions is performed by means of their descrip-

---

[1] https://www.shadowofmordor.com/

tions, whereas the actions' effects are measured by systems defining rules governing simulations built upon the results of polyhedral dice rolls.

The first electronic RPGs made their debut about a decade later.[2] Electronic RPGs, in general, share a similar context of dungeon exploration, but they lack an interpretative context. For example, players must explore an infinite dungeon in the pioneer RPG *Dungeon Master*. Evolved, modern games like New World Computing's *Might and Magic IV: Clouds of Xeen*[3] or recently Bioware's *Dragon Age*[4] have a strong interpersonal context in which players establish relationships with NPCs. An interpretative aspect is evident when the player faces social or decision-making situations.

Interactive digital storytelling, or simply *interactive storytelling* (IS), is a vast field of research that aims to build narratives supported by the use of interactive technologies found on multimedia. IS poses a complex challenge due to the mixture of knowledge needed for its implementation. Moreover, it is closely related to artificial intelligence (AI) because algorithms endowed with AI are necessary to model and implement narrative elements for computers. IS also demands tools for supporting the conception of enthralling stories capable of being influenced by players, especially in order to give way for game writers and designers expressing their artistry. It is important to consider such control because the complex underlying mechanisms driving the story can lead to unexpected situations. Therefore, a game may need some constraints as input to follow the general plot drawn up by the writer.

This chapter focuses on the design and implementation aspects of a general programming framework for supporting NPCs that behave according to their own personal traits. We resort to concepts from IS for tackling this challenge while considering electronic RPGs as an important test scenario. Although the *Dungeons & Dragons* (D&D) 3.5 system is adopted as a basis for this chapter, we recommend that readers use any systems they like or even to create RPG systems themselves. This programming framework is called "CordéIS" since this word combines IS and refers to a particular kind of popular literature from Northeastern Brazil.

---

[2] http://www.meanmachinesmag.co.uk/upload/media/scans/retrogamer_dungeonmaster.pdf
[3] http://might-and-magic.ubi.com/universe/en-gb/games/all-games/might-and-magic-rpg/index.aspx
[4] http://www.dragonage.com/

19.2 CordéIS Overview

We first present the main design goals considered for architecting a flexible programming framework for intelligent NPCs that fits modern game engines and can also benefit from emerging technologies and trends regarding interfaces for non-programmers. Therefore, our very first look at the framework is in connection with design patterns.

Design Goals

The following design goals were considered as requirements for CordéIS:

- Allow artists to feed the system somehow in addition to programmers. A data-driven design helps a lot during tests and also serves as a Pandora's box for building valuable tools. For example, data-driven systems are a few steps away from visual analytics and big data.
- Decouple planning from its effective implementations. Different algorithms are available in the literature for covering specific application scenarios.
- Consider that goal selection and planning can be fed with data provided by designers. Therefore, the framework should support the fact that portions regarding story and NPC behavior can be hard-coded when needed.
- Decouple actions from their actual execution. A specific game might adopt a measured pace with turn-based interaction while the needs of another game are better suited by real-time action.
- Consider that actions may fail, and consequently, replanning or even selecting a different goal might be necessary.
- Keep as simple and general as possible. Layers of extra information can be added to solve different domain-specific problems such as path planning.
- Support electronic RPGs. We deem this genre as an important validation scenario. Therefore, further simplifications are likely to be necessary when adapting the framework to other game genres.
- Ensure reusability at the expense of performance. This general framework can fit a number of games, but optimization is left as future work since it can produce better or quicker results for specific situations. Moreover, there are plenty of performance-related tools in the game development ecosystem that can produce effective results given how the framework splits the responsibilities.

Components

The framework was implemented to satisfy the design goals referred to above. The CordéIS core comprises the following main components (see Figure 19.1).

Game System

The game system represents the universe in which characters live and interact by means of actions that are implemented on top of the game's specific rules and mechanics. The game also defines central and accessory entities that allow various actions to occur, such as maps, places, items, weapons, and power-ups. Places are usually special entities that control events occurring in the game. Events are special actions because they do not fail, and they do not require complex

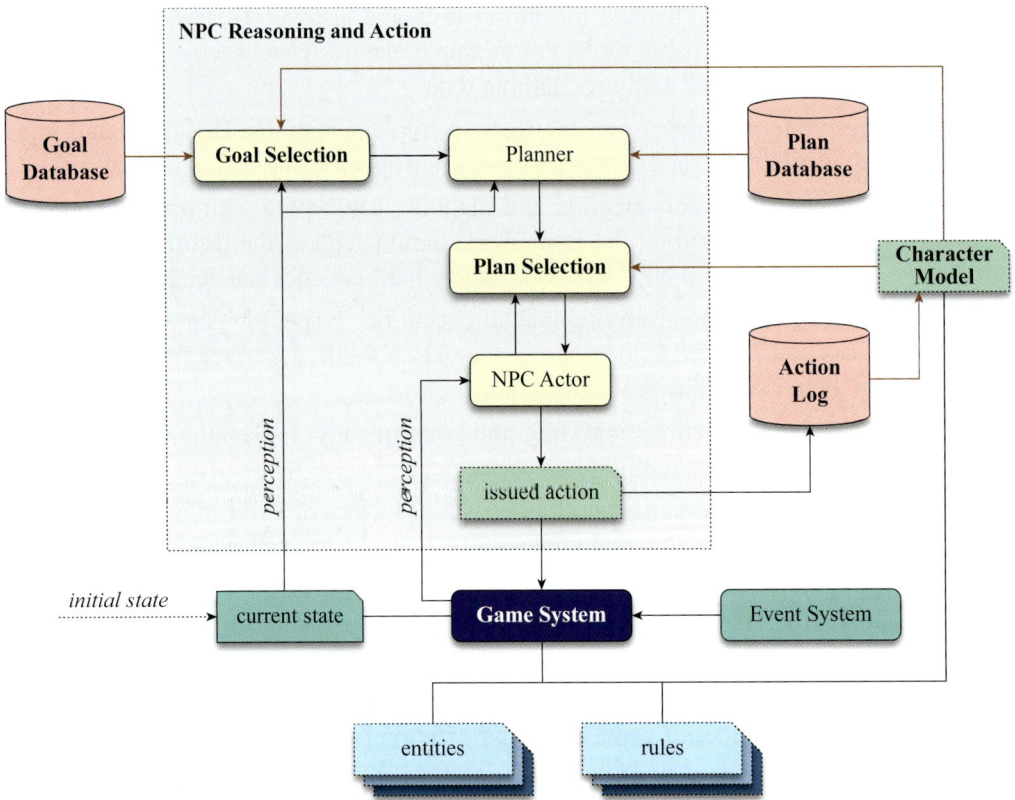

Figure 19.1. Overview of the core CordéIS framework for autonomous NPCs. This model covers decision making and controlling how the character actually performs in the game.

planning. Finally, the game system keeps track of the current state that is perceived and considered by each character's decision-making mechanism.

Character Model

Characters are a general representation for autonomous agents in the game. Characters have their personal characteristics driving them toward their own goals by means of action plans that are coherent within themselves. Other properties, like emotional state and relationships, may be considered in order to allow for a higher level of sophistication when performing goal selection and planning.

Goal Database

The goal database manages useful information when selecting goals for characters, groups, or even for character stereotypes. Designers can therefore influence what the goals are by fitting them to different characters' personalities and situations. Goals can be triggered when the right requirements are met in order to provide control over how the game plays, to unlock extras, etc. Optionally, such a goal can also provide metadata in order to force its usage by the underlying goal selection.

Goal Selection

Goal selection is the process that finds and selects goals according to the current game state for a given character based on its drives and its own knowledge about the world. What goals are applicable? What goals can lead to the NPC's satisfaction? This component determines when an NPC commits itself to achieving one or more goals, which is an important aspect since these outline a character's lifestyle and reasoning. Therefore, an NPC needs to keep track of such decision making. Recurrent, abnormal goal choices may indicate an upcoming personality transformation that can be detected and reinforced in the game.

Plan Database

Similar to the goal database, the plan database maintains information about actions and their respective effects, conditions, and duration. This component can be fed with explicit information from designers in order to build characters who tend to solve a given problem through a specific set of means (plans). Designers may describe general plans crafted to be considered in certain game states. Optionally, such a plan can also provide metadata in order to force its usage by the underlying plan selection component. This database assists planning and outlines agency, controlling how much a given NPC's automatic actions are allowed to affect the story.

Planner

The planner is a central component for autonomous decision making. It determines a (possibly unitary) set of applicable plans to achieve the NPC's goals. Within our framework, a planner does not necessarily make heavy usage of information from the character's drives because solving a problem can pose a complex task even without considering nuances from the NPC's nature. Also, multiple plans can be determined at once in order to allow for contingency when a plan fails. This approach decouples and delegates the problem of choosing a specific plan that suits the NPC's personality to another component. A planner can report back to goal selection when a goal is no longer feasible.

Plan Selection

Fundamentally the plan selection component chooses (and commits to the execution of) the best plan for that NPC's own drives. This component can also perform quick replanning by resorting to the remaining plans already evaluated when a given plan is considered unfeasible by the NPC actor. Moreover, an additional planning step can be executed after considering new information. A clever implementation can also plan adaptation strategies in order to avoid the costs of full replanning.

NPC Actor

The NPC actor performs the selected plan by issuing actions to be executed by the game system. This component keeps track of the execution status of each action and reports back to plan selection when any replanning is needed. Specialized actors can handle multiple characters, but this cannot be covered in detail here.

Action Log

The action log gathers raw data about actions performed by the game's characters with the specific purpose of being consulted by NPCs considering their levels of knowledge. Furthermore, the log may also contain additional information regarding goals and plans selected by characters. Given the central importance of actions in the game system's dynamic, this log provides starting materials to model reputation and interpersonal relationships between characters. The action log may also include a history preceding the moment when a player actually began to experience the game—partial logs crafted by designers or the players themselves can give hints about characters' drives. Switching between NPC and player control can also rely on this log. However, in order to obtain reliable data, a subtle or explicit mechanic might be included in the game for entrusting the player with goal and plan selection.

Practical Considerations

Each of the components described above considers a well-defined domain and can operate by processing slices of information. Their implementation requires an effective interface for describing characters, goals, plans, states, actions, entities, and rules. Defining an interface for each of these elements can be a time-consuming and error-prone task. Modern scripting languages are an attractive technology for implementation due to their flexible and powerful nature. We therefore point out that a general mechanism for manipulating game elements by means of scripts can lead to significant enhancements on reuse and faster prototyping in this case.

Practical usage in a game project demands tools capable of translating artist's designs crafted inside a high-level tool into those structures supported in the implementation in order to feed the game. A general implementation of this programming framework for electronic RPGs based on the D&D system is described in the next section. Readers are invited to devise their own implementations according to the broad lines laid down by CordéIS.

19.3 Implementing CordéIS for Electronic RPGs

Tools of the Trade

This section presents details regarding the application of the CordéIS programming framework to digital RPGs. C/C++ was chosen as the main programming language along with Lua for scripting due to its proven effectiveness for game development. Moreover, Lua's syntax and data description constructs are simple enough to suit the needs of nonprogrammers. A data-driven design can be supported by text files, scripts, virtual filesystems, and data exchange data formats like XML or JSON. SQLite is an attractive option for high-level programming because it provides a powerful, compact, cross-platform transactional SQL database engine supporting in-memory storage that can become helpful in implementing such a system.

Implementation Overview

D&D Game System

The game system implementation is inspired by traditional RPGs because their dynamic systems allow for interpretative aspects. Game elements are based on the D&D system due to its popularity and open licensing.[5] D&D's system comprises rules defining the variables that describe the entities found within the game world. Characters are modeled from six main variables (strength, dexterity, constitution, intelligence, wisdom, and charisma), and action execution is simulated using dice. Unfortunately, there is no room for showing all of the rules, but these can be found in official books and on related websites.[6] Other RPG systems are applicable given the necessary underlying adaptations.

Game Entities

A unified entity model was used for our implementation. This may look weird at a first glance since object-oriented programming practice causes us to think that specializations are often better. However, a unified model allows for flexibility and better reuse, as we stated earlier. Within RPGs, there is room to define items, places, collections, and characters using similar concepts. For example, a character can be seen as a place when such an interpretation seems useful.

Character Model

Emotional and relationship models are not included in our implementation for the sake of simplicity. Therefore, we focus on developing characters' drives, building on top of the concept of karma, which defines four attributes [Barbosa et al. 2010] in the $[-1,+1]$ range: sense of duty, material gain, pleasure seeking, and spiritual endeavor.

Regarding planning, we propose a similar approach, inspired by the personal attitude representation found on D&D's alignment [Franco et al. 2015]. Therefore, we derive five attributes belonging to the $[-1,+1]$ range: pleasing, cost, risk, moral, and order. Pleasing determines how much characters are ready to perform activities considered pleasant or unpleasant to themselves. Cost determines the extent to which characters are willing to spend their time and resources in order to achieve a goal. Risk defines how much characters can expose themselves to danger, harm, or loss. The last two variables are familiar to traditional D&D players—moral is represented by good, neutral, and evil; and order is represented

---

[5] See http://www.d20srd.org/ogl.htm
[6] Such as http://www.d20resources.com/

as lawful, neutral, and chaotic. An insane, erratic NPC, for example, can be represented by setting its moral to neutral and its order to chaotic.

Goal Selection

Goals are evaluated by calculating dot products between an NPC's karma attribute vector and an estimate of karma attribute vectors corresponding to each applicable goal. Therefore, artist-crafted goals must include a description of their preconditions as well as their karma attributes. Special goals can be devised in order to induce "artificial stupidity" on some characters, which gives room for players to drive the game story.

GOAP Planner

We reused the General Purpose GOAP[7] (goal-oriented action planning) as the planner of choice for our implementation. This planner is straightforward to use and can achieve interesting results for general purposes despite the fact that it reports only one plan per execution.

Plan Selection

In order to assist plan selection, actions may define general information regarding their plan selection attributes. Actually, most aspects of plan and goal selection can be implemented at a high-level for a general framework working over metadata. Therefore, actions are associated with plan selection attributes that allow the characteristics of individual actions to be summed up in order to obtain an attribute vector that represents an entire plan. A straightforward plan selection can be performed based on dot products of attribute vectors. More sophisticated selection mechanisms can utilize alternative measures for representing a given plan's attributes, such as average and standard deviation. Moreover, trivial actions are marked so they can be ignored during this process.

FSM-based NPC Actor

The actor operates the game system by controlling the actions found in the selected plan. We adopt the finite-state machine (FSM) proposed by [Franco et al. 2015] for implementing such control based on three fundamental states, shown in Figure 19.2. "Workaday" is the common state that comprises actions reflecting the character's daily routine that is built around predefined goals. Consequently, this state does not require goal selection until a conflict involving the character occurs. Such a situation corresponds to the "Unforeseen" state, in

---

[7] https://github.com/stolk/GPGOAP

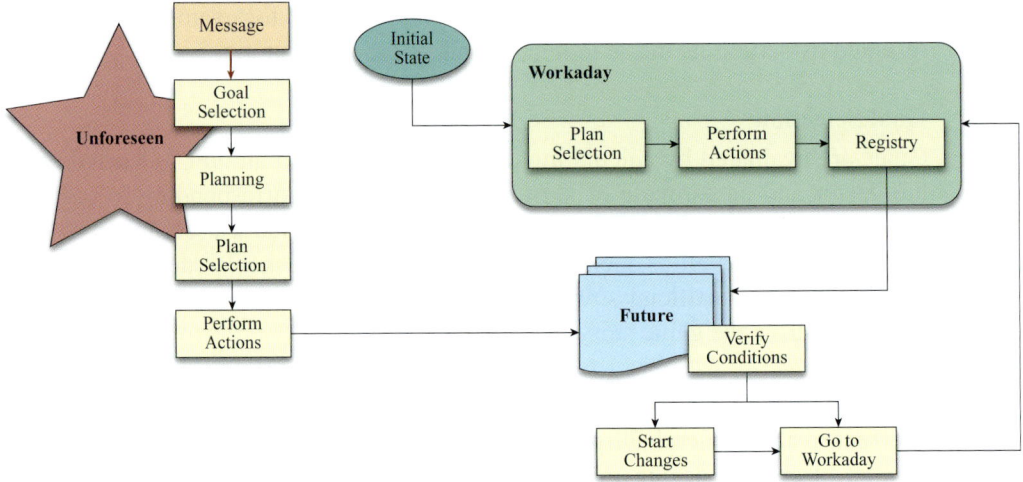

Figure 19.2. Overview of the FSM-based NPC actor implemented for electronic RPGs.

which the NPC resorts to goal and plan selection for responding to external stimuli. Finally, the "Future" state is responsible for maintaining characters' features based on the outcomes of their actions.

Additional Guidelines

There are additional considerations regarding integration of this framework into a game engine. Developers should consider a resource budget needed for delivering a subsystem that orchestrates data and checks whether goals and plans are achievable, especially for games featuring real-time action. Clever approaches such as resource pools and memory allocation strategies might be necessary for maintaining real-time performance. Another important question concerns the size of the NPC population. Level of detail can be used for behavior as long as any simplification can at least provide data for feeding back to the system's action log. Consideration of mechanisms for controlling character groups as a single NPC is also relevant for addressing performance issues. On the other hand, there is room for reducing the cost of simulating complex characters that hardly ever interact with players.

Moreover, obtaining goal selection mechanisms and planners capable of producing varied commitment possibilities is valuable for drawing attention to the game. This allows for a rich emulation of human behaviors, especially when a character undergoes personality transformations or resorts to alternative plans due to eventual execution failures.

19.4 About the Demo

The demo included with this chapter illustrates most parts of the framework and provides simple, textual output for a non-playable story about a foreigner arriving at a mysterious, small city to work on an abandoned gold mine that suddenly becomes profitable again. A few things were intentionally coded using different approaches in similar situations. The main idea behind this is to expose some options for readers wanting to implement their own framework.

Most plot metadata is retrieved from an SQLite database. Lua scripts are left as an alternative for nonprogrammers, and these are brought into C++11 by means of Selene.[8] The demo's source code and documentation contain more details regarding how to set things up. Up-to-date source code is being maintained on the project's website at http://tejo.virtual.ufc.br/cordeis/.

References

[Barbosa et al. 2010] S. D. J. Barbosa, A. L. Furtado, and M. A. Casanova. "A Decision-making Process for Digital Storytelling". *2010 Brazilian Symposium on Games and Digital Entertainment*.

[Franco et al. 2015] Artur O. R. Franco, Joaquim A. M. Neto, José G. R. Maia, and Fernando A. C. Gomes. "An Interactive Storytelling Model for Non-Player Characters on Electronic RPGs". *2015 Brazilian Symposium on Games and Digital Entertainment*.

---

[8] https://github.com/jeremyong/Selene

20

Beyond Smart Objects: Behavior-Oriented Programming for NPCs in Large Open Worlds

Martin Černý
Charles University in Prague

Tomáš Plch
Charles University in Prague, Warhorse Studios

Cyril Brom
Charles University in Prague

20.1 Introduction

A typical limitation of many open world games (OWGs) is their inability to make the world appear alive and purposeful. A major cause is that most non-player characters (NPCs) display only very basic ambient behaviors in which NPCs perform activities on their own without being triggered by the player. This is partly due to problems that arise in managing a large codebase required for the nontrivial ambient behaviors in a large-scale game. In this chapter, we present an approach called *behavior objects* (BOs) by which we manage the complexity of ambient behaviors in a large-scale OWG.

The general idea behind BOs is simple—apply the principles known from object-oriented programming to behavior development. BOs are thus focused on encapsulation of code and data together to promote natural behavior decomposition and reusability. We outline our approach with examples from our ongoing work on *Kingdom Come: Deliverance*.

Let us start with a simple scenario. In a village, there are two kinds of NPCs, farmers and shopkeepers. Farmers spend most of their day on a field and go shopping once they are either hungry, are coming from the fields, or are just missing some items for dinner. Shopkeepers spend most of their days in their shops selling goods. All NPCs have a daily routine (like most living things) where they sleep, eat, work, and get back to sleeping. The village is composed of houses for NPCs as well as shops and nearby fields.

A natural high-level decomposition is to separately develop behaviors occurring at individual locations (e.g., house, field, shop). A nice property of this decomposition is that the behaviors for individual locations are well encapsulated and conveniently located at their respective places. If there are no dependencies, all these locations can be created, scripted, and tested separately. Thus, the main logic of an NPC is reduced to choosing a behavior and the location where it should be executed.

On a finer level, some code is shared among the locations. For example, both shops and houses have doors, so it makes sense to encapsulate the door-traversing behavior and reuse it in both locations. The behaviors should also work across multiple instances of the given location (e.g., shops with storage racks and shops with storage chests). So if we encapsulate the individual types of "take-item-from-storage" behaviors, the code for all types of shops may be the same and simply reference an array of storage containers. We could also mix chests and racks in a single shop. This kind of gradual hierarchical decomposition of behaviors can have multiple levels and is an important feature of the BO approach.

While it is natural for NPCs to be explicitly connected to the houses they live in (and they should use the same house for the whole game), it is not necessary for them to know all the shops in the village. Instead, an entity associated with the whole village may be the only object aware of all shops (plus pubs, churches, etc.) that are available. The NPCs simply ask the village they are currently in to direct them to an available shop, making the addition of more shops to a village easy because they need to be connected only to the village object, and all NPCs can automatically start using them.

In our scenario, the individual villages, shops, houses, doors, racks, etc., are *BO instances*. Some, such as the storage rack, provide only a single behavior, while others provide multiple behaviors (e.g., the shop has behaviors for both a shopkeeper and a customer). Some BOs may also need to be active entities and have a *brain*, a behavior that the BO executes on its own. All instances of the same type share the same behavior and brain code that is specified in a *BO tem-*

plate. Every instance is connected to its own *environment data* and has its own *internal state*.

Environment data are references to in-game entities that the BO needs for its execution. For example, environment data might be the point where the shopkeeper should stand, or it might be a set of storage containers. Internal state consists of a set of variables that the brain uses for its execution. For example, a variable might reflect whether a shopkeeper is present in a shop, or it might hold a list of NPCs waiting to be served. Internal state also consists of references to all NPCs executing behaviors of the BO. This way, adding new houses or shops to the game requires only instantiating a BO and connecting it to the relevant environment data.

20.2 A Little Bit of Context

The idea behind BOs did not come out of nowhere. BOs are a natural extension of smart objects [Kallman 2002]. A smart object in its most simple and typical form is an in-game entity endowed with animation data that instructs any NPC that wants to "use" the object what animations to play and where they should be applied. This approach is typically employed to handle levers, buttons, and the like as well as for traversing obstacles during navigation (e.g., a fence together with an animation to crawl over it). In our scenario, the storage containers could be reasonably handled as simple smart objects.

Many games further extend this simple pattern. *The Sims* have successfully built their whole AI engine on advanced smart objects that provide complete scripts that the NPCs execute while interacting with objects, allowing for behavior nesting [Ingebretson and Rebuschatis 2014, Champandard 2007b]. Basically, all behaviors that characters display are encapsulated in smart objects. However, due to different gameplay requirements, the approach used in *The Sims* is not directly transferable to OWGs, as the NPCs in *The Sims* are not designed to immediately react to user actions.

In the context of OWGs and shooter games, there are smart terrains providing more complex behaviors to NPCs in the *S.T.A.L.K.E.R.* series [Iasenev and Champandard 2008] and special objects that provide hints to NPCs about how to cooperate in specific situations in *Hitman: Absolution* [Vehkala 2012]. In *BioShock: Infinite,* the AI behind the sidekick character Elizabeth makes heavy use of "opportunities", which are marked places in the environment that contain information on how Elizabeth may interact with it (e.g., inspect things, talk to people, etc.).[1]

Behavior objects have also been inspired by "smart materializations", which are in-game entities that broadcast to NPCs goals that they may help to achieve [Brom et al. 2006].

Because the AI system in our project is based on a variant of behavior trees (BTs) [Champandard 2007a], all of our examples are given using the BT formalism, but we also outline how BOs can be used with other AI formalisms.

20.3 Behavior Objects

Now let us dive deeper into the details of BOs and how they differ from smart objects. First, consider a simple BO representing a storage rack. The rack provides only a single "use" behavior—align the NPC to a helper point and play a "search and pickup" animation. Its environment data is the rack entity with the associated animation helper data, and its state is a simple boolean value indicating whether the rack is currently in use. The rack has no brain.

As we already noted, the storage rack could be reasonably handled as a simple smart object, as it is in state-of-the art AI engines. BOs can, however, be used for much higher-level behaviors, such as shopping. The shop in our scenario is a BO providing two behaviors, "customer" and "shopkeeper". The environment data consists of helper points marking the spots where the shopkeeper and the customer should stand during a transaction and a few other points for other customers that are standing in line. Additional environment data consists of the rack BOs (as above) that the shopkeeper behavior uses while satisfying the orders. The state consists of a boolean flag indicating whether there is a shopkeeper present and an array with references to NPCs waiting in line. The shop also has a brain that manages the line of customers. If the shopkeeper leaves, the shopkeeper behavior notifies the brain, which in turn notifies all the customers, causing their customer behaviors to fail. If a customer is served, all waiting customers are notified and move one step forward in the line. A diagram of the situation is shown in Figure 20.1.

Both the rack and shop BOs are now well encapsulated and thus easily reusable. Creating multiple racks with different contents or multiple shops with different layouts and customer line capacities is possible by simply instantiating the respective BO templates and connecting them to the appropriate environment data. Further, the NPCs can be completely oblivious to how the behaviors are

---

[1] See http://www.youtube.com/watch?v=2viudg2jsE8.

20.4 Integration Within an AI System

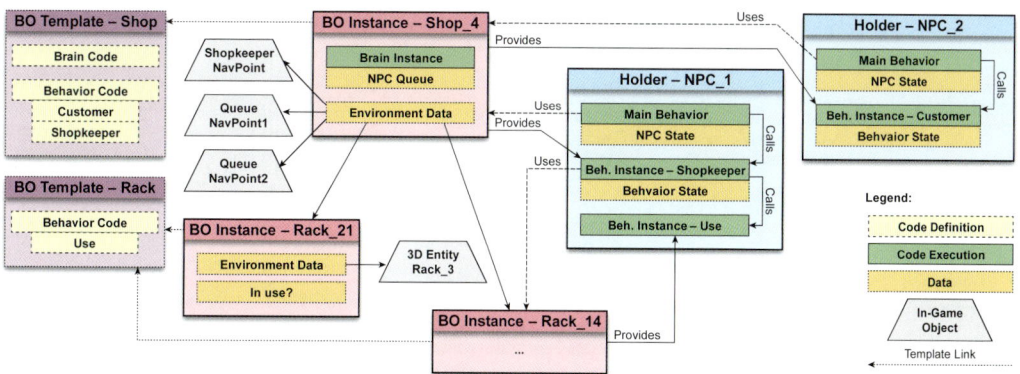

Figure 20.1. A diagram of the example usage of BOs in a shop with multiple racks. The code for individual behaviors and BO brains is provided in BO templates (purple, dotted) that are shared by multiple instances (pink, solid). The instances execute code and encapsulate state and environment data. NPC_1 represents a shopkeeper using the "Shopkeeper" behavior provided by the shop. NPC_2 is a customer using the "Customer" behavior provided by the shop, which further uses the "Sit" behavior provided by a chair.

actually executed, and all communication and synchronization is internal to the shop BO. This allows us to develop and test the shop independently of the rest of the game.

20.4 Integration Within an AI System

To provide any benefits, BOs need to be integrated with the rest of the AI system. Surely we want the NPCs executing a behavior from a BO to keep reacting to combat or other high-priority events, and it would not make much sense to include combat code in the BO. For this reason, the behaviors cannot simply override the main logic of the NPC. We have chosen the approach in which the behaviors are injected into the active behavior of the NPC, and the higher-level behavior still influences execution. In the context of BTs, injection is performed by inserting a subtree into the NPC's active behavior. In the simplest case, a special request node inserts the behavior tree as its only child when executed. The NPC then becomes a holder of the behavior. This lets the higher-level behavior keep its influence on the NPC. An example of this setup is shown in Figure 20.2.

Note that even though the behavior is executed in the context of the holder, it still needs access to BO data. For example, the shopkeeper behavior needs to know the point where the NPC should stand during a transaction. We have found

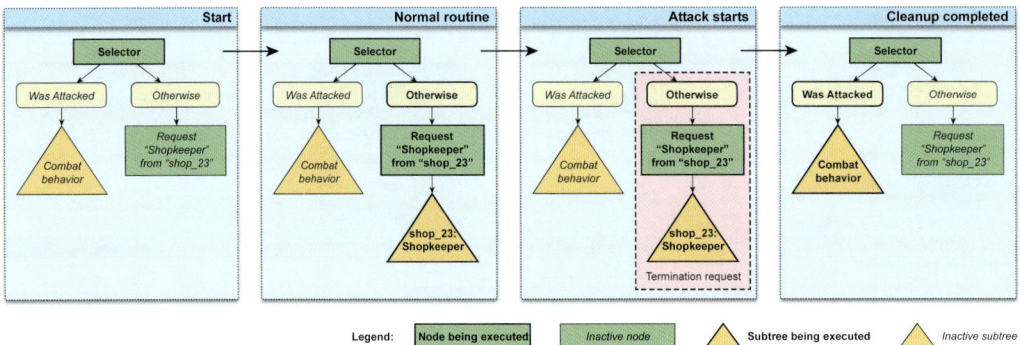

Figure 20.2. Injection of a behavior into a simplified main behavior tree belonging to a shopkeeper NPC. The selector node continually evaluates its child conditions and activates the subtree corresponding to the leftmost fulfilled condition. Since the selector node is still being evaluated when executing the "Shopkeeper" behavior, the NPC is able to react to combat situations.

it useful if the behavior has direct access to environment data because those are immutable, but the behavior cannot directly access the state of the BO to prevent race conditions when multiple holders work with the state concurrently. To access the state, the behavior has to send messages to the BO brain. The brain then handles those messages sequentially within its own updates.

A well designed object should ensure that its internal state stays consistent throughout behavior execution. To keep a BO in a consistent state even if a holder terminates an injected behavior prematurely, the injected behavior has to be allowed to always perform a cleanup procedure. In the shop example, a shopkeeper has to notify the shop brain that it has left the shop. The simplest way to achieve this is to develop the underlying AI system so that it enforces a consistent *init-work-done* lifecycle for all BT nodes. Every node that has completed its "init" phase is guaranteed to execute and complete its "done" phase before it stops receiving updates. Now, the behavior can be wrapped with a "Cleanup" node that executes a special subtree in its "done" phase, and scripters can perform any necessary cleanup behavior in this subtree. The downside is that in nontrivial cases, the "done" phase may take multiple frames (e.g., to correctly terminate a coordinated animation with another NPC), which makes the BT implementation more complex and possibly less reactive, but we consider it to be worth the consistency guarantees.

BOs should be useful even if your AI system is not based on BTs. For example, in the context of hierarchical finite state machines (FSMs) [Fu and Houlette 2004], an FSM may be injected in place of a state. Even if you code your AI directly in a scripting language or some graphical representation of a script (e.g., Blueprints in Unreal Engine 4), similar structuring is achievable. Clear init-work-done behavior lifecycles and an injection mechanism that keeps the higher-level reasoning in place will help you in all cases.

20.5 Implementation in *Kingdom Come: Deliverance*

The AI system in *Kingdom Come: Deliverance* (KC:D) is based on BTs with multiple improvements. A preproduction version of the system is described in [Plch et al. 2014]. An important additional feature of the AI system is a graph of named links between entities that can be searched from within the BTs. We use those links to connect BOs to their environment data. For example, the "shop-keeper" behavior in the "shop" BO may enumerate all objects linked to the shop with a link labelled "storage".

The most common types of BOs in KC:D are various types of *smart entities* (SEs) that include smart objects and their generalizations, such as navigation smart objects, quest smart objects, and smart areas. We also have *situations* as a very different type of BO.

All the BOs in our example scenario are SEs. SEs are attached directly to an entity in the game world. Behaviors from SEs are always injected upon explicit request from an NPC. To simplify the most common cases, SEs maintain an enabled state and a maximal number of holders for each behavior. These can be changed dynamically from within the SE brain (e.g., disabling the "customer" behavior when the shopkeeper leaves the shop). If an NPC requests a behavior that is not enabled or one for which the limit is exceeded, the request node fails. The request node may also specify a list of applicable behaviors, in which case the first available is used, or not specify any behavior at all, in which case any available behavior is used. If more complex decision making is needed to choose the correct behavior for the NPC (e.g., a rich man should behave differently in a shop than a peasant), the NPC requests a general "public" behavior that queries the NPC's properties, and this "public" behavior then requests an appropriate "private" behavior from the same smart entity (e.g., the shop has a public "customer" behavior which then requests either "customer-rich" or "customer-poor", which are private).

Another typical case is that the SE brain wants to execute code when an NPC injects or drops a behavior such as assigning or releasing a spot in the line. To handle this easily, the SE brain may contain *event trees*, small BTs that are executed automatically in those situations. The SE brain also has explicit references to all behavior holders and may thus easily send messages to all holders of a certain behavior or perform any kind of coordination needed.

We achieve a simple polymorphism by using duck typing semantics for SEs. The request node does not check the actual type of the SE but only checks whether it has a behavior with the given name. This way, the shopkeeper behavior may request a "use" behavior from a storage container and not care whether it is a rack or a chest.

Smart Objects and Their Variants

The simplest type of SEs are smart objects, and they are attached to specific objects in the game. Smart objects usually provide only few behaviors and usually have no active brains even though they frequently use event trees. Still, our smart objects may be much more complex than in other OWGs. For example, we have a bench with four seats. The bench itself manages free spots and the NPCs sitting on the bench. These NPCs must give way when an NPC wants to leave or use a spot in the middle.

We also use navigation smart objects. Those are smart objects that are connected to the navigation mesh and provide passage between two polygons (doors, stairs, etc.). Once again, as our navigation smart objects provide full-fledged behaviors, they are more powerful than their counterparts in contemporary games. For example, we have realistic doors on hinges including natural open and close animations for NPCs. A door also manages a queue of NPCs that want to use it, if necessary, and allows NPCs to react when it is locked. Unlike plain smart objects, the behaviors of navigation smart objects are injected as a child of the "move" BT node, and the NPC does not have direct control over what navigation smart objects are used to traverse a path.

We further use smart objects to handle quests. Quest smart objects are technically the same as plain smart objects but are used very differently. Whenever an NPC is scheduled to perform a quest-related activity (e.g., a boy keeps secretly visiting a girl in the evening, and the player may find this out), it requests the relevant behavior form the quest smart object. The brain of the quest smart object coordinates all NPCs participating in the quest, tracks progress of the quest, and communicates with the global quest system. Quest smart objects usually have a lot of environment data because they are connected to all in-game assets relevant to the quest. This way, all the behaviors related to a single quest and all relevant assets are accessible from one place, and the quest behaviors can be developed and tested independently.

Smart Areas

The most complex SEs we use are *smart areas*. Unlike smart objects, smart areas are connected to whole areas of the game, such as a shop, a house, or the whole village. This has the advantage that an NPC does not need an explicit reference to a smart area, but may request a behavior implicitly from "the smart area I am currently inside". Smart areas have explicit parent-child relationships. The child areas are fully contained within the bounds of the parent. This allows for both top-down and bottom-up redirects of behavior requests.

A top-down redirect occurs when an NPC is in a village and asks for a shopping behavior. All shops within the village are children of the village smart area, and it thus may choose an open and nearby shop for the NPC. In our implementation, the village smart area provides a "shopping" behavior that performs any necessary computation to find the correct shop and then requests the "customer" behavior of the shop. Note that the village is in no way restricted in redirecting the behavior. For example, if a fair just started in the village, it may redirect the NPCs requesting the "shopping" behavior to participate in the fair.

A bottom-up redirect occurs when an NPC is in a house and asks for a shopping behavior. As the house smart area does not provide such behavior, it asks its parent area (the village) and, if necessary, parents further up in the tree to the root smart area (the whole world). In our case, the village provides the behavior, including a redirect to an appropriate shop. This allows for greater flexibility because the NPC now does not need to know anything about locations of particular facilities. It may simply ask the smart area it is currently inside, and the redirects handle the rest.

Smart Entities in Practice

In our game, smart areas usually represent complex high-level behaviors and delegate a lot of tasks to smart objects that are part of their environment data. For example, when an NPC wants to eat in its house, the house delegates the behavior to a table smart object that manages several chair smart objects that the NPC may sit on. The table then uses a bowl smart-object for the actual eating behavior, further delegating some parts of it to a chicken smart object. This setup is very flexible because any smart object in the above chain can be transparently replaced with a different one as long as the new object provides a behavior with the same name.

Another interesting and frequent usage pattern is executing a piece of code while using a smart object. For instance, the shop smart area provides a behavior for the shopkeeper to sit on a chair and think aloud about business. It would not be sensible to have this behavior within the chair smart object. Instead, the chair smart object provides separate "sit" and "stand up" behaviors that are referenced from within the "init" and "done" logic of the "think-aloud" behavior. See Figure 20.3(a) for an example.

A different take on the same problem is forwarding the behavior request. If the smart object needs to retain more control over the behavior, then the smart area forwards the name of the behavior to be requested to the smart object behavior, which then requests the forward behavior as a part of its own execution. See Figure 20.3(b) for an example.

The fact that SEs keep track of the maximal number of available instances of behaviors can be exploited to use behavior requests as locks. Not only does this mechanism ensure that a single NPC can ever execute the shopkeeper behavior at a time, the SE may also expose an empty behavior with a limited number of

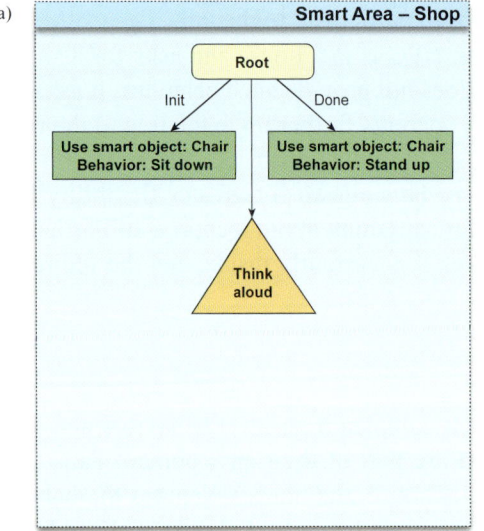 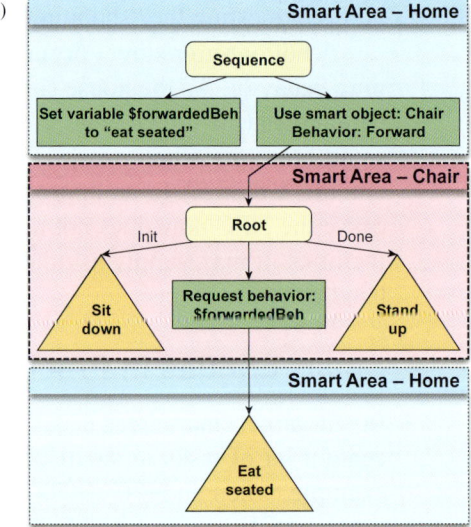

Figure 20.3. Two approaches to executing a piece of code while using a smart object. (a) The higher-level behavior retains main control and requests separate "init" and "done" behaviors from the smart object. (b) The behavior request is forwarded to the smart object, which gets control over the forwarded behavior. In the actual implementation, the node structure is a bit more complicated but is conceptually equivalent to the structure shown here.

available instances whose sole purpose is to serve as a lock. An NPC requests the behavior and then executes a critical behavior section in parallel while holding the behavior.

Empty behaviors may also be used as a communication mechanism. The NPC requests and immediately drops a behavior, resulting in the execution of an event tree in the SE.

External events (e.g., crimes or times of day) can also alter the enabled status of behaviors, allowing the NPCs to use previously unavailable context-specific reactions to those events. For example, when an NPC is notified of a crime, it tries to request an appropriate crime reaction behavior from the smart area it is in. During the night, the city also provides a specific behavior for handling movement of NPCs among smart areas in the city. NPCs try to acquire a lantern prior to moving and hide the lantern once they get inside.

Since NPCs may query the AI system for nearby SEs providing specific behaviors, the changes in the availability of the behaviors thus affect which SEs the NPCs end up using.

Since the player presents himself to the AI system as another NPC, he may also use smart entities. This is useful especially in the context of smart objects because the player avatar can execute the very same code as the NPCs to sit on a chair or open a chest.

Situations

Last but not least, we have a single type of BO that is different from SEs to demonstrate the wider applicability of the concept. We call those BOs *situations*, and they represent short scripted scenes occurring randomly on the streets of our cities. As opposed to SEs, situations do not have brains and are short-lived. Once the situation system decides that a situation should be executed, it chooses appropriate NPCs to enact the situation, instantiates the BO, and injects the respective behaviors into a special place in the NPC decision logic. Once the scene has been played, the BO is discarded. As situations are not gameplay-critical, a situation is stopped and discarded if any of the NPCs terminates the behavior prematurely (e.g., when it is attacked). A more detailed account of how situations work with the rest of the AI system and how appropriate NPCs are chosen is given in [Černý et al. 2014]. So far, situations are still in the preproduction phase.

20.6 Lessons Learned

We have now been using multiple variants of BOs for almost two years, so what have we learned? In general, BOs provide benefits similar to object-oriented programming (OOP) in that they do not enable programming anything fundamentally impossible without BOs, but they help greatly in managing the codebase. Taking inspiration from OOP best practices has helped us significantly in designing BOs. BOs also correspond well to designers' view of the game because designers naturally think in terms of places and quests.

Be aware, however, that implementing BOs in an AI system will very likely add a slight computational overhead due to more indirections in behavior evaluation, lower cache coherence, and managing the BOs. They also have a nontrivial memory footprint due to BO state and pooling of behavior trees for injection. Therefore, one has to consider whether the benefits of improved code structure outweigh the overhead costs for the particular project.

In KC:D, we found it useful to decompose heavily and to keep the individual behaviors small and highly hierarchical as in the eating in a house example above. As in OOP, decomposition promotes reusability and makes creating new environments quick. The only thing that is necessary is to properly set up the environment data. The downside is that after multiple levels of injection, the trees tend to grow large and we thus had to optimize our BT engine heavily to evaluate large trees quickly. Another possible way of handling the growing size would be to remove or deactivate parts of the trees that are no longer needed in a manner similar to a tail recursion optimization.

As with any AI technology, good debugging support is key to success. One problem we struggled with was that as the trees grow large, they become difficult to visualize on a single screen. We have yet to improve our tools to make this less of a nuisance.

Our implementation also does not allow for explicit parameter passing to behaviors. Instead, we share data through variables with agreed-upon names (as in Figure 20.3). This is far from optimal, but parameters are not needed often enough to justify investing development time in this feature.

There are also situations where BOs cannot help you. For example, we have a relatively large piece of code that properly prepares an NPC for a dialog with the player or another NPC. This code snippet is needed in many behaviors, but it makes no sense to encapsulate it in a BO. Good support for reusing code snippets is an important complement to BOs.

It also seems a good idea to provide more computation time to brains of BOs that are used heavily so that they can respond to all messages sent by their holders in a timely fashion.

Additional details about BOs and their implementation in KC:D are given in a more academically oriented description of BOs [Černý et al. 2015].

Acknowledgements

The research behind behavior objects is partially supported by the Czech Science Foundation under the contract P103/10/1287 (GAČR), by student grant GAUK No. 559813/2013/A-INF/MFF, and by SVV project number 260 224.

Special thanks belong to Warhorse Studios and its director Martin Klíma for making this research possible by their openness to novel approaches and by letting researchers work in close cooperation with the company.

References

[Brom et al. 2006] Cyril Brom, Jiří Lukavský, Ondřej Šerý, Tomáš Poch, and Pavel Šafrata. "Affordances and level-of-detail AI for virtual humans". *The Proceedings of Game Set and Match 2*, 2006, pp. 134–145.

[Černý et al. 2014] Martin Černý, Cyril Brom, Roman Barták, and Martin Antoš. "Spice it up! Enriching open world NPC simulation using constraint satisfaction". *Proceedings of Tenth Annual AAAI Conference on Artificial Intelligence and Interactive Digital Entertainment*, 2014, pp. 16–22.

[Černý et al. 2015] Martin Černý, Tomáš Plch, Matěj Marko, Jakub Gemrot, Petr Ondráček, and Cyril Brom. "Using Behavior Objects to Manage Complexity in Virtual Worlds". ArXiv preprint. Available at http://arxiv.org/abs/1508.00377.

[Champandard 2007a] Alex J. Champandard. "Understanding behavior trees". AIGameDev.com, 2007. Available at http://aigamedev.com/open/article/bt-overview/.

[Champandard 2007b] Alex J. Champandard. "Living with The Sims' AI: 21 Tricks to Adopt for Your Game". AIGameDev.com, 2007. Available at http://aigamedev.com/open/review/the-sims-ai/.

[Fu and Houlette 2004] Dan Fu and Ryan Houlette. "The ultimate guide to FSMs in games". *AI Game Programming Wisdom 2*, edited by Steve Rabin. Charles River Media, 2004.

[Iassenev and Champandard 2008] Dmitriy Iassenev and Alex J. Champandard. "A-Life, emergent AI and S.T.A.L.K.E.R.". AIGameDev.com, 2008. Available at http://aigamedev.com/open/interviews/stalker-alife/.

[Ingebretson and Rebuschatis 2014] Peter Ingebretson and Max Rebuschatis. "Concurrent interactions in The Sims 4". Game Developers Conference, 2014. Available at http://www.gdcvault.com/play/1020190/Concurrent-Interactions-in-The-Sims

[Kallmann 2002] Marcelo Kallmann and Daniel Thalmann. "Modeling behaviors of interactive objects for real-time virtual environments." *Journal of Visual Languages & Computing*, Vol. 13, No. 2 (April 2002), pp. 177–195.

[Plch et al. 2014] Tomáš Plch, Matěj Marko, Petr Ondráček, Martin Černý, Jakub Gemrot, and Cyril Brom. "An AI system for large open virtual world". *Proceedings of Tenth Annual AAAI Conference on Artificial Intelligence and Interactive Digital Entertainment*, 2014, pp. 44–51.

[Vehkala 2012] Mika Vehkala. "Crowds in Hitman: Absolution". AIGameDev.com, 2012. Available at http://aigamedev.com/ultimate/video/hitmancrowds/.

21

A Control System for Enhancing Entity Behavior

Mike Ramsey

Ramsey Research, LLC

We've all seen games where an alien soldier is running down a hallway, and as that soldier reaches the end of the hallway, he starts to blend in a turn animation to change his direction but ends up careening into a wall! Sure, we could have the level designer make the hallway wider in a vain attempt to fix the problem, but the real problem is that we're mixing statically generated assets with behavior that's driven or influenced by the game player. We need entities that can react to these types of situations, and one of the mechanisms that can help us modify that soldier's behavior is by taking feedback into consideration in an entity's control architecture.

Control and feedback are everywhere in our everyday interactions with the real world. We perceive and act according to a myriad of feedback from ourselves and the environment as well as social cues. One of the essential understandings we want to achieve is that we want to influence an entity's behavior specifically by its own output, rather than just brute world queries. We are seeking reliable behavior. Feedback within a control system is essentially perceiving or receiving suggestions about an action that we've performed within a specific set of contextual extents and using them in a manner that appropriately modifies an entity's behavior. What this chapter shows is how we can use a proportional integral differential (PID) controller to influence our entity's behavior through negative feedback.

The accompanying C++ implementation of a closed-loop controller is fairly straightforward and can be dropped into virtually any game engine. The field of process control theory has been generating literature for over fifty years, so by necessity this chapter is focused on the applicability and usefulness of negative feedback control to a specific set of problems that benefit from this approach. For a history and an in-depth guide to feedback, please consult [Janert 2013]. In this chapter, we'll discuss several examples for handling several common AI behavioral issues such as altering the urgency of an entity's response and animation variance as well as covering some general strategies that are useful when creating and tuning controllers for your own game. While the use of a PID controller can enhance an entity's response to a dynamic event in a game, you'll also need the required support systems to exist, such as collision sensors and a query space [Ramsey 2011] as well as the ability to translate the PID's correction into an appropriate corrective action.

21.1 Controller Basics

PID is an acronym for proportional, integrative, and derivative. A PID controller is a method to control feedback into our system in a linear manner. The formula for a traditional PID controller is

$$M(t) = K_p e(t) + K_i \int_0^t e(\tau) d\tau + K_d \frac{d}{dt} e(t),$$

where e denotes the error, i denotes the integral, and d denotes the derivative component. While this formula is how the majority of books represent the traditional PID formula, we can make this formula's translation into our actual C++ implementation a bit more amenable if we factor out the gain K to obtain

$$M_{PID}(t) = K \left[e(t) + \frac{1}{T_i} \int_0^t e(\tau) d\tau + T_d \frac{d}{dt} e(t) \right]$$

$$K = K_p$$

$$T_i = \frac{K_p}{K_i}$$

$$T_d = \frac{K_d}{K_p}.$$

The proportion (P) is the magnitude of the corrective action applied to the perceived error. The integral (I) is the history of perceived errors in addition to the momentary perceived error. Using an integral inside a PID controller allows us to effectively correct more quickly if we've had a large error in the past. The differential (D) is a prediction of future error, which is essentially our potential rate of change.

K_p is a constant that represents the controller gain, K_i is our integral constant, and K_d is our derivative constant. (While other books use "coefficient" in place of the "constant", we use the word "constant" here to make it clear that these three values traditionally do not change!) These constants are typically different for each context in which your PID controller is used. Perhaps one of the most useful characteristics of the PID controller is that it's actually multiple controllers in one. Depending on how you tune it (which again depends entirely on the context in which you use it), we can either have a proportional controller, a proportional integral controller, or a full-blown proportional integral derivative controller. The context determines which controller would be most beneficial by how we decide to tune the integral or derivative components. Figure 21.1 is an example graph of how a simple proportional controller can be used to reduce an error to near zero in a smooth manner. So we have a nice little formula that allows us to pick and choose whether to take the past, the present, and the future into consideration of our corrective action. Let's see how this maps to some source code and some common use cases.

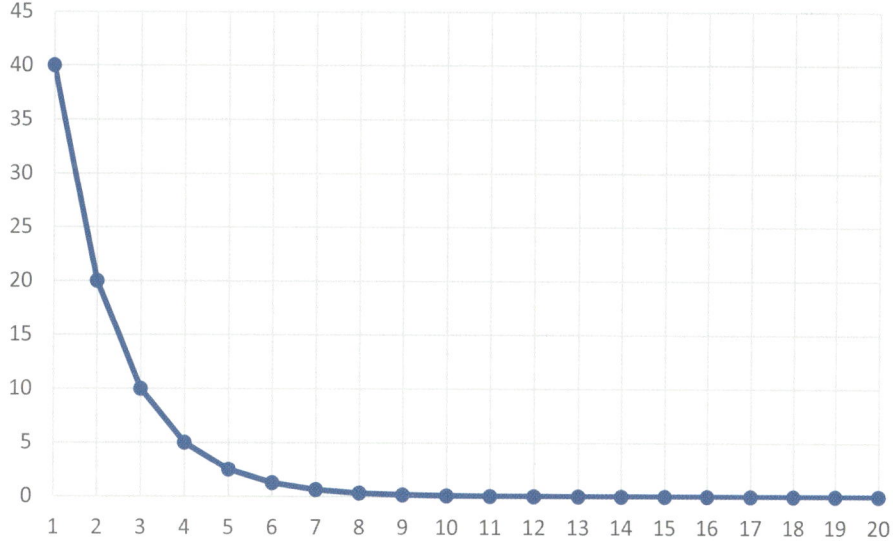

Figure 21.1. The sample PID (0.5, 0, 0) with no integral or derivative applied exhibits no oscillation below zero.

21.2 PID Implementation

In Listing 21.1, we have our implemented PID controller that operates on floating-point values. This is a useful starting point for our examples in this chapter; however, [Ramsey 2015] contains multiple implementations including one that operates on a traditional `vector3` that may be more specific to your use case. The implementation follows the formula rather closely, but it is helpful to step through it.

The first condition we want to test for is whether there's been no change in time. If there hasn't, then we exit. Assuming that we have a time delta, we calculate the error, which is the difference between our current and desired value or condition, and we then add it to our historic error after multiplying by the time delta. This is our integral. If we intend to use the predictive aspect of the PID controller, then we need to generate an error for the derivative component. This is the current error minus the previous error divided by the time delta. We then store this error for the next update cycle. The result is the sum of the proportional, integral (historic), and derivative (future) errors. This sum is then typically added to the current value by the caller of the controller update.

Listing 21.1. Core update function for a PID controller.

```
class PIDController
{
    public:

        PIDController(float p, float i, float d) : m_p(p), m_i(i), m_d(d)
        {
        }

        float update(const float& current, const float& desired,
                const float& dt)
        {
            float result = 0.0F;

            // If there's been no change in time, then exit.
            if (dt <= 0.0F)
            {
                return result;
            }
```

```cpp
            const float error = desired - current;
            m_historicError += (dt * error);

            const float derivativeError = (error - m_previousError) / dt;
            m_previousError = error;

            const float proportional = m_p * error;
            const float integral = m_i * m_historicError;
            const float differential = m_d * derivativeError;

            result = proportional + integral + differential;

            return result;
        }

        // Call this when context changes.
        void reset()
        {
            m_historicError = 0.0F;
            m_previousError = 0.0F;
        }

    private:

        float m_p = 0.5F, m_i = 0.2F, m_d = 0.001F;
        float m_historicError = 0.0F,
        m_previousError = 0.0f;
};
```

21.3 Use Cases and Strategies for a PID Controller

In modern game engines, animations do not solely drive an entity's movement. Character movement is influenced by many factors including the players desired direction of movement, the collision system, game logic, and the physics simulation. A typical game system expects the animations to be interruptible in order to react to unnatural game mechanics, e.g., zero-wind up jump, strafing, and more, but the perceived credibility of an entity when it transitions into that new state is expected to look plausible. Our goal of minimizing these obvious perceptual hitches, such as running into a wall as the collision response system rotates the character so that it eventually slides until it works itself free, is a typical game situation that we strive to avoid. It's situations like these where a PID controller with an integral value of zero can assist us. When an unnatural game mechanic is detected, the blend tree can use a PID controller to transition into the target state based on the desired corrective response. Let's dive into a couple examples of environmental feedback influencing an entity's behavior through a PID controller.

Dynamic Turn Tightening

Handling turning independently of locomotion is advantageous because it allows animators to avoid generating a large number of turn animations. Turning can be handled by using a target point, such as the next point along a navigation route or a point that is dynamically generated as seen in Figure 21.2. A turn angle is generated by taking the dot product between the alien soldier ant's heading and the target and using that to solve for the angle. This value is then used to twist the spine of the solider ant, and that's where our PID controller can assist us. Typically, a uniform twist would be applied to all bones in the spine, e.g., the alien ant soldier has four bones and our turn angle is 40 degrees. We would apply 10 degrees of twist to each bone. However, depending on the urgency of the situation, we can increase the proportional gain of the controller to tighten the turn (of course, within reason!) by twisting bones in different amounts.

Animation Variance

Subtle changes to animation can also be applied by controlling the additive blending through a PID. For example, suppose an incoming projectile will hit our alien ant soldier. How that soldier responds to the projectile is dependent upon the speed of the approaching projectile, and the soldier's surprise factor would lead to upper torso flinches or a transition to a new behavioral state. The flinch effect is visually very subtle, but subconscious of an animator or player will notice the increased sense of immersion.

One of the prototypical uses for a PID controller is when an entity is approaching a position. If our position is far away, we want to move quicker toward it, but if we're approaching our target point, we want to slow down so we don't overshoot it. If the target point is being dynamically altered (perhaps by the player), then the derivative component of the controller might be used to help anticipate the future error. However, one of the problems with using the derivative component is that if a set point change is too large, then there will a momentary spike in the output of the controller. This outwardly erratic behavior is usually

21.3 Use Cases and Strategies for a PID Controller

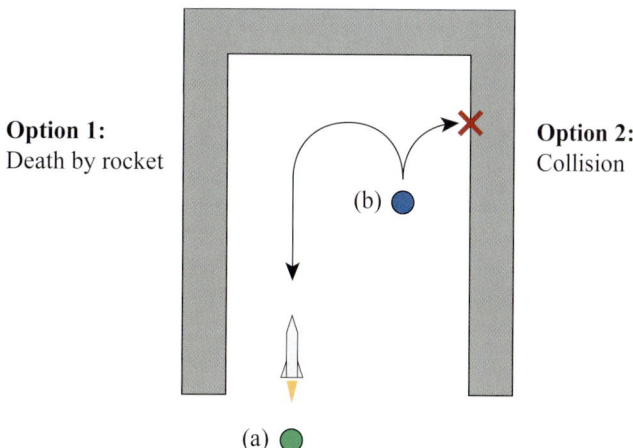

Figure 21.2. Turn tightening. The human player (a) is chasing an alien ant soldier into a hall. The AI system typically would generate a turn target for the ant soldier (b) to the left avoiding the wall while transitioning into an attack stance of some type. However, the human player has fired a rocket to the left of the soldier, so the soldier needs to execute a tight right turn. Choices for the AI are either death by rocket or perform a right turn and retaliate. The PID controller can dynamically tighten the soldier's right turn so that he won't collide with the wall. If the turn cannot be tightened sufficiently then the instigating system could alter the soldier's behavior appropriately (e.g., a rapid turn in place and fire).

labeled as a controller "explosion" because the managing system does not detect and handle such large spikes. Where the integral component is used to eliminate steady-state errors (see Figure 21.3) for PID controllers that are executing for extended periods without a context reset, the derivative component is typically avoided due this reason.

One of the last uses for our controller is the application to dynamic leaning. Dynamic leaning can also be handled in a relatively straightforward manner by adding some rotation to the affected bones as an entity makes its turn. Typically, at extreme speeds, this is would be handled by animators, but even an exaggerated lean can be initially handled by your controller and then tuned down to only handle lower angle turns.

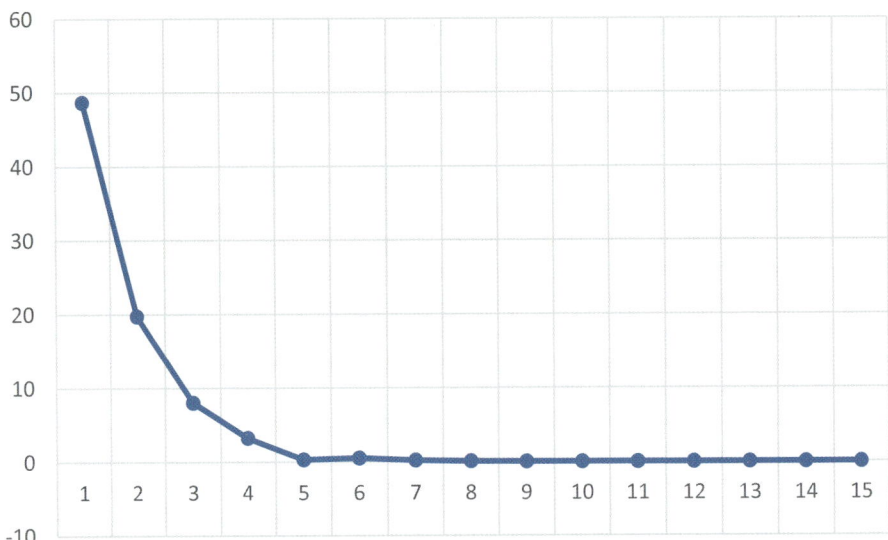

Figure 21.3. The sample PID (0.6, 0.25, 0) with a relatively small integral factor. This exhibits minor oscillation as the controller factors in past error in an effort to eliminate any steady state errors.

References

[Janert 2013] Philipp K. Janert. *Feedback Control for Computer Systems*. O'Reilly, 2013.

[Powers 2008] William T. Powers. *Living Control Systems III: The Fact of Control*. Benchmark Publications, 2008.

[Ramsey 2011] Michael Ramsey. "An Egocentric Motion Management System". *Game Engine Gems 2*, edited by Eric Lengyel. A K Peters, 2011.

[Ramsey 2012] Michael Ramsey. "PD Controllers for AI and Animation". 2012.

[Ramsey 2015] Michael Ramsey. "PID Numerical Companion". 2015.

22

A Control System Based Approach to Entity Behavior

Mike Ramsey

Ramsey Research, LLC

In the companion chapter "A Control System for Enhancing Entity Behavior", we dealt with one focused aspect of enhancing entity behavior in a nonspecific game engine. This was essentially detecting an error and generating a subsequent corrective action to a perceived discrepancy in the environment, such as an alien soldier being too close to a wall to execute an effective turn. This chapter focuses on a hierarchical control system to model an entity's AI. While many games' AI appear to exhibit nothing more than a simple stimulus and response mechanic, more robust behavior can be crafted through the use of control systems, ideally resulting in more compelling gameplay. Instead of coding for specific behaviors that may break under unknown game situations, we compose a hierarchical architecture of negative feedback systems to minimize disturbances between the entity and the environment, allowing it to exhibit purposeful behavior, even when those disturbances may be unknown.

22.1 A Single Control System

An individual control system fundamentally does four things: receives signals, analyzes signals, generates instructions to act on the analyzed signals, and finally uses these instructions to do something (see Figure 22.1). A typical example of a control system is how the cruise control of vehicle maintains a specific driving speed. When the cruise control is enabled with a particular speed, that speed becomes the control system's reference signal. As the vehicle's speed varies from the initial reference signal, the control system alters the vehicle's fuel intake

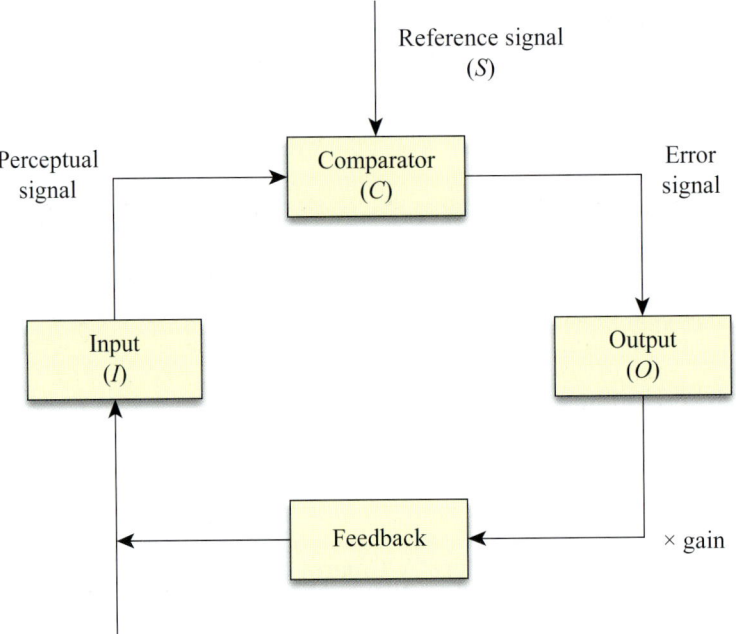

Figure 22.1. A single negative feedback control system.

accordingly. This variance compensation attempts to minimize the discrepancy through negative feedback [Jannert 2013].

The control system shown in Figure 22.1 is labeled with very general terms as the actual details of the boxes are application specific, but the principles are the same for all negative feedback control systems. The design of this single system is to minimize the variance between a perceived perceptual signal and a set reference signal. The reference signal can either be static (as set by a designer) or dynamically altered in a more hierarchically architected system. This negative feedback system has an input function that generates a perceptual signal from some world input. The comparator then compares this perceptual signal with a reference signal, which in turn generates an error signal. This error signal is then converted inside the output function into a compensatory action that attempts to reduce the initial variance. A gain factor can also be applied to increase the rate of change.

While operating on a single floating-point control variable inside cruise control is straightforward, our typical in-game entities are usually more complex and need more customized controllers that operate on coarse data structures and objects [Ramsey 2009, Ramsey 2010]. Some examples of coarse controllers include a personal space controller, a biological urge controller (e.g., nutrients, sleep [Toda 1982]), and a spatial orientation controller. Our gosling example later in this chapter uses a spatial controller in its following behavior.

22.2 Hierarchical Control System Basics

William Powers proposed a complex hierarchy of negative feedback control systems as the foundation for human and animal perception [Powers 1989]. While Powers' approach is indeed very detailed, the suggested hierarchy is physiologically based, and not all elements are practical when architecting an entity behavior system for a game. We focus on the general concept without diving into the full complexity of his proposed hierarchy. Our hierarchical system (see Figure 22.2) is composed of individual control systems that, instead of just consuming a reference signal, actually have that reference signal modified by a higher-order control system. The inputs of the lower-order control systems can also be directed into a higher-order control system. The perceptions in the higher-order control systems are typically informed by combinations of lower-order systems.

22.3 A Hierarchical Control System for Following

While our example focuses on a particular aspect of a larger gosling behavior system, it can provide the foundation for some interesting interactions in a dynamic virtual world that are translatable to a more typical game setting (e.g., alien ant soldier FPS). Tackling the engineering of a behavioral system for an entity is complex, but we can limit our focus on our virtual animal by addressing specific needs or urges [Toda 1982]. This gives our designers the tweakable parameters that allow us to influence the underlying control systems that make up our behavior. For our particular example, we detail a normal following behavior that a gosling exhibits.

A gosling's initial association for the setting of its contact distance is what Konrad Lorenz [Lorenz 1981] referred to as imprinting, whereby its innate closeness is associated to the first animate object that the gosling sees. This distance interval is initially defined by our game designer. The priming and subsequent distance requires a gosling to keep within that interval. This contact distance is in essence a comfort level for the gosling. Goslings do not typically follow a regimented schedule of always staying at their mother's side. They'll forage for food, explore, play with siblings, or sleep. Each of these are modeled with a negative

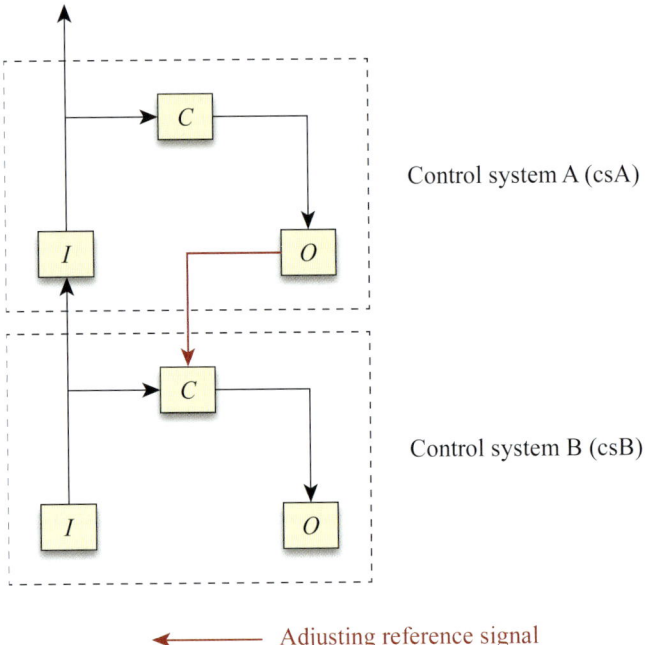

Figure 22.2. A simple hierarchical control system illustrating both the setting of a comparator's reference signal from a higher-order controller (red line from O into C) and the propagation of input into a higher-order control system (I into I). This system's architecture has a higher-order control system (csA) that adjusts a lower-order system's reference signal (csB). Then the input that is sensed by the lower-order system is propagated back into the higher-order system.

feedback control system that is added to our hierarchical tree (see Figure 22.3). In Figure 22.3, we see that the maximum contact distance is used as the initial reference signal for the distance control system. As the gosling's normal behavior moves it around the environment, the distance control system samples the distance to the mother and generates an error. It's also worth noting that all active control systems continuously step. If the error signal that comes out of the distance control system is too large then the spatial orientation controller informs the action manager to move the gosling toward its mother using the current velocity scale.

One of the issues that you may face during development is that groups of control systems may be active for longer than desired, which means that the action manager may have competing behaviors running. Traditional approaches of

22.3 A Hierarchical Control System for Following

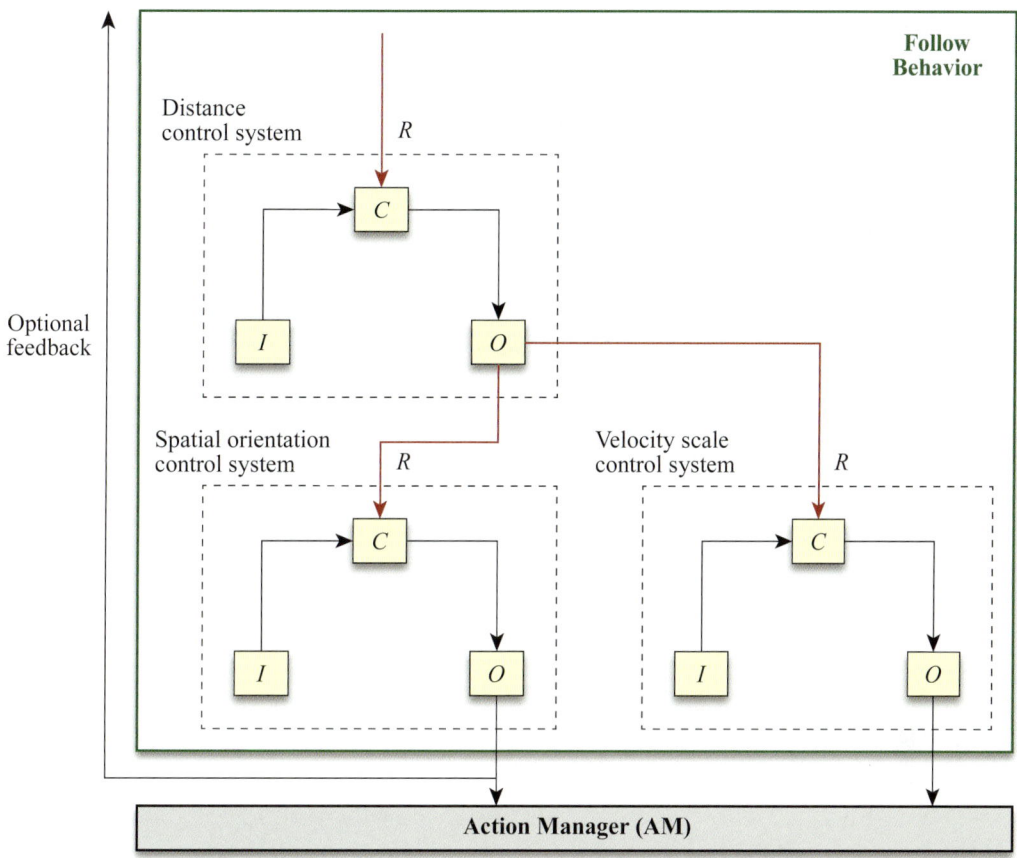

Figure 22.3. A hierarchical gosling behavior constructed out of three negative feedback controllers, allowing a gosling to follow at the side of a specified target.

brute force prioritization of one control system over another would break the dynamic usefulness of this approach, so we need an alternative. We can generate a controller's priority by normalizing the difference in the perceptual and reference signals. This may require some extra logic to get around the perceptual and reference signal comparison, but it's worth the effort. This allows the control systems to effectively prioritize themselves depending upon the situation in the game, and the action manager can just handle the system with the highest priority.

There are also situations where the error from the distance control system is very large. These are situations where the error could be fed back into the higher-order control system for invocation of another control system's behavior (e.g., random movement). One of the fundamental understandings in building a hierarchical control system is that no single component should do too much! When in doubt, feed back the error into a higher-order control system, and let it be the arbiter of what to do, which would likely include suppressing or deactivating the control system that has effectively caused a transition to another control block.

References

[Janert 2013] Philipp K. Janert. *Feedback Control for Computer Systems*. O'Reilly, 2013.

[Powers 1989] William T. Powers. *Behavior: The Control of Perception*. Benchmark Publications, 1989.

[Powers 2008] William T. Powers. *Living Control Systems III: The Fact of Control*. Benchmark Publications, 2008.

[Ramsey 2011] Michael Ramsey. "An Egocentric Motion Management System". *Game Engine Gems 2*, edited by Eric Lengyel. A K Peters, 2011.

Contributor Biographies

Cyril Brom
brom@ksvi.mff.cuni.cz

Cyril Brom is an Assistant Professor at Charles University in Prague. He is one of the fathers of GameDev @ mff.cuni.cz.

Martin Černý
cerny@gamedev.cuni.cz

Martin is interested in (not only reactive) planning techniques and in applying symbolic AI techniques in game worlds. He is working part time for Warhorse Studios, helping them with the creation of magnificent AI for *Kingdom Come: Deliverence*.

Fernando Antonio de Carvalho Gomes
fernandocarv@gmail.com

Fernando Antonio de Carvalho Gomes is a professor of Artificial Intelligence in the Department of Computing at the Federal University of Ceará (UFC) in Brazil. He received his PhD in Computer Science from the Université de Montpellier II in 1993. He was also a Postdoctoral Visiting Professor at SITE from 2000 to 2001. In both the PhD and the postdoc he worked with machine learning. His current research interests are optimization, big data, and games. He also works with telecommunication policies, optimization, and computer vision. He has been the coordinator of several government and industry-sponsored applied research projects.

Marc Fauconneau Dufresne
marc.fauconneau.dufresne@intel.com

Marc is a graphics software engineer with Intel's Visual Computing Engineering group. He received a MEng. degree from Ecole Centrale de Lille and a MEng. degree from Doshisha University. At Intel, he works on pre-enabling for future Intel GPUs. He also occasionally contributes software such as the Fast ISPC Texture Compressor.

Teófilo Bezerra Dutra
teofilo.dutra@gmail.com

Teófilo Dutra obtained his PhD in Computer Graphics from Universidade Federal do Ceará (UFC) in 2015. He is currently a postdoctoral researcher at UFC, and he participates in the research group CRAb (Computer Graphics, Virtual and Augmented Reality, and Animation) with an emphasis on crowd simulation. In his master's, he developed a model based on potential fields and social forces for simulating crowds with secondary (local) goals. His current research started during his PhD and is focused on crowd simulation based on synthetic vision.

Nicolas Guillemot
nlguillemot@gmail.com

Nicolas is a software engineering student at the University of Victoria, and he is currently working in Intel's Advanced Technology Group. Nicolas spends his cycles thinking about C++, computer graphics, and game development. He participates in the standard C++ community through Study Group 14, the ISO C++ study group for game development & low latency. Nicolas is a regular speaker at UVGD, the University of Victoria Game Development Club.

Contributor Biographies

Frank Kane
fkane@sundog-soft.com

Frank Kane is the owner of Sundog Software, LLC, makers of the SilverLining SDK for real-time rendering of skies and the Triton Ocean SDK for real-time rendering of 3D oceans (see www.sundog-soft.com for more information).

Frank's game development experience began at Sierra Online, where he worked on the system-level software for a dozen classic adventure game titles including *Phantasmagoria*, *Gabriel Knight II*, *Police Quest: SWAT*, and *Quest for Glory V*. He's also an alumnus of Looking Glass Studios, where he helped develop *Flight Unlimited III*. Frank developed the C2Engine scene rendering engine for SDS International's Advanced Technology Division, which is used for virtual reality training simulators by every branch of the US military. He currently lives with his family outside Orlando.

Josh Klint
joshklint@leadwerks.com

Josh Klint is the founder of Leadwerks Software, a company dedicated to making game development tools aimed at beginners. His career in game technology began while performing behavioral experiments at the UC Davis Department of Neurological Surgery. He left science to pursue entrepreneurship and then earned a Masters of Business Administration at Sacramento State University. Josh is also a GDC speaker and avid snowboarder.

Manny Ko
man961@yahoo.com

Manny Ko is currently working in the graphics R&D group at Activision Blizzard. Prior to that, he worked in the Rendering Group for DreamWorks Animation and on the ICE team for Naughty Dog, where he worked on next-generation lighting and GPU technologies.

Eric Lengyel
lengyel@terathon.com

Eric Lengyel is a veteran of the computer games industry with over 21 years of experience writing game engines. He has a PhD in Computer Science from the University of California, Davis, and he has an MS in Mathematics from Virginia Tech. Eric is the founder of Terathon Software, where he currently leads ongoing development of the Tombstone Engine.

Eric was the Lead Programmer for *Quest for Glory V* at Sierra Online, he worked on the OpenGL team for Apple, and he was a member of the Advanced Technology Group at Naughty Dog, where he designed graphics driver software used on the PlayStation 3. Eric is the author of the bestselling book *Mathematics for 3D Game Programming and Computer Graphics* and several chapters in other books including the *Game Programming Gems* series. His articles have also been published in the *Journal of Game Development*, in the *Journal of Graphics Tools*, and on *Gamasutra.com*.

Khaled Mamou
kmamou@gmail.com

Khaled Mamou received a PhD degree in Applied Mathematics and Computer Science from the University of Paris V in 2008. Currently, he is a Senior Member of Technical Staff on the AMD Software Multimedia Drivers Team, working on designing and optimizing multimedia solutions. Dr. Mamou has been a member of the ISO/IEC MPEG Standard Committee since 2005, focusing on 3D graphics compression. He chaired the MPEG Ad-Hoc Group on MR3DMC (Multi-Resolution 3D Mesh Coding) and significantly contributed to the standardization of the SC3DMC (Scalable Complexity 3D Mesh Compression) and FAMC (Frame-based Animated Mesh Compression) CODECs for static and animated 3D meshes. Dr. Mamou is a holder of several patents and prestigious awards, such as the first prize in the 2015 AMD Innovation Showcase, the 2013 AMD spotlight award, and the ISO/IEC award for the "special contribution" as a project editor in the international MPEG standard (MPEG-4 Part 16). He is the author of several books, book chapters, and peer-reviewed conference and journal papers on multimedia content compression and processing. He also has over 40 contributions to the MPEG standards.

Contributor Biographies

Ricardo Marques
ricardo.marques@upf.edu

Ricardo Marques received his MSc degree in Computer Graphics and Distributed Parallel Computation from Universidade do Minho, Portugal, in Fall 2009, after which he worked as a researcher at the same university. He joined INRIA (Institut National de Recherche en Informatique et Automatique) and the FRVSense team as a PhD student in Fall 2010 under the supervision of Kadi Bouatouch. His thesis work has focused on spherical integration methods applied to light transport simulation. He defended his PhD thesis in Fall 2013 and joined the Mimetic INRIA research team as a research engineer in 2014, where he worked in the field of crowd simulation. In Fall 2015, he joined the Interactive Technologies Group (GTI) of Universitat Pompeu Fabra (UPF) in Barcelona.

Muhammad Mobeen Movania
mobeen.movania@dsu.edu.pk

Dr. Muhammad Mobeen Movania received his PhD degree in Advanced Computer Graphics and Visualization from Nanyang Technological University (NTU), Singapore in 2012. He carried out research in biomedical volume rendering and visualization in collaboration with the National Cancer Centre of Singapore (NCCS). After his graduation, he joined Institute for Infocomm Research (I^2R), a division of A-Star Singapore, as a research scientist. His responsibilities there were research and development in the areas of advanced computer graphics, augmented reality, and 3D animation.

Dr. Movania has published several international conference and journal papers in the area of computer graphics and visualization including a poster at SIGGRAPH 2013. He has contributed chapters in *WebGL Insights* and *OpenGL Insights*, and he has reviewed several recent OpenGL books including *OpenGL 4 Shading Language Cookbook* (Second Edition) and a video course *Building Android Games with OpenGL ES*. He has also written the book *OpenGL Development Cookbook*, which details several applied recipes on using modern OpenGL. He is the author of the open source cloth simulation library, OpenCloth (http://github.com/mmmovania/opencloth).

Dr. Movania is currently serving as an Assistant Professor in the Department of Computer Science at DHA Suffa University in Karachi, Pakistan. More information about his current research activities may be obtained from his research group web page (http://cgv.dsu.edu.pk).

Artur de Oliveira da Rocha Franco
arturfhtagn@gmail.com

Artur de Oliveira da Rocha Franco is an indie game developer, an HTML5 enthusiast, and a junior researcher in the TEJO laboratory at the Federal University of Ceará (UFC) in Brazil. He received a BS in Digital Systems and Media from the Virtual University Institute at UFC in 2015. His current research interests are interactive storytelling, electronic RPGs, and multivariate data analysis. He also works with JavaScript technologies, artificial intelligence for games, and education.

Jan Ondřej
jan.ondrej@gmail.com

Jan Ondřej is a Postdoctoral Associate at Disney Research, Los Angeles. He obtained his PhD in 2011 from INSA/INRIA Rennes in France, supervised by Julien Pettré. He was a postdoctoral researcher at Trinity College Dublin, headed by Professor Carol O'Sullivan. His research interests focus on real-time simulation, visualization and validation of crowds and autonomous virtual humans, computer animation, and virtual reality.

Julien Pettré
julien.pettre@inria.fr

Julien Pettré has been a research scientist at INRIA, the French National Institute for Research in Computer Science and Control (www.inria.fr) since 2006. He prepared his thesis under the supervision of Jean-Paul Laumond and obtained his PhD in 2003 from the University of Toulouse III in France. He then spent 18 months as a postdoc at VRlab, EPFL, Switzerland, headed by Daniel Thalmann. At INRIA in Rennes, he joined the Bunraku team headed by G. Dumont. His research interests are crowd simulation, motion planning, autonomous virtual humans, computer animation, and virtual reality.

Tomáš Plch
tomas.plch@gmail.com

Tom has programmed computer games since he entered collage in 2002. After finishing his Bachelor's degree, he continued his studies in the field of operating systems. However, after few years, he got back into the field of computer games, focused on artificial intelligence for believable agents. His vision was to develop agent techniques to get more complex and large-scale worlds to work more interactively and believably. After finishing his Master's thesis in the field of Believable Agent Behavior via Behavior Trees, he continued as a PhD candidate at the Charles University (Faculty of Mathematics and Physics) and shifted into the AI planning domain and aerial robotics. He continued to work on various technologies to integrate large-scale worlds, but was more focused on robotics AI of assisted drone piloting. In 2012 came the offer to collaborate between the faculty and Warhorse on enriching the virtual world in *Kingdom Come: Deliverance*. After a short period, Tom quickly got more and more involved in designing and programming the completely new AI system for the game, which is based on ideas from his Master's thesis. After being put in charge of the AI Team, Warhorse was engaged in the quest of having a completely open-world simulated AI system. He continues to work on his PhD thesis, which is based on the work he does at Warhorse, bridging the industry/academia gap.

Michael Ramsey
mike@ramseyresearch.com

Mike Ramsey is the principle programmer on the GLR AI Engine. Mike has developed core technologies for Xbox 360, PC, and Wii at various companies. He has also shipped a variety of games, including *World of Zoo* (PC and Wii), *Men of Valor* (Xbox and PC), *Master of the Empire*, several *Zoo Tycoon 2* products, and other titles. Mike has contributed multiple articles to both the *Game Programming Gems* and *AI Game Programming Wisdom* series, and he has presented at the AIIDE conference at Stanford on uniform spatial representations for dynamic environments. Mike has a BS in Computer Science from Metropolitan State College of Denver, and his publications can be found at http://www.masterempire.com/. He also has a forthcoming book entitled *A Practical Cognitive Engine for AI*. When Mike isn't working, he enjoys playing speedminton, drinking mochas, and having thought-provoking discussions with his fantastic wife and daughter, Denise and Gwynn!

João Lucas Guberman Raza
jraza@microsoft.com

João Lucas Guberman Raza is a Program Manager at Microsoft's Direct 3D team. An avid gamer, he has been working on the game industry for over six years, having shipped multiple titles, SDKs, and platforms. He holds a Bachelor of Computer Science from Universidade Federal de São Carlos (UFSCar) and runs the blog www.versus-software.com, where he writes about his main interests in game design, graphics, and networking.

Stefan Reinalter
stefan.reinalter@molecular-matters.com

Stefan Reinalter is the founder of Molecular Matters, which is the developer of the Molecule Game Engine and development tools. He holds an MS in Computer Science, and specializes in low-level programming, engine architecture, and optimization. In his more than a decade in the games industry, he has contributed to a variety of titles on most platforms. Stefan loves to share his knowledge and experience on his blog and as a lecturer at the University of Applied Sciences in Vienna, where he teaches C++, game engine design, and console programming.

José Gilvan Rodrigues Maia
gilvan.maia@gmail.com

José Gilvan Rodrigues Maia is a professor of Game Development in Digital Systems and Media at the Virtual University Institute of the Federal University of Ceará (UFC) in Brazil. He received his PhD in Computer Science from the Department of Computing at UFC in 2010. He spent many years working with computer game technologies, especially game engine development and collision detection. His current research interests are computer games, computer vision, machine learning, and computer graphics. Gilvan enjoys programming retro games, and he has been working for at least 15 years on research projects at UFC.

Contributor Biographies

Rahul Sathe
sathe.rahul@gmail.com

Rahul works as a Sr. Software Engineer at Intel Corporation. His current role involves defining and prototyping the next-generation technologies in the Intel Graphics Performance Analyzer. Prior to this role, he has worked in various capacities in research and product groups at Intel. He is passionate about all aspects of 3D graphics and its hardware underpinnings. He holds several patents in rendering and game physics. Prior to joining Intel, he studied at Clemson University and the University of Mumbai. While not working on the rendering related things, he likes running and enjoying good food with his family and friends.

Gino ven den Bergen
gino@dtecta.com

Gino has been involved professionally with interactive physics since the beginning of this century. He developed the SOLID collision detection library that has been applied in top-selling game console titles, such as the *Formula One* series for PlayStation 2. He currently works as an independent consultant picking up physics programming contracts. Among his clients are companies involved in game development, medical devices, robotics, and CAD/CAM. Gino is a frequent speaker at the GDC main event, and has shared his ideas in a number of influential publications on game physics.

Don Williamson
dwilliamson_coder@hotmail.com

Don entered game development at the age of 16, when he published his first shareware game. After entertaining offers from the likes of Lionhead after A-Levels, he accepted his first job writing PlayStation emulators to port games to PC in a few days. *The Flintstones*, *Lucky Luke*, and several canceled games later, Don got the opportunity to rewrite the *Splinter Cell* engine for Xbox 360 from the ground up. The next destination was the *Fable* franchise, where Don lead the engine team, working on *Fable 2* and *Fable 3* and co-creating *Fable Heroes*. A specialist in finding performance where none can be found, Don runs Celtoys, a contracting company that can optimize and grow the pretties for any ship's engine.

Kin-Ming Wong
kmwong@cse.cuhk.edu.hk

Kin-Ming Wong is an award-winning visual effects professional and the owner of artixels, a boutique visual effects software developer that focuses on plug-in development for high-end motion pictures. He has recently joined Professor Tien-Tsin Wong's research group to pursue his PhD degree, where he works on photorealistic rendering problems with a strong interest in high-performance sampling and filtering techniques. He is also a computational artist with his works exhibited in SIGGRAPH and GRAPHITE (predecessor of SIGGRAPH Asia).

Tien-Tsin Wong
ttwong@cse.cuhk.edu.hk

Tien-Tsin Wong is a Professor in the Department of Computer Science and Engineering in the Chinese University of Hong Kong (CUHK) and served as head of the committee advisory board of the Computer Game Technology Centre in the department. He has been coding in the area of computer graphics for over 20 years, and he has written publicly available code, libraries, demos, and toolkits (check his home page) as well as code for all his graphics research. He works on GPU techniques, rendering, image-based relighting, natural phenomenon modeling, computational manga, and multimedia data compression. He is a SIGGRAPH author and has published in *Graphics Gems V*, the *ShaderX* series, and the Game Developers Conference.

Index

3ds Max, 3

A
animation structure, 18–21
anisotropic diffusion, 118
Arneson, Dave, 255
artificial intelligence (AI), 256, 271–73, 289
atlas packing, 115–18
atmospheric scattering, 23
autonomous NPC, 255–65

B
ball-and-socket joint, 124
barycentric interpolation, 175
behavior object, 267–78
bending constraint, 164
Bézier curve, 19
BioShock: Infinite (game), 269
Bioware, 256
Blender, 3
bone, 13, 15, 124
Boost library, 186
buffer-free rendering, 85–89

C
C++11, 185, 186, 193, 199, 204, 207, 208
C++14, 186, 208, 209
camera object, 18
character animation, 123
chart segmentation, 113–14

cloth, 160, 169–72
clouds, 30–31
collision avoidance, 239–52
concavity measure, 146–48
constraint
    bending, 164
    tetrahedral, 162
    triangular, 163
    volume/area conservation, 165
control system, 289–94
    hierarchical, 291–94
controller, PID, 281–88
convex decomposition, 141–56
convex hull, 142–54
    merging, 150
    resampling, 151
CordéIS, 257–65

D
`ddx_coarse()` function, 103
`ddy_coarse()` function, 103
degrees of freedom (DOFs), 123
delegate, 185–95
Direct3D, 101
Dragon Age (game), 256
Dungeon Master (game), 256
Dungeons & Dragons (D&D), 256

E
Euler angle, 125, *126*
Euler integration
    semi-implicit, 161

Euler's rotation theorem, 124
Eulerian circuit, 89
event tree, 274
exponential map, 127, 129

F
finite-state machine (FSM), 263, 272
FNV 1a hash function, 198, 199, 200
fog, 23–34, 37–52
Fresnel equations, 31

G
Gauss-Seidel iteration, 160, 161, 166
G-buffer, 102, 104
GCN architecture, 88
geometry object, 14–15
Gigax, Gary, 255
gimbal lock, 126
GJK algorithm, 138
GLSL, 43, 82
goal-oriented action planning (GOAP), 263
gosling, 291
Grassmann algebra, 37
Green-St Venant strain tensor, 162
guided image filtering, 91–97

H
hashing
 string, 197–205
hierarchical control system, 291–94
Hitman: Absolution (game), 269
horizon map
 generation, 75–79
 rendering, 79–82
horizon mapping, 73–82

I
infinite geometry, 43–44
Intel SPMD Program Compiler (ISPC), 219–28
interactive storytelling (IS), 256

J
JavaScript, 207
joint
 ball-and-socket, 124
joint limit, 123–38
JSON, 207, 210, 211, 212, 214, 215, 261

K
Kingdom Come: Deliverance (game), 267, 273–77

L
Laplacian diffusion, 118
Leadwerks Game Engine 4, 55
least-square conformal mapping (LSCM), 112
light object, 18
limit
 swing-twist, 130–37
 volumetric, 137–38
LLVM, 219
Lorenz, Konrad, 291
Lua, 261

M
material, 15, 17–18
Maya, 3, 111, 112, 119
mesh structure, 14
microedge, 118
Middle-earth, Shadow of Mordor (game), 255
Mie scattering, 26
Might and Magic IV, Clouds of Xeen (game), 256
`min10float` data type, 103, 104, 107
`min16float` data type, 103, 104
Monolith Productions, 255
morphing, 17

N
name, in OpenDDL, 9

Index

negative feedback, *290*
network array, shared, 229–36
New World Computing, 256
Newton Game Dynamics library, 65
Newton's method, 49, 50, 136, 137, 138
node, in OpenGEX, 12
non-player character (NPC), 239, 255
    autonomous, 255–65
normal mapping, 73
Nvidia, 111

O

object, in OpenGEX, 12
ocean, 31–33
Open Data Description Language
    (OpenDDL), 4, 8–12
Open Game Engine Exchange
    (OpenGEX) format, 3–21
open world game (OWG), 267
optimal reciprocal collision avoidance
    (ORCA), 241

P

path planning, 240–41
Phong shading, 18
PID controller, 281–88
pixel shading
    variable precision, 101–9
PlayStation 4, 220
position based dynamics, 160–62
Powers, William, 291
Preetham model, 23, 27
primitive data type, 9
property, in OpenDDL, 11

Q

quaternion, 128–33

R

railroad diagram, 8
Rayleigh scattering, 26, 30
reference, in OpenDDL, 11

reflection, static, 207–17
role playing game (RPG), 255
rotation, 124–27
RTTI, 215

S

S.T.A.L.K.E.R. (game), 269
sandwich product, 129
semi-implicit Euler integration, 161
shadow, 73–81
shared network array (SNA), 229–36
SilverLining Sky SDK, 27
situation, 273, 277
skinning, 15–17
sky, 26–31
smart area, 275
smart entity (SE), 273
smoothing filter, 91–99
soft body, 159–80
Sony, 111
SQL, 215, 261
standard template library (STL), 186
static reflection, 207–17
strain based dynamics, 159–80
Streaming SIMD Extensions (SSE),
    219, 220
string hashing, 197–205
structure, in OpenDDL, 8
summed area table, 91
swing-twist limit, 130–37

T

tension-continuity-bias (TCB) curve, 19
tetrahedral constraint, 162
tetrahedral mesh, 160, 172–75
tetrahedralization, 146
Tetris algorithm, 112
texture atlasing, 111–20
texture mapping, 111
The Sims (game), 269
tile, 103
transformation structure, 12–14

triangular constraint, 163
tuple, 208–10
type erasure, 186

U
Unity, 244

V
variable precision pixel shading, 101–9
vegetation management, 53–71
velocity obstacle, 241
visibility culling, in fog, 44–52

vision based collision avoidance, 239–52
vision based local path planning (VBLPP), 242–44
volumetric hierarchical convex decomposition (V-HACD), 141, 145–56
volumetric limit, 137–38
voxelization, 146

W
wedge product, 37
Winsock, 230